LEVEL 3 PRACTICE EXAMS

HOW TO USE THE LEVEL 3 PRACTICE EXAMS

From many years of working with Level 3 candidates, we have compiled the following suggestions, which should help you get the most out of these exams.

Save the Practice Exams for last. A good strategy is to take one exam in each of the three weeks prior to the exam. Plan ahead (i.e., actually schedule the exam and take it on the scheduled day) and do your best to mimic actual exam conditions. For example, time yourself, have someone work on a computer in the same room, and for distractions, have that person leave the room occasionally, turn the temperature in the room up and down, and talk to him- or herself. Remember, no matter how challenging we make our Practice Exams, the actual exam will be different, because you and everyone else in the room will be nervous and fidgety with the pressures of the day. Also, mainly due to the exam experience, your perception will be that the actual exam was much more difficult than our practice exams or even old exam questions you have seen.

Be ready for essay and multiple-choice questions. The morning session (3 hours and 50% of the exam) is entirely constructed response essay format. The afternoon session (3 hours and 50%) is 10 selected response item sets, each worth 18 points. *For the 2008 exam, expect any topic (e.g., portfolio management, derivatives, GIPS®) in either format.* The 2008 Level 3 topic area weights, exactly as presented by CFA Institute® on their website, are shown in Figure 1:

Figure 1: Topic Area Weights for the 2008 CFA Exam

Topic Area	Level 3 Weight
Ethical and Professional Standards (total)	10%
Investment Tools (total)	0%
Quantitative Methods	0%
Economics	0%
Financial Reporting and Analysis	0%
Corporate Finance	0%
Asset Classes (total)	35–45%
Equity Investments	5–15%
Fixed Income	10–20%
Derivatives	5–15%
Alternative Investments	5–15%
Portfolio Management and Wealth Planning (total)	45–55%
Total	100%

* Note: These weights are intended to guide the curriculum and exam development processes. Actual exam weights may vary slightly from year to year.

Please note that some topics are combined for testing purposes.

Figure 2 below shows the topic areas by study session. When you compare Figure 2 to Figure 1, the topic area weights in Figure 1 are a little confusing. For example, you will notice in Figure 2 that Study Session 6 is titled *Economic Concepts for Asset Valuation in Portfolio Management*. Then, you will notice that the weight for Economics in Figure 1 is zero. As explained to me by a representative of CFA Institute, this is because Economics is tested as part of Portfolio Management. In fact, Study Sessions 3 through 18 all fall under the umbrella of Portfolio Management. Just how the individual topics will be tested is somewhat of an unknown, so your focus for 2008 is exactly the same as that for prior years' candidates; you must learn the entire Level 3 curriculum.

Figure 2: 2008 Level 3 Topic Areas by Study Session

Study Session	Topic Area	Title
1	Ethics and Standards	Code of Ethics and Professional Standards
2	Ethics and Standards	Ethical and Professional Standards in Practice
3	Portfolio Management	Behavioral Finance
4	Portfolio Management	Private Wealth Management
5	Portfolio Management	Portfolio Management for Institutional Investors
6	Portfolio Management	Economic Concepts for Asset Valuation in Portfolio Management
7	Portfolio Management	Asset Allocation
8	Portfolio Management	Management of Passive and Active Fixed Income Portfolios
9	Portfolio Management	Portfolio Management of Global Bonds and Fixed Income Derivatives
10	Portfolio Management	Equity Portfolio Management
11	Portfolio Management	Alternative Investments for Portfolio Management
12	Portfolio Management	Risk Management
13	Portfolio Management	Risk Management Applications of Derivatives
14	Portfolio Management	Execution of Portfolio Decisions
15	Portfolio Management	Monitoring and Rebalancing
16	Portfolio Management	Performance Evaluation and Attribution
17	Portfolio Management	Portfolio Management in a Global Context
18	Portfolio Management	Global Investment Performance Standards

Don't underestimate Level 3. Many candidates believe Level 2 is the hardest exam and Level 3 is the most enjoyable. However, this does not mean you should take Level 3 lightly. Your best strategy is to come to the exam as prepared and confident as you can be. There is a lot of new material every year at Level 3, so relying on the comments of those who took the exam last year, or even relying on last year's study notes, could be a prescription for disaster.

Write effective answers to the essay questions. CFA Institute's guideline answers for old exam questions are "perfect answers" (i.e., the one you would write if you had enough time). Also, CFA Institute typically gives you much more answer space than you need (often several pages for a one-paragraph answer), so don't think you are expected to fill all the answer space provided. Your responses should be concise, to the point, and most importantly, address the command words. This way, there can be no doubt that you are addressing the question.

Give the CFA answer. Graders use an answer key and don't give points for creative thought, either yours or theirs! That is, they are not allowed to read anything into your answer, so you must be precise. Also, organize your work and think before you write. If the graders can't find or decipher your work, you will receive no credit. Make sure to use the template for your answer, if one is provided. If you don't use the template, your answer will still be graded. Logic tells us, however, that using the template makes it easier for the grader, and that should always be your focus. The clearer your answer, the higher the probability of receiving at least partial credit.

New feature for 2008. To help make these exams a true learning experience, this year there are two answers for every constructed response essay question. The first answer is labeled **For the Exam**. These short, to-the-point answers would be awarded full credit on the exam. The second answer is labeled **Discussion**. This answer is more of an explanation to help you fully understand why you were correct or incorrect.

Be prepared. It should go without saying that you should get plenty of sleep the night before the exam. Bring all necessary items (including food) with you, and arrive early enough at the test site to get a decent parking space. In fact, I recommend thoroughly checking out the site before exam day. *Important!* Be sure to read the CFA Institute guidelines for test day, which can be found on the CFA Institute website. Also, remember to answer *every* question, even if it means guessing. Graders can only award points; they cannot deduct points for wrong answers.

My thanks to the Schweser team. I would like to thank all of my colleagues at Schweser, especially my content specialist, Eric Smith, CFA, FRM, for their incredible work ethic and commitment to quality. Schweser would not be the company it is, nor could it provide the quality products you see, without all the Schweser content and editing professionals.

Best regards,

Bruce Kuhlman

Dr. Bruce Kuhlman, CFA, CAIA
Vice President and Level 3 Manager
Schweser, a Kaplan Professional Company

PRACTICE EXAMS VOL. 2 ANSWERS AND EXPLANATIONS ARE ONLINE AT WWW.SCHWESER.COM

Letter answers for self-grading Practice Exam item sets are included at the end of this book. Explanations and calculations for the item sets are available online at schweser.com. They have been expanded and contain embedded links to supporting curriculum material for the relevant Learning Outcome Statements. You also have online access to Performance Tracker, a tool that will provide you with exam diagnostics to target your study and review effort, and allow you to compare your scores on Practice Exams to those of other candidates.

JUST USE YOUR SCHWESER *ONLINE ACCESS* ACCOUNT

All purchasers of Schweser Study Notes are sent login information for Online Access in an email. This is your login to view the 2008 Kickoff Seminar, to view video volumes in the Schweser Library, to use the Schweser Study Planner, to get Practice Exam item set answer explanations, to use Performance Tracker, and (if you purchased the Essential or Premium Solution) to get your questions answered during Office Hours. Simply log in at www.schweser.com and select Online Access to use any of these features. Access Practice Exam answers and explanations with the Practice Exams Vol. 2 left-hand menu item. If you need password help, go to www.schweser.com/password or use the Password Help link that appears if your login is unsuccessful.

PRACTICE EXAM ONLINE FEATURES AT A GLANCE

Answer Explanations
Our new format contains expanded Practice Exam answer explanations to help you understand why one answer is the best of all the choices. When using Performance Tracker, you can choose to get detailed explanations for only those questions you missed or for all questions.

Links to Curriculum
Within the answer explanations, we have embedded links to the relevant content for review. This can include multiple Learning Outcome Statements, concepts, definitions, or formulas.

Exam Diagnostics
When you enter your answers in our Performance Tracker utility, you can request a breakdown of your overall score on the afternoon session of any exam. You can even get the Learning Outcome Statement references for questions you answered incorrectly to help you focus your review efforts.

Performance Comparison

Log in today and enjoy the benefits of the Kickoff Seminar, the Schweser Library, Office Hours*, the Schweser Study Planner, expanded Practice Exam item set answers, and Performance Tracker.

* Included with either the Essential or Premium Solution.

LIST OF OLD EXAM QUESTIONS BY TOPIC

These old Level 3 exam questions include 2005 and 2006 questions that are currently available online on the CFA website, as well as older questions that are in the 2008 Level 3 curriculum volumes. Together they represent the majority of available questions from study sessions 3, 4, 5, and 7. As we progress through the season, look for old exam questions from the other study sessions in the Level 3 blog.

I strongly recommend that you first attempt the 2005 and 2006 questions as if you were taking an exam. That is, try not to peek at the answers. Peeking can lead to the "that's what I would say" syndrome, which can be quite counter-productive.

The questions that are included as part of the Level 3 curriculum are generally not indicative of actual exam questions, which will be far more focused. Instead of treating them like exam questions, then, I strongly recommend you use them as the basis for discussions with fellow Level 3 candidates.

In the 2005 and 2006 exam question answers, you will find Professor's Notes, which are designed to give additional information to help you understand the question and answer. You will also find *For the Exam* notes, which provide tips for the exam.

Study Session 3

QUESTION 10 (2005) HAS THREE PARTS FOR A TOTAL OF 9 MINUTES.

10. Five years ago, Crown Airlines, an Irish airline company, merged with a major Dutch airline company to form C-K Air. The companies had equal market capitalization at the time of the merger. As a result of the merger, Crown Airlines stock (CRO) now represents 50% of the share capital of C-K Air, and a Dutch stock listing (KNV) represents the remaining 50%.

CRO is currently trading substantially below its intrinsic value, primarily because of selling on pessimism by a group of irrational investors. KNV, which is a perfect substitute for CRO, is also currently trading below its intrinsic value. Within the Irish airline sector, C-K Air has only one major competitor, Atlantic Airways, whose stock (ATL) is currently trading at its intrinsic value.

ATL and CRO are not perfect substitutes. Joshua Lavinsky, portfolio manager of a domestic Irish equity market-neutral fund, follows both CRO and ATL. He is considering the following long-short position:

*   A long position in CRO
*   An equal and opposite short position in ATL

Sam Blake, portfolio manager of a Pan-European equity market-neutral fund, also follows CRO. Because CRO is currently trading at a premium relative to KNV, Blake is considering the following short-long position:

*   A short position in CRO.
*   An equal and opposite long position in KNV.

A. **Identify** the specific risk that both Lavinsky and Blake would face in establishing their respective positions. **Explain** how that risk would limit both Lavinsky and Blake in seeking to exploit a mispricing.

(3 minutes)

B. **Identify** the specific risk that Lavinsky would face but that Blake would not face in establishing their respective positions. **Explain** how that risk would limit Lavinsky in seeking to exploit a mispricing.

Six months later, Lavinsky and Blake have liquidated their respective positions. CRO is now trading at a 1% premium relative to KNV. The cost of trading Dutch and Irish equities is approximately 35 basis points (bps) each way. The total cost of borrowing Dutch and Irish equities is an additional 40 bps.

(3 minutes)

C. **Determine** if an opportunity to exploit a mispricing now exists with respect to CRO and KNV. **Support** your response with *one* reason.

(3 minutes)

Study Session 4

QUESTION 1 (2006) HAS FOUR PARTS FOR A TOTAL OF 34 MINUTES.

1.   Rodolfo Serra is a professional soccer player with FA Milan, a leading soccer team in Italy's Series A league. He has been well paid over his career including an initial, one-time signing bonus of €2 million, which he immediately invested in a start-up company designing training equipment. This aggressive venture eventually went bankrupt. At 34 years old, Serra is now at his professional peak with an annual pre-tax salary of €5 million: €4 million paid throughout the year and a €1 million year-end bonus. His salary is taxed at 40%.

Since the beginning of his career Serra has managed his own investments. He has had mixed results in his growth equity portfolio. One of his worst performing equity holdings is B&K, an investment he initially made three years ago. On several occasions, in reaction to an extended decline in B&K's share price, Serra used a portion of his year-end bonus to acquire additional shares in an effort to lower his average cost per share. He avoids the technology sector after incurring severe investment losses in the late 1990's. The remainder of his growth equity portfolio has performed satisfactorily. He also has commercial real estate investments that are expected to be cash-flow neutral this year. A summary of his personal assets is shown in Exhibit 1.

Exhibit 1: Rodolfo Serra: Personal Assets (all amounts in €)

Cash savings	4,000,000
Growth equity portfolio*	40,000,000
Commercial real estate investments	14,000,000

* All dividends are reinvested

Serra expects the annual after-tax interest income on his cash savings to be €100,000 at the end of the year.

Serra will retire from professional soccer one year from now at the age of 35. He will pay cash for a personal home costing €4.5 million when he receives his year-end bonus. Having grown up in poverty, Serra recently established a children's welfare foundation. He will legally gift all his commercial real estate investments to the foundation upon his retirement. After retirement, Serra intends to volunteer all of his time to the foundation and does not expect to receive any compensation from other sources.

Serra has been divorced for two years and has a 7-year-old son who lives with his mother in Italy. He makes annual family support payments amounting to €800,000. The annual family support payments will stop when his son reaches age 18. Serra's living expenses are expected to be €1.2 million this year. Both family support payments and living expenses will grow at an average annual inflation rate of 4%. All income net of expenses is currently reinvested in his growth equity portfolio. Serra has expressed his desire to maintain the real value of his portfolio during retirement, which is expected to last a minimum of 40 years.

Serra recently hired a portfolio manager, Patrick Schneider, CFA, who expects the after-tax nominal annual return for growth equity to be 8.5%.

A.   i.   **Formulate** the return objective in Serra's investment policy statement.

        ii. **Calculate** the *after-tax* nominal rate of return that is required during his first year of retirement. **Show** your calculations.

Note: Assume there are no tax benefits or tax liabilities related to Serra's gifting commercial real estate, or paying family support and living expenses.

(13 minutes)

B.   i. **Identify** *two* factors in Serra's personal situation that increase his ability to take risk.

      ii. **Identify** *two* factors in Serra's personal situation that decrease his ability to take risk.

      iii. **Judge**, considering all factors, whether Serra has below-average, average, or above-average ability to take risk.

(6 minutes)

Answer Question 1-B in the Template provided below.

Identify *two* factors in Serra's personal situation that increase his ability to take risk.
1.
2.
Identify *two* factors in Serra's personal situation that decrease his ability to take risk
1.
2.
Judge, considering all factors, whether Serra has below-average, average, or above-average ability to take risk (circle one)
Below-average   Average   Above-average

C.   **Formulate** *each* of the following constraints in Serra's investment policy statement:

   i.   Liquidity requirement

   ii. Time horizon

   Support *each* response with *one* reason based on Serra's specific circumstances.

(6 minutes)

Answer Question 1-C in the Template provided below.

Constraint	Formulate *each* of the following constraints in Serra's investment policy statement. Support *each* response with *one* reason based on Serra's specific circumstances.
i. Liquidity requirement	
ii. Time horizon	

QUESTION 2 (2006) HAS THREE PARTS FOR A TOTAL OF 12 MINUTES.

2.   Lucinda Kennedy, a 65-year-old retiree, has accumulated investment assets of $3 million and has a life expectancy of 20 years. Kennedy meets with Richard Bulloch, CFA, to develop an asset allocation that will provide for her retirement spending needs. Her needs are significant and it would be very difficult to reduce her spending. Kennedy informs Bulloch that her biggest fear is outliving her assets because she has no other sources of income. Kennedy and Bulloch agree to use a life expectancy of 20 years for planning purposes. Bulloch presents Kennedy with three alternative portfolio allocations shown in Exhibit 1. Kennedy believes that a conservative allocation will provide the safety she needs. However, she wonders whether a more aggressive allocation to increase the value of the portfolio would be better over the long term.

Exhibit 1: Alternative Portfolio Allocations (%)

Asset Class	Conservative	Moderate	Aggressive
U.S. equities	10	30	40
Non-U.S. equities	10	30	40
Global fixed income	60	30	15
Cash equivalents	20	10	5

Bulloch states:

"Given your circumstances, an asset-liability management approach to strategic asset allocation is more appropriate than an asset-only approach."

A.   **Explain** *two* advantages of using an asset-liability management approach in Kennedy's situation.

(4 minutes)

Bulloch decides to use Monte Carlo simulation to determine the most appropriate asset allocation for Kennedy's portfolio.

B. **Explain** *two* ways that Monte Carlo simulation differs from mean-variance analysis in a multi-period setting.

(4 minutes)

Bulloch prepares a Monte Carlo simulation using his capital markets expectations. The likely outcomes for the conservative, moderate, and aggressive portfolio allocations are shown in Exhibit 2. Bulloch explains Exhibit 2 to Kennedy. Using the conservative allocation as an example, there is a 75% probability that the terminal value will be less than or equal to $986,000 and a 25% probability that the terminal value will be greater than $986,000.

Exhibit 2: Monte Carlo Simulation Results

Projected Portfolio Terminal Values at 20 Years			
	Terminal Values		
Percentile	*Conservative*	*Moderate*	*Aggressive*
95th	1,701	5,936	11,938
90th	1,313	3,972	7,243
75th	986	3,064	4,818
50th	621	1,632	2,271
25th	343	718	777
10th	3	98	0
5th	0	13	0

* After Kennedy's retirement spending needs have been met

C. **Recommend** the *most* appropriate portfolio allocation for Kennedy based upon the results of the Monte Carlo simulation. **Justify** your response with *one* reason. (Study Session 7)

(4 minutes)

QUESTION 7 (2005) HAS THREE PARTS FOR A TOTAL OF 25 MINUTES.

7.   Elizabeth Yeo, aged 55, will retire one year from now as managing director of Sawit Palm Oil Industries, a Malaysia-based palm oil plantation company. At retirement, Yeo will receive a MYR450,000 taxable lump sum cash payment from Sawit and a MYR500,000 tax-exempt lump sum cash payment from the Employees' Provident Fund, the country's retirement savings plan. Upon retirement, Yeo will also receive MYR8.5 million as proceeds from the sale of her stock in Sawit. Her original investment in the Sawit stock was MYR1.5 million.

Yeo is widowed and has a son, Jonathan Lok, who will be attending a foreign university. She intends to pay all expenses associated with his four-year undergraduate education. She estimates the first year's expenses will be MYR150,000 payable one year from now, and that these expenses will increase approximately 6% annually as a result of inflation in educational costs.

Yeo maintains a money market fund currently valued at MYR1.2 million and earning 2.5% annually. To honor her late husband, she plans to make a non-tax deductible fixed donation of MYR100,000 annually, beginning one year from now, to a Malaysian charity. Yeo's current after-tax salary is equal to her current living expenses of MYR250,000 annually. Both she and Lok currently reside in the family home, which has a current value of MYR1.4 million. She intends to give the house to Lok as part of her estate upon her death. She has expressed a desire to maintain the real value of her investable assets.

Yeo is taxed at 28% on salary, benefits, and investment income. Capital gains are not taxable under Malaysian tax law.

Her living expenses are expected to grow at an annual inflation rate of 3% throughout her retirement period, which is expected to be 25 years given her family's mortality history.

Yeo is working with Ismail Hamid, her financial advisor, to prepare an investment policy statement for her retirement period.

A.   **Formulate** the return objective in Yeo's investment policy statement. **Calculate** the after-tax nominal rate of return that is required to achieve this objective for her first year of retirement. **Show** your calculations.

(10 minutes)

©2008 Schweser

In an interview with Hamid, Yeo admits to having little knowledge about investing, as evidenced by her preference to maintain all excess cash reserves in the money market fund. She tells Hamid that she also views the money market fund as a way to safeguard the wealth she has "worked so hard for." She adds that regardless of her wealth situation, she is habitually conservative in all decisions except where she believes she has control. Citing a case in point, Yeo told Hamid about her aggressive leveraging of Sawit to expand capacity in order to guarantee a customer's purchase order. In contrast she describes two different occasions where she did not take advantage of potentially attractive personal investment opportunities because she could not be certain of the outcomes.

B.   **Characterize** Yeo as below average, average, or above average with respect to *each* of the three components of the risk objective in her investment policy statement:

    i.   Ability to take risk

    ii. Willingness to take risk

    iii. Overall risk tolerance

Justify *each* of your responses with *one* reason based on Yeo's specific circumstances and/or her interview with Hamid.

(9 minutes)

Answer Question 7-B in the Template provided below.

Component	Characterize Yeo as below average, average, or above average with respect to each of the three components of the risk objective in her investment policy statement (circle one)	Justify each of your responses with one reason based on Yeo's specific circumstances and/or her interview with Hamid
i. Ability to take risk	Below average Average Above average	
ii. Willingness to take risk	Below average Average Above average	
iii. Overall risk tolerance	Below average Average Above average	

C.   **Formulate** *each* of the following constraints in Yeo's investment policy statement:

i.   Time horizon

ii. Tax

Justify *each* of your responses with *one* reason based on Yeo's specific circumstances and/or her interview with Hamid.

(6 minutes)

Answer Question 7-C in the Template provided below.

Constraint	Formulate *each* of the following constraints in Yeo's investment policy statement	Justify *each* of your responses with one reason based on Yeo's specific circumstances and/or her interview with Hamid
i. Time horizon		
ii. Tax concerns		

QUESTION 8 (2005) HAS ONE PART FOR A TOTAL OF 12 MINUTES.

8.   Three years have passed and Elizabeth Yeo is meeting with Ismail Hamid for their annual review of her investment portfolio. Yeo has committed to make a one-time donation of MYR2 million to a Malaysian charity, with payment to be made 10 years from now. She also wants to maintain a cash reserve equal to six months of living expenses. With these facts in mind, Hamid estimates that a minimum nominal after-tax rate of return of 7% annually is now required. Yeo and Hamid agree that Yeo's overall risk tolerance has increased somewhat compared with three years ago. Yeo is still taxed at 28% on investment income, and capital gains remain nontaxable under Malaysian tax law. Hamid prepares a summary of asset class characteristics, shown in Exhibit 8-1.

Exhibit 8-1: Elizabeth Yeo Asset Class Characteristics

Asset Class	Expected Annual Return (%)	Expected Annual Standard Deviation of Returns (%)	Expected Interest Rate or Dividend Yield (%)
Money Market	2.5	0.3	2.5
Domestic Bond	5.2	2.1	5.2
Domestic Equity: Income	13.5	13.7	7.5
Domestic Equity: Growth	12.5	13.9	0.0

For the purposes of preparing a strategic asset allocation, Hamid asks Yeo to consider the asset class allocation ranges shown in Exhibit 8-2.

Exhibit 8-2: Elizabeth Yeo Asset Class Allocation Ranges

Asset Class	Allocation Ranges
Money Market	0% to 10% 11% to 20% 21% to 30%
Domestic Bond	31% to 40% 41% to 50% 51% to 60%
Domestic Equity: Income	0% to 10% 11% to 20% 21% to 30%
Domestic Equity: Growth	0% to 10% 11% to 20% 21% to 30%

Recommend for Yeo the *most* appropriate allocation range for *each* of the asset classes in Exhibit 8-2. **Justify** *each* of your responses with *one* reason based on Yeo's specific circumstances.

(12 minutes)

Answer Question 8 in the Template provided below.

Asset	Recommend for Yeo the most appropriate allocation range for each of the asset classes in Exhibit 8-2 (circle one)	Justify *each* of your responses with *one* reason based on Yeo's specific circumstances
Money Market (Cash)	0% to 10% 11% to 20% 21% to 30%	
Domestic Bonds	31% to 40% 41% to 50% 51% to 60%	
Domestic Equity-Income	0% to 10% 11% to 20% 21% to 30%	
Domestic Equity-Growth	0% to 10% 11% to 20% 21% to 30%	

Question 9, 2008 Level 3 curriculum, volume 2, page 198.

9.   **[Adapted from the 2001 CFA Level III Examination]**

James Stephenson, 55 years old and single, is a surgeon. He has accumulated a $2.0 million investment portfolio with a large concentration in small-capitalization U.S. equities. During the last five years, his portfolio has averaged a 20 percent annual total return on investment. Stephenson's current portfolio of $2.0 million is invested as shown in Exhibit P-1.

Exhibit P-1 Summary of Stephenson's Current Portfolio

	Value	Percent of Total	Expected Annual Return	Annual Standard Deviation
Short-term bonds	$200,000	10%	4.6%	1.6%
Domestic large-cap equities	$600,000	30%	12.4%	19.5%
Domestic small-cap equities	$1,200,000	60%	16.0%	29.9%
Total portfolio	$2,000,000	100%	13.8%	23.1%

His newly hired financial advisor, Caroline Coppa, has compiled the following notes from her meetings with Stephenson:

Stephenson hopes that long term, his investment portfolio will continue to earn 20 percent annually. For the remainder of this year, he would like to earn a return greater than the 5 percent yield to maturity currently available from short-term government notes. When asked about his risk tolerance, he described it as "average."

He was surprised when informed that U.S. small-cap portfolios have historically experienced extremely high volatility.

Stephenson does not expect to retire before age 70. His current annual income from his surgical practice is $250,000, which is more than sufficient to meet his current yearly expenses of $150,000. Upon retirement, he plans to sell his surgical practice and use the proceeds to purchase an annuity to cover his post-retirement cash flow needs. He could not state any additional long-term goals or needs.

Stephenson's income and realized capital gains are taxed at a 30% rate.

No pertinent legal or regulatory issues apply. He has no pension or retirement plan but does have sufficient health insurance for post-retirement needs.

Stephenson soon expects to receive an additional $2.0 million from an inheritance and plans to invest the entire amount in an index fund that best complements the current portfolio. Coppa is evaluating the four index funds shown in Exhibit P-2 for their ability to produce a portfolio that will meet the following two criteria relative to the current portfolio:

- maintain or enhance expected return
- maintain or reduce volatility

Each fund is invested in an asset class that is not substantially represented in the current portfolio.

Exhibit P-2: Index Fund Characteristics

Index Fund	Expected Annual Return	Expected Annual Standard Deviation	Correlation of Returns with Current Portfolio
A	15%	25%	+0.80
B	11%	22%	+0.60
C	16%	25%	+0.90
D	14%	22%	+0.65

A.   **Formulate** the following elements of Stephenson's investment policy statement and justify your response for each element with two arguments:

i.   Return objective

ii.   Risk tolerance

iii.   Liquidity requirements

iv.   Time horizon

B.   State which fund Coppa should recommend to Stephenson. Justify your choice by describing how your chosen fund best meets both of the criteria set forth by Coppa. (No calculations are required.)

Question 10, 2008 Level 3 curriculum, volume 2, page 199.

10.   Adapted from the 2000 CFA Level III Examination]

Robert Taylor, 50 years old and a U.S. resident, recently retired and received a $500,000 cash payment from his employer as an early retirement incentive. He also obtained $700,000 by exercising his company stock options. Both amounts are net of tax. Taylor is not entitled to a pension; however, his medical expenses are covered by insurance paid for by his former employer. Taylor is in excellent health and has a normal life expectancy.

Taylor's wife died last year after a long illness, which resulted in devastating medical expenses. All their investments, including a home, were liquidated to fully satisfy these medical expenses.

Taylor has no assets other than the $1,200,000 cash referenced above, and he has no debts. He plans to acquire a $300,000 home in three months and insists on paying cash given his recent adverse experience with creditors. When presented with investment options, Taylor consistently selects the most conservative alternative.

After settling into his new home, Taylor's living expenses will be $2,000 per month and will rise with inflation. He does not plan to work again.

Taylor's father and his wife's parents died years ago. His mother, Renee, is 72 years old and in excellent physical health. Her mental health, however, is deteriorating and she has relocated to a long-term care facility. Renee's expenses total $3,500 per month. Her monthly income is $1,500 from pensions. Her income and expenses will rise with inflation. She has no investments or assets of value. Taylor, who has no siblings, must cover Renee's income shortfall.

Taylor has one child, Troy. Troy and a friend need funds immediately for a start-up business with first-year costs estimated at $200,000. The partners have no assets and have been unable to obtain outside financing. The friend's family has offered to invest $100,000 in the business in exchange for a minority equity stake if Taylor agrees to invest the same amount.

Taylor would like to assist Troy; however, he is concerned about the partners' ability to succeed, the potential loss of his funds, and whether his assets are sufficient to support his needs and to support Renee. He plans to make a decision on this investment very soon. If he invests $100,000 in Troy's business, he insists that this investment be excluded from any investment strategy developed for his remaining funds.

With the above information, portfolio manager Sarah Wheeler prepared the investment policy statement for Taylor shown in Exhibit P-3.

Exhibit P-3: Robert Taylor Investment Policy Statement

Return objective:	Income requirement is $2,000 monthly. Total return requirement is 2.7% annually ($24,000/$900,000).
Risk tolerance:	Substantial asset base and low return requirement provide ample resources to support an aggressive, growth-oriented portfolio.
Time horizon:	Client is 50 years old, recently retired, and in excellent health. Time horizon exceeds 20 years.
Liquidity needs:	$300,000 is needed in three months for purchase of home. Modest additional cash is needed for normal relocation costs. $100,000 may be needed for possible investment in son's business. A normal, ongoing cash reserve level should be established.
Tax concerns:	There is little need to defer income. Mother's expenses may have an effect.
Legal and regulatory factors:	No special considerations exist.
Unique circumstances:	Client desires to support mother. Client insists that any investment in son's business be excluded from long-term planning. Client has strong aversion to debt.

A.   **Evaluate** the appropriateness of Taylor's investment policy statement with regard to the following objectives:

   i.   Return requirement

   ii. Risk tolerance

   iii. Time horizon

   iv. Liquidity requirements

After revising the investment policy statement and confirming it with Taylor, Wheeler is now developing a long-term strategic asset allocation for Taylor. Wheeler will use the following revised information to recommend one of the allocations in Exhibit P-4.

- Taylor has decided to invest $100,000 in his son's business but still insists that this investment be disregarded in making his allocation decision.
- Taylor's total cash flow needs have changed to $4,200 a month.
- The available asset base is $800,000.
- Wheeler estimates that the inflation rate will be 1 percent next year.
- Taylor is determined to maintain the real value of his assets because he plans to set up a charitable foundation in the future.
- Taylor insists on taking no more risk than absolutely necessary to achieve his return goals.

Exhibit P-4: Potential Long-Term Strategic Asset Allocations

	Allocation			
	A	B	C	D
Asset Class				
Stocks	20%	40%	60%	80%
Bonds	75%	55%	35%	15%
Cash	5%	5%	5%	5%
Total	100%	100%	100%	100%
Expected Return	6.7%	7.5%	8.2%	9.1%
Standard deviation	9.0%	11.5%	15.3%	19.0%
Potential for Growth				
Asset growth	very low	low	moderate	high
Income growth	very low	low	moderate	high
Current income	high	high	low	very low
Stability	very high	high	moderate	low

B.   Select the strategic asset allocation that is most appropriate for Taylor and justify your selection with two supporting reasons related to the revised information shown above.

Question 11, 2008 Level 3 curriculum, volume 2, page 202.

11.   **[Adapted from the 1999 CFA Level III Examination]**

Mark and Andrea Mueller, U.S. residents, are reviewing their financial plan. The Muellers, both 53 years old, have one daughter, 18 years old. With their combined after-tax salaries totaling $100,000 a year, they are able to meet their living expenses and save $25,000 after taxes annually. They expect little change in either their incomes or expenses on an inflation-adjusted basis other than the addition of their daughter's college expenses. Their only long-term financial goal is to provide for themselves and for their daughter's education. The Muellers both wish to retire in 10 years.

Their daughter, a talented musician, is now entering an exclusive five-year college program. This program requires a $50,000 contribution, payable now, to the college's endowment fund. Thereafter, her tuition and living expenses, to be paid entirely by the Muellers, are estimated at $40,000 annually.

The Mueller's personal investments total $600,000, and they plan to continue to manage the portfolio themselves. They prefer "conservative growth investments with minimal volatility." One-third of their portfolio is in the stock of Andrea's employer, a publicly traded technology company with a highly uncertain future. The shares have a very low-cost basis for tax purposes. The Muellers, currently taxed at 30 percent on income and 20 percent on net realized capital gains, have accumulated losses from past unsuccessful investments that can be used to fully offset $100,000 of future realized gains.

In 10 years, Mark will receive a distribution from a family trust. His portion is now $1.2 million and is expected to grow prior to distribution. Mark receives no income from the trust and has no influence over, or responsibility for, its management. The Muellers know that these funds will change their financial situation materially but have excluded the trust from their current financial planning.

A.   Construct the objectives and constraints portion of an investment policy statement for the Muellers, addressing each of the following:

   i.   return objective

   ii. risk tolerance

   iii. time horizon

   iv. liquidity requirements

   v.   tax concerns

   vi. unique circumstances

Ten years have passed. The Muellers, now both aged 63, will retire this year. The distribution from Mark's family trust will occur within the next two weeks. The Muellers' current circumstances are summarized below:

Personal Circumstances and Assets
- Pension income will total $100,000 a year and will not increase with inflation.
- Annual expenses will total $180,000 initially and will increase with inflation.
- Inflation is expected to be 2 percent annually.
- Their personal investments now total $1,000,000 (excluding trust distribution).
- The Muellers will rely on this $1,000,000 portfolio to support their lifestyle and do not wish to reduce their level of spending.
- The Muellers have health problems and neither is expected to live more than 10 years. All health care expenses will be covered by employer-paid insurance.
- The Muellers' daughter is now financially independent, and the Muellers' sole investment objective is to meet their spending needs.
- The Muellers are not concerned with growing or maintaining principal. The income deficit may be met with both investment income and by invading principal.

Trust Distribution Assets
- The trust distribution totals $2,000,000 and will occur within the next two weeks. No tax liability is created by the distribution.
- The Muellers will maintain separate accounts for their personal assets and the trust distribution.
- They do not plan to withdraw income or principal.
- Tax liabilities produced by these assets will be paid from this portfolio.
- The Muellers plan to donate these assets to an arts society when the surviving spouse dies. They have made a minimum pledge of $2.6 million toward construction of a new building.
- An after-tax annual return of 5.4 percent is required over five years to meet the minimum pledge.
- The Muellers are concerned only that a minimum gift of $2.6 million is available. The Muellers assume that at least one of them will live at least five years and that neither will live more than 10 years.
- Alternative portfolios for the Muellers' consideration appear in Exhibit P-5.

Exhibit P-5

Asset Allocation	Portfolio			
	A	B	C	D
Domestic large-cap stocks	14%	30%	40%	30%
Domestic small-cap stocks	3%	5%	10%	25%
Foreign stocks	3%	5%	10%	25%
Intermediate-term fixed income	70%	60%	30%	20%
Cash Equivalents	10%	0%	10%	0%
Total	100%	100%	100%	100%
Expected annual return*	4.2%	5.8%	7.5%	8.5%
Annual standard deviation	6.0%	8.0%	13.0%	18.0%

* Nominal after-tax returns

B. Select and justify with three reasons the most appropriate of the four portfolios from Exhibit P-5 as an asset allocation for the Muellers' $1,000,000 in personal assets.

C. Select and justify with three reasons the most appropriate of the four portfolios from Exhibit P-5 as an asset allocation for the Muellers' $2,000,000 in trust distribution assets.

Question 12, 2008 Level 3 curriculum, volume 2, page 204.

12. **[Adapted from the 1997 CFA Level III Examination]**

John Mesa, CFA, is a portfolio manager in the Trust Department of BigBanc. Mesa has been asked to review the investment portfolios of Robert and Mary Smith, a retired couple and potential clients. Previously, the Smiths had been working with another financial advisor, WealthMax Financial Consultants (WFC). To assist Mesa, the Smiths have provided the following background information:

Family We live alone. Our only daughter and granddaughter are financially secure and independent.

Health We are both 65 years of age and in good health. Our medical costs are covered by insurance.

Housing Our house needs major renovation. The work will be completed within the next six months, at an estimated cost of $200,000.

Expenses Our annual after-tax living costs are expected to be $150,000 for this year and are rising with inflation, which is expected to continue at 3 percent annually.

Income In addition to income from the Gift Fund and the Family Portfolio (both described below), we receive a fixed annual pension payment of $65,000 (after taxes), which continues for both of our lifetimes.

Financial Goals Our primary objective is to maintain our financial security and support our current lifestyle. A secondary objective is to leave $1 million to our grandchild and $1 million to our local college. We recently completed the $1 million gift to the college by creating a "Gift Fund." Preserving the remaining assets for our granddaughter is important to us.

Taxes Our investment income, including bond interest and stock dividends, is taxed at 30 percent. Our investment returns from price appreciation (capital gains) are taxed at 15 percent, at the time of sale. We have no other tax considerations.

General Comments We needed someone like WFC to develop a comprehensive plan for us to follow. We can follow such a plan once it is prepared for us. We invest only in companies with which we are familiar. We will not sell a security for less than we paid for it. Given our need for income, we invest only in dividend-paying stocks.

Investments We benefit from two investment accounts:

- The Gift Fund ($1 million) represents our gift to the college. During our lifetimes, we will receive fixed annual payments of $40,000 (tax free) from the Gift Fund. Except for the annual payments to us, the Gift Fund is managed solely for the benefit of the college-we may not make any other withdrawals of either income or principal. Upon our deaths, all assets remaining in the Gift Fund will be transferred into the college's endowment.
- The Family Portfolio ($1.2 million) represents the remainder of our lifetime savings. The portfolio is invested entirely in very safe securities, consistent with the investment policy statement prepared for us by WFC as shown in Exhibit P-6.

Exhibit P-6: WFC Investment Policy Statement for Smith Family Portfolio

The Smith Family Portfolio's primary focus is the production of current income, with long-term capital appreciation a secondary consideration. The need for a dependable income stream precludes investment vehicles with even modest likelihood of losses. Liquidity needs reinforce the need to emphasize minimum-risk investments. Extensive use of short-term investment-grade investments is entirely justified by the expectation that a low-inflation environment will exist indefinitely into the future. For these reasons, investments will emphasize U.S. Treasury bills and notes, intermediate-term investment-grade corporate debt, and select "blue chip" stocks with assured dividend distributions and minimal price fluctuations.

To assist in a discussion of investment policy, Mesa presents four model portfolios used by BigBanc; Exhibit P-7 applies the bank's long-term forecasts for asset class returns to each portfolio.

Exhibit P-7: BigBanc Model Portfolios

				Portfolio		
Asset Class	Total Return	Yield	A	B	C	D
U.S. large-cap stocks	13.0%	3.0%	0%	35%	45%	0%
U.S. small-cap stocks	15.0%	1.0%	0%	5%	15%	0%
Non-U.S. stocks	14.0%	1.5%	0%	10%	15%	10%
U.S. corporate bonds (AA)	6.5%	6.5%	80%	20%	0%	30%
U.S. Treasury Notes	6.0%	6.0%	0%	10%	5%	20%
Non-U.S. government bonds	6.5%	6.5%	0%	5%	5%	0%
Municipal bonds (AA)*	4.0%	4.0%	0%	10%	0%	10%
Venture capital	20.0%	0.0%	0%	0%	10%	25%
U.S. Treasury Bills	4.0%	4.0%	20%	5%	5%	5%
Total			100%	100%	100%	100%
After-tax expected return			4.2%	7.5%	13.0%	6.4%
Sharpe ratio			0.35	0.50	0.45	0.45
After-tax yield			4.2%	2.9%	1.9%	3.3%
Expected inflation: 3.0%						

* Tax-exempt

A. Prepare and justify an alternative investment policy statement for the Smiths' Family Portfolio.

B. Describe how your IPS addresses three specific deficiencies in the WFC investment policy statement.

C. Recommend a portfolio from Exhibit P-7 for the Family Portfolio. Justify your recommendation with specific reference to:

   i. three portfolio characteristics in Exhibit P-7 other than expected return or yield; and

   ii. the Smiths' return objectives. Show your calculations.

Question 13, 2008 Level 3 curriculum, volume 2, page 206.

13. **[Adapted from the 2004 CFA Level III Examination]**

Louise and Christopher Maclin live in London, United Kingdom, and currently rent an apartment in the metropolitan area. Christopher Maclin, aged 40, is a supervisor at Barnett Co. and earns an annual salary of £80,000 before taxes. Louise Maclin, aged 38, stays home to care for their newborn twins. She recently inherited £900,000 (after wealth-transfer taxes) in cash from her father's estate. In addition, the Maclins have accumulated the following assets (current market value):

- £5,000 in cash
- £160,000 in stocks and bonds
- £220,000 in Barnett common stock

The value of their holdings in Barnett stock has appreciated substantially as a result of the company's growth in sales and profits during the past ten years. Christopher Maclin is confident that the company and its stock will continue to perform well.

The Maclins need £30,000 for a down payment on the purchase of a house and plan to make a £20,000 non-tax deductible donation to a local charity in memory of Louise Maclin's father. The Maclins' annual living expenses are £74,000. After-tax salary increases will offset any future increases in their living expenses.

During discussions with their financial advisor, Grant Webb, the Maclins express concern about achieving their educational goals for their children and their own retirement goals. The Maclins tell Webb:

- They want to have sufficient funds to retire in 18 years when their children begin their four years of university education.
- They have been unhappy with the portfolio volatility they have experienced in recent years. They state that they do not want to experience a loss in portfolio value greater than 12 percent in any one year.
- They do not want to invest in alcohol and tobacco stocks.
- They will not have any additional children.

After their discussions, Webb calculates that in 18 years the Maclins will need £2 million to meet their educational and retirement goals. Webb suggests that their portfolio be structured to limit **shortfall risk** (defined as expected total return minus two standard deviations) to no lower than a negative 12 percent return in any one year. Maclin's salary and all capital gains and investment income are taxed at 40 percent and no tax-sheltering strategies are available. Webb's next step is to formulate an investment policy statement for the Maclins.

A. i. Formulate the risk objective of an investment policy statement for the Maclins.

    ii. Formulate the return objective of an investment policy statement for the Maclins. Calculate the pre-tax rate of return that is required to achieve this objective. Show your calculations.

B. Formulate the constraints portion of an investment policy statement for the Maclins, addressing *each* of the following:

    i. time horizon

    ii. liquidity requirements

    iii. tax concerns

    iv. unique circumstances

    Note: Your response to Part B should not address legal and regulatory factors.

Study Session 5

QUESTION 4 (2006) HAS FOUR PARTS FOR A TOTAL OF 24 MINUTES.

4.   American Cruise Lines (ACL) is a leading global cruise ship company
     with few major competitors and a market capitalization of $10 billion. The
     assets of the ACL Defined Benefit Pension Plan (ACLP) have a current
     market value of $100 million. Using a 5% discount rate (the current yield
     to maturity on a long-term U.S. Treasury bond), ACLP's actuary calculates
     the value of its Projected Benefit Obligation to be approximately $100
     million with a duration of 15 years. ACLP has an early retirement feature
     which includes annuity and lump sum pay-out options for long-term
     employees over 50 years old. Few employees are currently planning to
     retire early. ACLP is directed and managed by an independent investment
     committee that is subject to a fiduciary obligation to act in the best interests
     of its beneficiaries. ACLP's investment committee has recruited Emily
     Wilson, CFA, to manage ACLP's investment portfolio. Wilson conducts
     research on ACL and concludes the company is financially sound with a
     stable workforce. Compared to the averages for the cruise industry, ACL
     has a lower debt/equity ratio and a higher return on equity. Wilson prepares
     Exhibit 1 which summarizes the workforce characteristics of ACL and the
     cruise industry.

Exhibit 1: Comparison of ACL and the Cruise Industry

Workforce Characteristics	ACL Cruise	Industry Average
Average age of active employees	33 years old	40 years old
Active long-term employees over age 50	14%	17%
Active employees/Retired employees	85%/15%	90%/10%

Wilson meets separately with ACLP's investment committee and with
ACLP's President John Johnson to listen to their ideas on ACLP's
investments. Investment Committee: "Our investment objective is to build
a pension surplus in ACLP by setting a return objective that is 200 basis
points above ACLP's minimum required return. We have determined that
this investment objective is consistent with ACLP's current risk tolerance."
Johnson: "In today's environment, ACLP should be able to produce returns
of at least 10% per year. In addition, according to industry analysts, the
increasing popularity of cruises should translate into increased growth and
profitability for the cruise industry over the next 10 to 15 years. The
investment committee should increase ACLP's investment in cruise
industry equities from its current level of 10% to at least 15% of plan
assets."

Wilson's first task is to draft an ACLP investment policy statement (IPS) to present to its investment committee.

A. **Formulate** the return objective of an IPS for the American Cruise Line's Defined Benefit Pension Plan (ACLP). **Show** your calculation.

(3 minutes)

B. **Indicate** whether ACLP has a below-average, average, or above-average ability to take risk compared with the average for the cruise industry with respect to *each* of the following risk factors:
    i.   Sponsor financial status and profitability
    ii. Workforce age
    iii. Retired employees

Justify *each* response with *one* reason.

(9 minutes)

Answer Question 4-B in the Template provided.

Risk factor	Indicate whether ACLP has a below-average, average, or above average ability to take risk compared with the average for the cruise industry with respect to *each* of the following risk factors (circle one)	Justify *each* response with *one* reason.
i. Sponsor financial status and profitability	Below average Average Above average	
ii. Workforce age	Below average Average Above average	
iii. Retired employees	Below average Average Above average	

C.   **Indicate** whether *each* of the following factors increases, leaves unchanged, or decreases ACLP's ability to take risk:
   i.   Sponsor (ACL) and pension fund (ACLP) common risk exposures
   ii. Retirement plan features

Justify *each* response with *one* reason.

(6 minutes)

Answer Question 4-C in the Template provided.

Factor	Indicate whether *each* of the following factors increases, leaves unchanged, or decreases ACLP's ability to take risk (circle one)	Justify *each* response with *one* reason
i. Sponsor (ACL) and pension fund (ACLP) common risk exposures	Increases Leaves unchanged Decreases	
ii. Retirement plan features	Increases Leaves unchanged Decreases	

D.   **Formulate** *each* of the following constraints in ACLP's investment policy statement:
   i.   Liquidity requirement
   ii. Time horizon

Justify *each* response with *one* reason.

Note: Your answer should specifically address ACLP's circumstances.

(6 minutes)

Answer Question 4-D in the Template provided.

Constraint	**Formulate** *each* of the following constraints in **ACLP's investment policy statement. Justify** *each* response with *one* reason. Note: Your answer should specifically address ACLP's circumstances.
i. Liquidity requirement	
ii. Time horizon	

QUESTION 6 (2006) HAS ONE PART FOR A TOTAL OF 12 MINUTES.

6. Vrieland Foundation is an independent foundation with the objective to fund children's music education programs. Sophie Arnold is interviewing for the position of portfolio manager at Vrieland. Arnold previously managed her former employer's defined benefit pension plan.

   During her interview, Arnold makes the following statements:

   "The sole return objective of both Vrieland and a defined benefit pension plan is to maintain purchasing power."

   "Vrieland, unlike a defined benefit pension plan, does not need to consider the correlation between plan sponsor financial performance and the performance of the portfolio."

   "Like a defined benefit pension plan, the liquidity needs of Vrieland fluctuate over time."

   "The primary objective of both Vrieland and a defined benefit pension plan is to exist in perpetuity, resulting in an infinite investment time horizon."

   Determine whether you agree or disagree with *each* of the four statements made by Arnold. If you disagree, **support** your opinion with *one* reason related to portfolio management.

   Note: Supporting your opinion by simply reversing an incorrect statement will receive no credit.

Answer Question 6 in the Template provided.

Template for Question 6

Statement	Determine whether you agree or disagree with *each* of the four statements made by Arnold (circle one)	If you disagree, support your opinion with *one* reason related to portfolio management Note: Supporting your opinion by simply reversing an incorrect statement will receive no credit.
"The sole return objective of both Vrieland and a defined benefit pension plan is to maintain purchasing power."	Agree Disagree	
"Vrieland, unlike a defined benefit pension plan, does not need to consider the correlation between plan sponsor financial performance and the performance of the portfolio."	Agree Disagree	
"Like a defined benefit pension plan, the liquidity needs of Vrieland fluctuate over time."	Agree Disagree	
"The primary objective of both Vrieland and a defined benefit pension plan is to exist in perpetuity, resulting in an infinite investment time horizon."	Agree Disagree	

QUESTION 1 (2005) HAS THREE PARTS FOR A TOTAL OF 18 MINUTES.

1. Jonathan Fiertz is a U.K.-based investment manager whose institutional clients include a defined benefit pension plan sponsored by British Chemical Plc (BC Plc), a mature U.K.-based multinational firm. The BC Plc defined benefit pension plan is not available to new employees, who are only eligible to participate in a recently established defined contribution scheme. Fiertz is aware that the pension plan has experienced a declining ratio of plan assets to plan liabilities, and he has decided to compare workforce, pension plan, and company information for BC Plc with similar information for an average company in the FTSE 350 Index; his comparison is given in Exhibit 1-1.

Exhibit 1-1: BC Plc Comparison with Average FTSE 350 Company Workforce, Pension Plan, and Company Information

	Workforce Information		Pension Plan Information		Company Information	
	Average Age (years)	*Average Service (years)*	*Ratio of Plan Assets to Plan Liabilities*	*Ratio of Retired Lives to Active Lives Relative to Average*	*Profitability Relative to Average*	*Debt Ratio Relative to Average*
BC Plc	48	24	0.83	Higher	Lower	Higher
Average FTSE 350 Company	43	17	0.97	—	—	—

Assets and liabilities of the pension plan are legally separate from BC Plc. The pension plan is managed by a board of trustees whose duty under trust law is to act solely in the best financial interests of the beneficiaries. The pension plan portfolio is invested in U.K. gilts (bonds) and U.K. equities. Dividends paid to the portfolio are taxable. An extended period of low interest rates and weak equity markets has resulted in poor returns recently.

For actuarial purposes, the assumed long-term rate of return on plan assets is 8% annually and the current discount rate applied to the plan liabilities is 7%.

The trustees have asked Fiertz to examine the pension plan's current investment policy statement. They are particularly concerned about the plan's risk tolerance and two of the plan's constraints: the liquidity requirement and the time horizon. The trustees have also asked Fiertz to evaluate the plan's actuarial assumptions.

A.   **Judge** whether the BC Plc pension plan has below average, average, or above average risk tolerance compared with the average FTSE 350 company pension plan. **Support** your response with *four* reasons based on the specific circumstances of BC Plc and/or the BC Plc pension plan.

(9 minutes)

B.   **Characterize**, for the BC Plc pension plan relative to the average FTSE 350 company pension plan, *each* of the two plan constraints of concern to the trustees:
i.   Liquidity requirement
ii.   Time horizon

Justify *each* of your responses with *two* reasons.

(6 minutes)

Answer Question 1-B in the Template provided.

Constraint	Characterize, for the BC Plc pension plan relative to the average FTSE 350 company pension plan, *each* of the two plan constraints of concern to the trustees (circle one)	Justify *each* of your responses with *two* reasons
i. Liquidity requirement	Lower Similar Higher	
ii. Time horizon	Shorter Similar Larger	

©2008 Schweser

C.   **Judge** whether a change to 6% in the discount rate applied to the plan liabilities would cause the funded status of the BC Plc pension plan to deteriorate or improve, given that the assumed long-term rate of return on plan assets remains unchanged. **Support** your response with specific reference to the BC Plc pension plan.

(3 minutes)

Question 2, 2008 Level 3 Curriculum, Volume 2, page 371.

2. **[Adapted from the 2000 CFA Level III Examination]**

Light Speed Connections:

Hugh Donovan is chief financial officer of Lightspeed Connections (LSC), a rapidly growing U.S. technology company with a traditional defined-benefit pension plan. Because of LSC's young workforce, Donovan believes the pension plan has no liquidity needs and can thus invest aggressively to maximize returns. He also believes that U.S. Treasury bills and bonds, yielding 5.4 percent and 6.1 percent, respectively, have no place in a portfolio with such a long time horizon. His strategy, which has produced excellent returns for the past two years, has been to invest the portfolio as follows:

- 50 percent in a concentrated pool (15 to 20 stocks) of initial public offerings in technology and Internet companies, managed internally by Donovan;
- 25 percent in a small-capitalization growth fund;
- 10 percent in a **venture capital fund**;
- 10 percent in an S&P 500 index fund; and
- 5 percent in an international equity fund.

Working with LSC's Investment Committee, the firm's president, Eileen Jeffries has produced a formal investment policy statement, which reads as follows:

"The LSC Pension Plan's return objective should focus on real total returns that will fund its long-term obligations on an inflation-adjusted basis. The "time-to-maturity" of the corporate workforce is a key element for any defined pension plan; given our young workforce, LSC's Plan has a long investment horizon and more time available for wealth compounding to occur. Therefore, the Plan can pursue an aggressive investment strategy and focus on the higher return potential of capital growth. Under present U.S. tax laws, pension portfolio income and capital gains are not taxed. The portfolio should focus primarily on investments in businesses directly related to our main business to leverage our knowledge base."

A.   Evaluate Donovan's investment strategy with respect to its effect on each of the following:

i.   LSC's pension plan beneficiaries

ii.   Managing pension assets in relation to LSC's corporate strength

B.   Evaluate LSC's investment policy statement in the context of the following:

i.   Return requirement.

ii.   Risk tolerance

iii. Time horizon

iv.   Liquidity

Question 4, 2008 Level 3 Curriculum, Volume 2, page 373.

4.   **[Adapted from the 1994 CFA Level III Examination]**

Food Processors, Inc.:

Food Processors Inc. (FPI) is a mature U.S. company with declining earnings and a weak balance sheet. Its defined-benefit pension plan (which is subject to ERISA) has total assets of $750 million. The plan is underfunded by $200 million by U.S. standards-a cause for concern by shareholders, management, and the board of directors.

The average age of plan participants is 45 years. FPI's annual contribution to the plan and the earnings on its assets are sufficient to meet pension payments to present retirees. The pension portfolio's holdings are equally divided between large-capitalization U.S. equities and high-quality, long-maturity U.S. corporate bonds. For the purpose of determining FPI's contribution to the pension plan, the assumed long-term rate of return on plan assets is 9 percent per year; the discount rate applied to determine the present value of plan liabilities, all of which are U.S.-based, is 8 percent. As FPI's Treasurer, you are responsible for oversight of the plan's investments and managers and for liaison with the board's Pension Investment Committee.

At the committee's last meeting, its chair observed that both U.S. stocks and U.S. bonds had recorded total returns in excess of 12 percent per year over the past decade. He then made a pointed comment: "Given this experience, we seem to be overly conservative in using only a 9 percent future return assumption. Why don't we raise the rate to 10 percent? This would be consistent with the recent record, would help our earnings, and should make the stockholders feel a lot better."

Exhibit P-4 Capital Markets Data

Asset Class 2000	Total Return 1929–1993	Total Return 1984–1993	Annualized Monthly Standard Deviation 1984–1993	Consensus Forecast Total Return 1994–2004
U.S. Treasury bills	3.7%	6.4%	2.2%	3.5%
Intermediate-term Treasury bonds	5.3%	11.4%	5.6%	5.0%
Long-term Treasury bonds	5.0%	14.4%	11.7%	6.0% ~
U.S. corporate bonds (AAA rated)	5.6%	14.0%	8.9%	6.5%
U.S. common stocks (S&P 500)	9.5%	14.9%	18.0%	8.5%
U.S. inflation rate (annual rate)	3.2%	5.5%	N/A	3.3%

You have been directed to examine the situation and prepare a recommendation for next week's committee meeting. Your assistant has provided you with the background information shown in Exhibit P-4.

Assume that consensus forecast total returns for bonds are at least approximately equal to the bonds' yields.

A. Explain what is meant when a pension plan is said to be "underfunded" and use FPI to illustrate.

B. Discuss the risk-return dilemma that FPI faces.

C. Explain a rationale for reducing the discount rate from its current level of 8 percent.

D. Explain how the underfunded condition of FPI's plan would be affected if the discount rate were reduced to 7 percent from the current 8 percent.

Question 5, 2008 Level 3 Curriculum, Volume 2, page 374.

5.   **[Adapted from the 1993 CFA Level III Examination]**

Medical Research Foundation:

The Medical Research Foundation (MRF), based in the United States, was established to provide grants in perpetuity. MRF has just received word that the foundation will receive a $45 million cash gift three months from now. The gift will greatly increase the size of the foundation's endowment from its current $10 million. The foundation's grant-making (spending) policy has been to pay out virtually all of its annual net investment income. Because its investment approach has been conservative, the endowment portfolio now consists almost entirely of fixed-income assets. The finance committee understands that these actions are causing the real value of foundation assets and the real value of future grants to decline because of inflation effects. Until now, the finance committee believed it had no alternative to these actions, given the large immediate cash needs of the research programs being funded and the small size of the foundation's capital base. The foundation's annual grants must at least equal 5 percent of its assets' market value to maintain MRF's U.S. tax-exempt status, a requirement that is expected to continue indefinitely. The foundation anticipates no additional gifts or fund raising activity for the foreseeable future.

Given the change in circumstances that the cash gift will make, the finance committee wishes to develop new grant-making and investment policies. Annual spending must at least meet the 5 percent of market value requirement, but the committee is unsure how much higher spending can or should be. The committee wants to pay out as much as possible because of the critical nature of the research being funded; however, it understands that preserving the real value of the foundation's assets is equally important in order to preserve its future grant-making capabilities. You have been asked to assist the committee in developing appropriate policies.

A.   Identify and discuss the three key elements that should determine the foundation's grant-making (spending) policy.

B.   Formulate and justify an investment policy statement for the foundation.

Question 6, 2008 Level 3 Curriculum, Volume 2, page 374.

6.   **[Adapted from the 1998 CFA Level III Examination]**

James Children's Hospital:

The James Children's Hospital (JCH), based in Washington, DC, has an operating budget of $15 million and has been operating at a budget surplus for the last two years. JCH has a $20 million endowment (JCHE) whose sole purpose is to provide capital equipment for the hospital. The endowment's long-term expected total return is 8.6%, which includes a 3.3% income component. JCHE has no minimum payout requirement and expects no future contributions. Traditionally, the JCHE board of directors has determined the annual payout based on current needs. Payouts have been rising steadily-to $1,375,000 two years ago and to $1,400,000 last year.

Michelle Parker, chief financial officer of JCHE, has asked the board's guidance in establishing a long-term spending policy for JCHE. She has received $1,600,000 in requests to buy equipment and is concerned about the inflation rate for medical equipment prices, which is 4%, versus 2.5% for the U.S. Consumer Price Index.

A.   Discuss the implications of the current pressure on JCHE to increase spending.

B.   Discuss how JCHE's time horizon affects its risk tolerance.

C.   Determine a long-term spending policy for JCHE, including a spending rate as a percentage of assets, and justify the policy.

Question 7, 2008 Level 3 Curriculum, Volume 2, page 375.

7. **[Adapted from the 2000 CFA Level III Examination]**

    Donner Life:

    Susan Leighton, treasurer for U.S.-based Donner Life Insurance, has just joined the board of a charitable organization that has a large endowment portfolio. She is researching how the investment policy for an endowment differs from that of life insurance companies and has thus far reached the following conclusions:

    1. Both endowments and life insurance companies have aggressive return requirements.

    2. Endowments are less willing to assume risk than life insurance companies because of donor concerns about volatility and loss of principal.

    3. Endowments are less able to assume risk than life insurance companies because of expectations that endowments should provide stable funding for charitable operations.

    4. Endowments have lower liquidity requirements than life insurance companies because endowment spending needs are met through a combination of current income and capital appreciation.

    5. Both endowments and life insurance companies are subject to stringent legal and regulatory oversight.

        Evaluate each of Leighton's statements in terms of accuracy and justify your conclusions.

Study Session 7

QUESTION 5 (2006) HAS TWO PARTS FOR A TOTAL OF 10 MINUTES.

5.   Several years have passed. American Cruise Line's Defined Benefit
      Pension Plan (ACLP) now has $200 million in assets and has a funding
      surplus due to the successful execution of the policies adopted by ACLP's
      investment committee.

      American Cruise Lines (ACL) has experienced a decline in sales related to
      a sustained downturn in travel. The company is now faced with material
      restructuring expenses. As part of the restructuring, ACLP will be required
      to make lump-sum payments averaging $200,000 to each of 100 retiring
      employees over the next 12 months. Because of these changes and
      considering current market conditions, the investment committee adopts
      the following policy objectives:
      - a return requirement of 8.5%.
      - a shortfall risk objective of –8.0%. Shortfall risk is defined as the
        portfolio expected return minus two standard deviations.
      - match assets and liabilities in the short and long term.
      - reduce exposure to equities highly correlated with the plan sponsor.

      Emily Wilson, CFA, is instructed to reassess the portfolio's asset allocation
      and recommend any necessary changes. Wilson's analysis results in the
      asset allocation alternatives shown in Exhibit 1.

Exhibit 1 - Alternative Asset Allocations and Return/Risk Measures

Asset Class	Portfolio Allocations (%)				
	A	B	C	D	E
Cash equivalents	3	10	4	10	5
Global fixed income	45	30	40	35	35
U.S. equities	17	30	16	35	30
Non-U.S. equities	15	15	20	10	15
Cruise industry equities	15	5	0	0	0
Real estate	5	10	20	10	15
Total	100	100	100	100	100

Portfolio Measures	Return and Risk Measure (%)				
	A	B	C	D	E
Expected total return	9.25	9.06	8.59	9.04	9.07
Expected standard deviation	8.43	8.83	7.83	8.19	8.57

Wilson notes that all the portfolios have an expected return that meets the policy objectives of ACLP. She is considering other reasons for making her selection.

A. **Select** the *most* appropriate portfolio for ACLP. **Discuss** how the selected portfolio satisfies *two* investment committee policy objectives, other than meeting the return requirement.

(6 minutes)

B. **State**, for *each* of the four portfolios not selected, *one* reason why it is *not* the most appropriate.

(4 minutes)

QUESTION 7 (2006) HAS THREE PARTS FOR A TOTAL OF 9 MINUTES.

7.   Hartej Chanrai is a consultant to the board of directors of Vrieland Foundation. The board asks Chanrai to recommend an asset allocation for Vrieland. Chanrai reviews the current Vrieland investment policy statement, key aspects of which are shown in Exhibit 1.

Exhibit 1: Vrieland Foundation Key Aspects of Investment Policy Statement

Return objective:

The required rate of return on the investment portfolio is 9.5%.

Risk objectives:

1.   Diversify the portfolio consistent with prudent investment practices.

2.   A maximum standard deviation of portfolio returns of 10.6% is acceptable.

Constraint: Liquidity is needed to fund the annual contribution to the operating budget. (There are no other relevant constraints.)

For the strategic asset allocation analysis, Chanrai has generated the corner portfolios shown in Exhibit 2.

Exhibit 2 - Corner Portfolios (Risk-free Rate = 4.0%)

Corner Portfolio Number	Expected Return (%)	Expected Standard Deviation (%)	Sharpe Ratio	Asset Classes (Portfolio Weights, in %)					
				U.S. Equities	Non-U.S. Equities	Long-term U.S. Bonds	Intermediate-term U.S. Bonds	Non-U.S. Bonds	Real Estate
1	10.8	16.1	0.42	100.0	0.0	0.0	0.0	0.0	0.0
2	10.4	14.2	0.45	82.4	0.0	0.0	0.0	0.0	17.6
3	10.3	13.6	0.46	74.1	4.0	0.0	0.0	0.0	21.9
4	9.1	9.1	0.55	33.7	12.0	36.7	0.0	0.0	17.6
5	8.9	8.7	0.56	31.4	12.0	26.7	13.0	0.0	16.9
6	8.5	7.4	0.60	25.0	11.8	0.0	45.3	3.4	14.5
7	7.3	5.2	0.62	0.0	13.7	0.0	53.0	27.1	6.2
8	7.2	5.1	0.61	0.0	11.2	0.0	53.0	31.5	4.3

Answer Parts A, B, and C using mean-variance analysis:

A.   **Select** the two adjacent corner portfolios to be used in finding the most appropriate strategic asset allocation for Vrieland's investment portfolio, assuming that the purchase of securities using borrowed money (margin) is not allowed.

(3 minutes)

B.   **Determine** the most appropriate strategic asset allocation between the two adjacent corner portfolios selected in Part A, assuming that the purchase of securities using borrowed money (margin) is not allowed.

(3 minutes)

C.   **Determine** the percentage amount of the most appropriate strategic asset allocation (determined in Part B) that should be invested in U.S. equities.

(3 minutes)

QUESTION 3 (2005) HAS TWO PARTS FOR A TOTAL OF 9 MINUTES.

3.   The Lourie Foundation is also an institutional client of Jonathan Fiertz. Lourie is a small U.K.-based philanthropic organization whose stated goal is to enrich the lives of disadvantaged children. Fiertz has developed an investment policy statement for Lourie, whose risk tolerance and return requirement are summarized in Exhibit 3-1.

Exhibit 3-1 - Lourie Foundation - Risk Tolerance and Return Requirement

Risk Tolerance:	Above average (maximum 15% annual standard deviation of returns).
Return Requirement:	To earn an average annual return to meet a spending rate of 7.5% (including expected inflation) and management/administration fees of 0.6%.

To help Lourie's directors assess the appropriate strategic asset allocation for Lourie's portfolio, Fiertz has prepared Exhibit 3-2, which describes eight corner portfolios and a risk-free portfolio.

Exhibit 3-2: Lourie Foundation Corner Portfolios

Corner Portfolio	Portfolio Weights					Expected Return (%)	Expected Standard Deviation (%)	Sharpe Ratio
	U.K. Equities	Ex-U.K. Equities (%)	U.K. Intermediate-term Bonds (%)	U.K. Long-term Bonds (%)	U.K. Real Estate (%)			
1	100.0	0.0	0.0	0.0	0.0	8.9	18.0	0.272
2	76.2	23.8	0.0	0.0	0.0	8.7	16.8	0.280
3	64.6	24.0	0.0	0.0	11.4	8.5	16.0	0.281
4	55.6	22.6	0.0	9.5	12.3	8.2	14.9	0.282
5	53.2	24.7	13.3	0.0	8.8	8.0	14.1	0.284
6	32.6	26.2	41.2	0.0	0.0	7.1	11.0	0.282
7	0.0	24.8	75.2	0.0	0.0	5.7	7.7	0.221
8	0.0	15.5	84.5	0.0	0.0	5.5	7.5	0.200

Note: A risk-free portfolio is available and is expected to return 4%.

Lourie's charter prohibits short positions or the use of margin, but allows investment in any portfolio, or combination of portfolios, described in Exhibit 3-2. In addition to satisfying the risk tolerance and return requirement, Lourie's directors consider the Sharpe ratio to be a dominant factor in asset allocation decisions.

A.   Using mean-variance analysis:

i. Select the portfolios to be combined in the optimal strategic asset allocation for the Lourie Foundation. Justify your response with one reason other than meeting Lourie's return requirement.

ii. Determine the appropriate portfolio weights for U.K. equities and U.K. intermediate-term bonds in the optimal strategic asset allocation.

(6 minutes)

One of Lourie's directors asks Fiertz about the sensitivity of the strategic asset allocation to changes in key variables: "How would the strategic asset allocation change, for instance, if the return requirement for the endowment, including expected inflation and management/administration fees, was only 6% and the endowment's risk tolerance was consistent with a maximum 12% annual standard deviation of returns?"

B.   Select, using mean-variance analysis, the portfolios to be combined in a new strategic asset allocation based on the information in the director's question. Justify your response with specific reference to the tangency portfolio.

(3 minutes)

LEVEL 3 OLD QUESTION REVIEW ANSWERS (FROM PREVIOUS CFA EXAMS)

Study Session 3

Question 10 (2005) Answer:

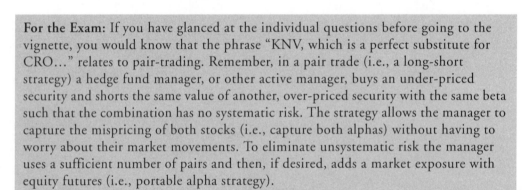

Professor's Note: Irrational investors are also known as "noise traders," because of the noise they produce in the capital markets. They base trades on non-fundamental factors, and their irrational trading can cause a stock's price to vary from its intrinsic value. When a stock varies from its intrinsic value, the astute manager can capitalize on the mispricing by taking the appropriate position (i.e., short if overpriced; buy if underpriced). When the mispricing is caused by noise traders, however, the stock may only very slowly return to its intrinsic value; it may move farther away from its intrinsic value; or it may never get back to its intrinsic value. That is, noise traders can make it very difficult for the manager to capture the mispricing.

For the Exam: If you have glanced at the individual questions before going to the vignette, you would know that the phrase "KNV, which is a perfect substitute for CRO…" relates to pair-trading. Remember, in a pair trade (i.e., a long-short strategy) a hedge fund manager, or other active manager, buys an under-priced security and shorts the same value of another, over-priced security with the same beta such that the combination has no systematic risk. The strategy allows the manager to capture the mispricing of both stocks (i.e., capture both alphas) without having to worry about their market movements. To eliminate unsystematic risk the manager uses a sufficient number of pairs and then, if desired, adds a market exposure with equity futures (i.e., portable alpha strategy).

Since neither Lavinsky nor Blake holds a significant number of pairs, both of their strategies are exposed to the unsystematic risks of the individual stocks. If the individual stocks are not perfect substitutes, they can be affected by firm-specific news and move independently of one another. If they are perfect substitutes, we can assume that they have the same beta and are not subject to different unsystematic factors. That is, they have the same macro- and microeconomic risk exposures and, when priced correctly, will always move together.

10.   Both Lavinsky and Blake face noise trader risk. Noise trader risk arises from the possibility that the mispricing being exploited worsens in the short run.

For Lavinsky, the risk is that the investors who have depressed the price of CRO will become even more pessimistic about CRO, worsening the undervaluation in the short run. Or, conversely, investors become irrationally optimistic about ATL.

For Blake, the risk is that, even though KNV is a perfect substitute for CRO, the investors who have caused KNV to trade at a discount relative to CRO become even more pessimistic about KNV, further widening the discount. Or conversely, investors in CRO become less irrationally pessimistic.

Part B

Lavinsky, but not Blake, faces fundamental risk. Fundamental risk arises from the possibility that, when securities are imperfect substitutes, additional relevant information/news will adversely effect a position.

Lavinsky's position involving ATL and CRO protects Lavinsky somewhat from adverse news about the airline industry as a whole. ATL is an imperfect substitute for CRO, however, so he still faces the risk associated with his position being vulnerable to news that is specific to ATL or CRO. In particular, adverse news about only CRO, or positive news about only ATL, may result in smaller profits or even losses from his position. Blake's position involves two securities that are perfect substitutes.

Part C

An opportunity to exploit a mispricing does NOT exist, because the implementation costs (110 bps*) of exploiting the mispricing exceed the 1% (100 bps) divergence that now exists between CRO and KNV.

*35 bps each for taking positions in CRO and KNV = 70 bps, plus 40 bps for borrowing CRO stock to short, for a total implementation cost of 110 bps

Study Session 4

Question 1 (2006) Answer:

> **For the Exam:** The questions in this case follow very closely the patterns established in 2005. Note first that you are asked to formulate Serra's return objective. Don't be afraid to simply list his required objectives as presented in the case.* Then you are asked to calculate his required return over his first year of retirement. In other words, rather than calculating the required return over the first time horizon, you are asked for the return during a very specific year.
>
> In calculating the required return, you can readily detect the pattern that must be followed: calculate the value of the portfolio at the beginning of the year and the required expenses for the year. The required return is just the ratio of the two.
>
> * You will notice that Serra's stated return objective is almost generic. With the possible exception of the family support payments, his return objective would be applicable to just about anyone.

1. **Part A**

    i. Return Objective: The return objective for Serra's portfolio is to earn a total rate of return on an after-tax basis that maintains the real value of his portfolio, and supports his annual living and family support expenses during retirement.

    ii. Calculation of after-tax nominal rate of return that is required at age 35:

Year	0 (year before retirement)	1 (first year of retirement)
Age at beginning of year	34	35
Inflows		
Salary	€5,000,000	
Interest income from cash savings (after-tax)	100,000	
Growth equity portfolio (after-tax)*	3,400,000	
Total Inflows	€8,500,000	
Outflows		
Income tax (@40%)*	€2,000,000	
Living Expenses+	1,200,000	€1,248,000
Family support payments+	800,000	832,000
Purchase of personal home	4,500,000	0
Total Outflows	€8,500,000	€2,080,000
Net Inflows/(Outflows)	0	€(2,080,000)

> **For the Exam:** If this figure is positive (i.e., inflows > outflows), the excess is added to the ending value of Serra's portfolio. If negative, it reduces the ending value of the portfolio.

Notes:

* Growth equity portfolio: €40,000,000 ×8.5%

× Income tax: €5,000,000 × 40%

+ Living and family support expenses adjusted for 4% inflation

Investable Assets at age 34	
Cash savings (beginning year 0)	€4,000,000
Growth equity portfolio (beginning year 0)	40,000,000
Total investable assets (beginning of year 0)	€44,000,000
Add: Net cash flows during age 35 year 0	0
Total investable assets (at retirement)	€44,000,000

For the Exam: Here we determined Serra's total portfolio at the beginning of his first year of retirement. Note the line where you would add/subtract the net inflow or outflow from the previous year, which was calculated above.

Outflows during first year of retirement	**€2,080,000**
Required after-tax real rate of return = 2,080,000/44,000,000	4.73%
Add: Inflation rate	4.00%
Required after-tax nominal rate of return	8.73%

Note: Real estate assets will not generate cash flow in the current year and are not investable due to the pledge to children's welfare foundation.

Personal home is not included in investable assets.

Required after-tax nominal rate of return = 8.73% [4.73%+4.00] (arithmetic)
Required after-tax nominal rate of return = 8.92% [(1.0473) (1.04)−1] (geometric)

Part B

Template for Question 1-B

Identify *two* factors in Serra's personal situation that increase his ability to take risk

The following factors could act to increase Serra's ability to take risk:
- He has a long time horizon and thus more ability to recover from any intermediate investment shortfalls.
- He has investable assets that are more than sufficient to cover his retirement objectives.
- He could pursue a second career or pursue endorsement deals.
- He could reduce his living expenses.

Identify *two* factors in Serra's personal situation that decrease his ability to take risk.

The following factors could act to decrease Serra's ability to take risk:
- His only source of income is his investment portfolio.
- He desires to maintain the real value of the portfolio.
- He could decide to increase his spending needs during retirement.
- He is at the peak of his career and earnings power. He is unlikely to be able to achieve comparable earnings power in the future.

For the Exam: Notice that only the first two factors in each case are actually from the vignette. You should also note that Serra's willingness to tolerate risk is not addressed in the question or the guideline answer and that, in judging his overall ability to tolerate risk, his wealth is the determining factor.

Judge, considering all factors, whether Serra has below-average, average, or above-average ability to take risk (circle one)

Below-average   Average   **Above Average**

Part C

Constraint	Formulate *each* of the following constraints in Serra's investment policy statement. Support *each* response with *one* reason based on Serra's specific circumstances.
i. Liquidity requirement	Serra's portfolio is required to provide sufficient liquidity to meet near-term spending needs during retirement. Liquidity is required for the following: • Annual family support payments • Ongoing living expenses during retirement • One-time liquidity need for house purchase

For the Exam: Under liquidity requirement, list only those expenses and other cash flows that must be met by the portfolio. For example, in some cases the client's salary covers a portion of his living expenses, and the portfolio must cover the remaining expenses. Only the expenses covered by the portfolio would be listed.

ii. Time horizon	Serra's time horizon is basically long-term but consists of two stages. This formulation is justified by the following: • The first stage consists of Serra's initial 10 years in retirement until he reaches age 45, when he stops making family support payments. • The second stage encompasses the rest of his time in retirement, which could be 30 years or more according to Serra's mortality expectations.

For the Exam: In this case, since Serra will have already retired, his time line is broken into two segments by the cessation of the family support payments. A common scenario for a morning case involves a client who is not retired. In that case, the client will have at least two stages: pre-retirement years and retirement years. Whether either of those two stages is further broken down will depend upon whether there are any events significant enough to cause the IPS to change along with a possible reallocation of the portfolio. With Serra, that event involved the family support payments.

Question 2 (2006) Answer:

2. **Part A**

Professor's Note: An asset-only approach focuses on maximizing the future value of the portfolio within stated risk parameters. We typically think of ALM approaches as being better suited to institutional investors. When an individual's spending needs are stated in monetary terms, however, an ALM approach will provide a better focus on meeting them.

By taking Kennedy's future liabilities and/or quasi-liabilities into account, the asset-liability approach controls risk better than the asset-only method by providing an asset allocation that (1) meets her retirement spending needs and (2) focuses on not outliving her assets.

Part B

Professor's Note: Monte Carlo simulation continues to receive considerable attention in the Level 3 curriculum.

The Monte Carlo simulation takes into account the cash flows into and out of the portfolio over time while standard mean–variance analysis does not. Because investment returns can vary significantly from year to year, the timing of these inflows and outflows can create major differences in the final result. In a situation where there will be varying cash flows over the investment period, the ending value of the portfolio is path dependent. (The sequence of the returns and the sequence of the changes in liabilities can be considered in a Monte Carlo simulation, demonstrating the probable range of results. Multiple scenarios can be considered.)

Part C

Moderate Portfolio. The foremost objective of the portfolio is to have funds available to provide for the spending needs for Kennedy's 20-year planning horizon. It is not necessary to achieve the lowest level of risk or the highest return. The Moderate Portfolio is the only portfolio that gives a positive terminal value under all scenarios.

Question 7 (2005) Answer:

7.   **Part A**

Return Objective:

Yeo's return objective is to earn a total rate of return that is sufficient to maintain the real value of the portfolio, while meeting her son's educational expenses and her annual charitable contributions, as well as support her ongoing living expenses during retirement.

Calculation of after-tax nominal rate of return:

> **For the Exam:** Notice that the question again asks you to calculate the required return over a very specific year (i.e., first year of retirement). On the exam, you could be asked to calculate the return for any single year, before or during retirement. The calculation is always the same. You must determine the cash outflows (from the portfolio) over that year and the value of the portfolio at the beginning of the year.

	One year from now (retirement)	*Two years from now (end of 1st year of retirement)*
Inflows	MYR	MYR
Retirement gratuity (taxable)	450,000	—
Interest income from money market fund (taxable)[a]	30,000	—
Sale of Sawit stock (non-taxable)	8,500,000	—
Redemption of provident fund savings (tax-exempt)	500,000	—
Total inflows	9,480,000	—
Outflows		—
Income tax (28%)[b]	(134,400)	
Living and miscellaneous[c]		(257,500)
Education for Lok[d]	(150,000)	(159,000)
Donation to Malaysian charity[e]	(100,000)	(100,000)
Total outflows	(384,400)	(516,500)
Net additions/withdrawals	**MYR9,095,600**	**(MYR516,500)**

Notes:

[a] MYR1,200,000 × 0.025

[b] (MYR450,000 + MYR30,000) × 0.28. Capital gain of MYR7m (MYR8.5m − MYR1.5m) from sale of Sawit stock is not taxable

[c] Assumed to increase with inflation of 3% per year.

[d] Assumed to increase with education inflation of 6% per year (MYR150,00 × 1.06)

[e] Fixed annual donation

Investable Assets and Required Return

Investable Assets at Retirement	(MYR)
Year 0 Net Cash Flow	9,095,600
Money Market Fund	<u>1,200,000</u>
	MYR 10,295,600
Distributions in Year 1	MYR 516,500)
Required After-Tax Real Rate of Return	<u>5.0167%</u>

Note:

The Yeo's family home is their primary residence, and is not considered to be an investable asset.

Required After-Tax Real Rate of Return = 5.0167%

Plus: 3% annual inflation rate = 3.0000%

Required After-Tax Nominal Rate of Return = 8.0167%

Proof:

$10,295,600 \times (1.080167) = 11,120,968$

$11,120,968 - 516,500 = 10,604,468$

$10,604,468 / 1.03 = 10,295,600$

Alternate return calculation:

Investable Assets and Required Return

Investable Assets at Retirement	(MYR)
Year 0 Net Cash Flow	9,095,600
Money Market Fund	1,200,000
	MYR 10,295,600
Distributions in Year 1	**(MYR 516,500)**
Required After-Tax Real Rate of Return	5.0167%

$10,295,600 \times 0.03$	= 308,868 to maintain portfolio value
	<u>= 516,500 year 1 distribution</u>
	= 825,368

$825,368 / 10,295,600 = 8.0167\%$

Part B

Component	Characterize Yeo as below average, average, or above average with respect to each of the three components of the risk objective in her investment policy statement (circle one)	Justify each of your responses with one reason based on Yeo's specific circumstances and/or her interview with Hamid
i. Ability to take risk	Above average	Yeo has on above-average ability to take risk given the: 1. long expected time horizon associated with her retirement (life expectancy). 2. large asset base that she will have amassed following the sale of the stake in Sawit, which is more than sufficient to cover her financial objectives.
ii. Willingness to take risk	Below average	Yeo is strongly below average in her willingness to assume risk in her personal investments. 1. She states that she is habitually conservative when faced with decisions where the future outcome is uncertain. 2. Further evidence is provided by her holding of all cash surpluses in a low-risk, low-return asset. 3. Although she has stated a desire to maintain the real value of the investable assets, she also implies an unwillingness to sustain losses in her statement about the money market fund safeguarding her wealth. 4. She has been unwilling to take advantage of attractive personal investment opportunities because of the perceived risks.
iii. Overall risk tolerance	Below average	Yeo has below-average risk tolerance, as she is clearly very risk-averse when faced with uncertain outcomes associated with investing. Her current conservative investment preferences, both stated and implemented, outweigh her above-average ability to assume risk.

For the Exam: In this case, you are asked to determine the client's ability, willingness, and overall tolerance for risk. I recommend the following process for answering this question. First, start at "average" for ability and then look for reasons to ramp it up or down a notch. Ability is best addressed by looking at the size of the portfolio, the client's time horizon, and the liquidity requirements:

• As portfolio increases, ability increases.
• As time horizon increases, ability increases.
• As liquidity requirements* increase, ability decreases.

Generally, whenever the portfolio must meet part of the client's living expenses, you will drop ability down a notch to below average. When the client's salary covers living expenses and future goals are small relative to the portfolio, ramp ability up a notch to above average.

Willingness to tolerate risk is based on psychological characteristics. Again, start at average and look for reasons to ramp it up or drop it down. Look for statements as well as actions. For example, any reference to risk generally indicates above average aversion to risk (below average tolerance). However, if the client's statements seem to indicate significant aversion to risk, but past investment actions contradict the statements, go with the aversion indicated by the actions. Remember, actions speak louder than words!

In selecting overall tolerance, always select the more conservative of the two. For example, if willingness > ability, go with ability. If ability > willingness, go with willingness. In either case, you should also state that counseling is recommended to reconcile the difference.

> * Remember, liquidity requirements are expenditures that must be met by the portfolio.

Part C

Constraint	Formulate *each* of the following constraints in Yeo's investment policy statement	Justify *each* of your responses with one reason based on Yeo's specific circumstances and/or her interview with Hamid
i. Time horizon	Yeo's time horizon is long-term and consists of two main stages.	This formulation is justified by the following: • The first stage consists of Yeo's initial four years in retirement, which include Lok's university expenses. • The second stage encompasses the rest of her time in retirement, which could be 21 years or more according to Yeo's mortality expectations.
ii. Tax concerns	Malaysia's tax structure differentiates between ordinary income and capital gains.	Because capital gains are not taxable, there is a preference for investment returns from capital gains versus taxable interest and dividend income.

Question 8 (2005) Answer:

Asset	Recommend for Yeo the most appropriate allocation range for each of the asset classes in Exhibit 8-2 (circle one)	Justify *each* of your responses with *one* reason based on Yeo's specific circumstances
Money Market (Cash)	0% to 10%	Yeo's need for money market assets is minimal as the only liquidity need mentioned is her desire for a cash reserve of six months of living expenses. In addition, the lowest allocation to money market is justified as its return will drag down total portfolio return. NOTE: The MYR2 million donation is 10 years from now and is not a current liquidity requirement. **For the Exam:** Your exam answer: "Limit cash to six months of living expenses."
Domestic Bonds	51% to 60%	Yeo's overall risk tolerance has only increased somewhat, and it remains below average. As such, the highest allocation to bonds is most suitable. NOTE: Bonds have a lower standard deviation than equities. This will provide Yeo with lower overall volatility. While expected bond return is lower than equities, it is higher than money market. As such, bond return should contribute more to the 7% after-tax return objective than money market. **For the Exam:** Your exam answer: "Risk tolerance remains below average."
Domestic Equity-Income	0% to 10%	The lowest allocation to this asset class is recommended. *After-tax* expected return is lower than domestic equity growth while the risk (standard deviation) is virtually identical. NOTE: The *after-tax* expected return from domestic equity income is 11.4% [7.5% × (100%−28%) + 6.0%], which is 1.1% lower than the after-tax expected return of 12.5% from domestic equity growth. Because the standard deviation of these two classes is similar, domestic equity growth is preferable. **For the Exam:** Your exam answer: "Same risk as domestic equity growth, but lower return."
Domestic Equity-Growth	21% to 30%	The maximum allocation to domestic equity growth is warranted. This is one of two asset classes which exceed the 7% required rate of return. The after-tax return for this asset class is higher than that for domestic equity income, but the standard deviation is almost the same. As a result, domestic equity growth has the superior risk-adjusted return. **For the Exam:** Your exam answer: "Higher return and same risk as domestic equity income."

> **For the Exam:** The following calculations are not required by the question. On the exam, you might do a quick mental calculation to see that your suggested allocations would yield the necessary required return.

Sample allocation in correct ranges:

After-tax expected annual returns:

Money Market: $2.5\% \times (1 - 0.28) = 1.80\%$

Domestic Bond: $5.2\% \times (1 - 0.28) = 3.74\%$

Domestic Equity Income: $[7.5\% \times (1 - 0.28)] + 6.0\% = 11.40\%$

Domestic Equity Growth: $[0\% \times (1 - 0.28)] + 12.5\% = 12.50\%$

Funds	Fund Allocation (%)	After-tax Annual Return	Weighted Return (%)
Money Market	5	1.80	0.09
Domestic Bond	55	3.74	2.06
Domestic Equity: Income	10	11.40	1.14
Domestic Equity: Growth	30	12.50	3.75
Portfolio Expected Return			7.04

Answer: Question 9, 2008 Level 3 Curriculum, Volume 2, page 198

9. A.

   i. *Return objective*. Stephenson's expressed desire for 20% average annual return is unrealistic. Coppa should counsel Stephenson on the level of return he can reasonable expect from the financial markets over long time periods and to define an achievable return objective. Nevertheless, Stephenson's circumstances support an above-average return objective that emphasizes capital appreciation. This formulation is justified by the following:
   - Because Stephenson has a sizable asset base and ample income to cover his current spending, focus should be on growing the portfolio.
   - Stephenson's low liquidity needs and long time horizon support a long-term capital appreciation approach.
   - Stephenson is in the consolidation phase of his life cycle and does not rely on the portfolio to meet living expenses.

   Stephenson stated that he wants a return in excess of 5.0% for the remainder of the year. This short-term goal needs to be considered to the extent possible but should not be a significant factor in the IPS, which focuses on the client's long-term return objective.

   To maintain his lifestyle after retirement, Stephenson needs approximately $234,000 in inflation-adjusted after-tax income annually when he retires in 15 years [$150,000 × $(1.03)^{15}$ = $233,695]. Assuming he can achieve a 7% return (3% inflation + 4% real return = 7%), Stephenson will have $5.5 million in 15 years [$2 million × $(1.07)^{15}$ = $5.52 million]. Generating $234,000 from a $5.52 million asset base requires a 4.2% after-tax return.

   > **For the Exam:** The question asks you to *formulate* the return objective, so no calculations are required unless specifically requested. However, pay attention to the calculation in the guideline answer. On the exam, they might provide enough data (e.g., the 7% return before retirement) to calculate a future required annual return.

   ii. *Risk tolerance*. Stephenson has an above-average risk tolerance.
   - Although Stephenson describes his risk tolerance as "average," his current investment portfolio indicates an apparent above-average willingness to take risk.
   - His financial situation (large current asset base, ample income to cover expenses, lack of need for liquidity or cash flow, and long time horizon) indicates an above-average ability to assume risk.

    Professor's Note: This is a good example of how clients' actions speak louder than their words.

iii. *Liquidity requirements.* Stephenson's liquidity needs are low.
  • Stephenson has no regular cash flow needs from the portfolio because the income from his medical practice meets all current spending needs.
  • No large, one-time cash needs are stated. It would be appropriate, however, to keep a small cash reserve for emergencies.

For the Exam: Your exam answer: "Income covers expenses. Only requirement is minimum amount to cover emergencies."

iv. *Time horizon.* Stephenson's time horizon is long term and consists of two stages:
  • Time until retirement, which he expects to be 15 years; and
  • His lifetime following retirement, which could range from 15 to 20 years.

For the Exam: Your exam answer: "Two stages: 15 years to retirement; retirement ~ 20 years."

B. Fund D represents the single best addition to complement Stephenson's current portfolio, given his selection criteria. First, Fund D's expected return (14.0%) has the potential to increase the portfolio's return somewhat. Second, Fund D's relatively low correlation coefficient with his current portfolio (+0.65) indicates that it will provide larger diversification benefits than any of the other alternatives except Fund B. The result of adding Fund D should be a portfolio with about the same expected return and somewhat lower volatility compared with the original portfolio.

For the Exam: Your exam answer: "Fund D. Low correlation with existing assets. *D* dominates *B* because same risk, higher return."

The three other funds have shortcomings in either expected return enhancement or volatility reduction through diversification benefits:
  • Fund A offers the potential for increasing the portfolio's return but is too highly correlated to provide substantial volatility reduction benefits through diversification.
  • Fund B provides substantial volatility reduction through diversification benefits but is expected to generate a return well below the current portfolio's return.
  • Fund C has the greatest potential to increase the portfolio's return but is too highly correlated to provide substantial volatility reduction benefits through diversification.

For the Exam: In this case, they did not ask you to explain why the others were inappropriate. They might on your exam, however.

Answer: Question 10, 2008 Level 3 Curriculum, Volume 2, page 199

10. A.

i. The IPS's *return objective* section is inadequate.
   - Although Wheeler accurately indicates Taylor's personal income requirement, she has not recognized the need to support Renee.
   - Wheeler does not indicate the need to protect Taylor's purchasing power by increasing income by at least the rate of inflation over time.
   - Wheeler does not indicate the impact of income taxes on the return requirement.
   - Wheeler calculates required return based on assets of $900,000, appropriately excluding Taylor's imminent $300,000 liquidity need (house purchase) from investable funds. However, Taylor may invest $100,000 in his son's business. If he does, Taylor insists this asset be excluded from his plan. In that eventuality, Taylor's asset base for purposes of Wheeler's analysis would be $800,000.
   - Assuming a $900,000 capital base, Wheeler's total return estimate of 2.7% is lower than the actual required after-tax real return of 5.3% ($48,000/$900,000).

> **For the Exam:** This is not indicative of an exam question. On the exam, you would probably be asked to state one or two reasons why each is inappropriate.

ii. The *risk tolerance* section is inappropriate.
   - Wheeler fails to consider Taylor's below-average willingness to assume risk as exemplified by his aversion to loss, his consistent preference for conservative investments, his adverse experience with creditors, and his desire not to work again.
   - Wheeler fails to consider Taylor's below-average ability to assume risk, which is based on his recent life changes, the size of his capital base, high personal expenses versus income, and expenses related to his mother's care.
   - Wheeler's policy statement implies that Taylor has a greater willingness and ability to accept volatility (higher risk tolerance) than is actually the case. Based on Taylor's need for an after-tax return of 5.3%, a balanced approach with both a fixed-income and growth component is more appropriate than an aggressive growth strategy.

iii. The *time horizon* section is partially appropriate.
   - Wheeler accurately addresses the long-term time horizon based only on Taylor's age and life expectancy.
   - Wheeler fails to consider that Taylor's investment time horizon is multistage. Stage 1 represents Renee's life expectancy, during which time Taylor will supplement her income. Stage 2 begins at Renee's death, concluding Taylor's need to supplement her income, and ends with Taylor's death.

iv. The *liquidity* section is partially appropriate.
   - Wheeler addresses potential liquidity events.
   - Wheeler fails to specifically consider ongoing expenses ($2,000/month for Taylor's living expense and $2,000/month to support his mother) relative to expected portfolio returns.
   - The reference to a "normal, ongoing cash reserve" is vague. The reserve's purpose and size should be specified.

B. Allocation B is most appropriate for Taylor. Taylor's nominal annual return requirement is 6.3%, based on his cash flow (income) needs ($50,400 annually), to be

---

generated from a current asset base of $800,000. After adjusting for expected annual inflation of 1.0%, the real-return requirement becomes 7.3%. To grow to $808,000 ($800,000 × 1.01), the portfolio must generate $58,400 ($50,400 + $8,000) in the first year ($58,400/$800,000 = 7.3%).

Allocation B meets Taylor's minimum return requirement. Of the possible allocations that provide the required minimum real return, Allocation B also has the lowest standard deviation of returns (i.e., the least volatility risk) and by far the best Sharpe ratio. In addition, Allocation B offers the balance of high current income and stability with moderate growth prospects.

Allocation A has the lowest standard deviation and best Sharpe ratio but does not meet the minimum return requirement when inflation is included in that requirement. Allocation A also has very low growth prospects.

Allocation C meets the minimum return requirement and has moderate growth prospects but has a higher risk level (standard deviation) and a lower Sharpe ratio, as well as less potential for stability, than Allocation B.

Answer: Question 11, 2008 Level 3 Curriculum, Volume 2, page 202

11. A.   The Muellers' investment policy statement should include the following objectives and constraints:

   i.   *Return objective.* The Muellers' return objective should reflect a total return approach that combines capital appreciation and capital preservation. After retirement, they will need approximately $75,000 (adjusted for inflation) annually to maintain their current standard of living. Given the Muellers' limited needs and asset base, preserving their financial position on an inflation-adjusted basis may be a sufficient objective. Their long life expectancy and undetermined retirement needs, however, lead to the likely requirement for some asset growth over time, at least to counter any effects of inflation.

   Although the Muellers wish to exclude the future trust distribution from their current planning, that distribution will substantially increase their capital base and dramatically alter the return objective of their future IPS, primarily by reducing their needed return level.

   ii.   *Risk tolerance.* The Muellers are in the middle stage of the investor life cycle. Their income (relative to expenses), total financial resources, and long time horizon give them the ability to assume at least an average, if not an above-average, level of investment risk. Their stated preference of "minimal volatility" investments, however, apparently indicates a below-average willingness to assume risk. The large realized losses they incurred in previous investments may contribute to their desire for safety. Also, their need for continuing cash outflow to meet their daughter's college expenses may temporarily and slightly reduce their risk-taking ability. In sum, the Muellers' risk tolerance is average.

   Two other issues affect the Muellers' ability to take risk. First, the holding of Andrea's company stock represents a large percentage of the Muellers' total investable assets and thus is an important risk factor for their portfolio. Reducing the size of this holding or otherwise reducing the risk associated with a single large holding should be a priority for the Muellers. Second, the future trust distribution will substantially increase their capital base and thus increase their ability to assume risk.

   > **For the Exam:** This is an example of a large holding of a low cost basis stock. You are likely to see a similar situation on your exam, only you will probably be asked how to deal with it. Be ready to discuss possible diversification techniques such as selling part of the position, using exchange funds or completion portfolios, or hedging the position.

   iii.   *Time horizon.* Overall, the Muellers' ages and long life expectancies indicate a long time horizon. They face a multistage horizon, however, because of their changing cash flow and resource circumstances. Their time horizon can be viewed as having three distinct stages: the next five years from now (some assets, negative cash flow because of their daughter's college expenses), and beyond 10 years (increased assets from a sizable trust distribution, decreased income because they plan to retire).

   > **For the Exam:** Your exam answer: "Long time horizon with three stages: five years while daughter is in school; five years after that until trust received and retire; retirement years."

iv. *Liquidity.* The Muellers need $50,000 now to contribute to the college's endowment fund. Alternatively, they may be able to contribute $50,000 of Andrea's low-cost-basis stock to meet the endowment obligation. In addition, they expect the regular annual college expenses ($40,000) to exceed their normal annual savings ($25,000) by $15,000 for each of the next five years. This relatively low cash flow requirement of 2.7% ($15,000/$550,000 asset base after $50,000 contribution) can be substantially met through income generation from their portfolio, further reducing the need for sizable cash reserves. Once their daughter completes college, the Muellers' liquidity needs should be minimal until retirement because their income more than adequately covers their living expenses.

> **For the Exam:** Your exam answer: "$50,000 contribution to school. Annual $15,000 music school expenses for five years."

v. *Tax concerns.* The Muellers are subject to a 30% marginal tax rate for ordinary income and a 20% rate for realized capital gains. The difference in the rates makes investment returns in the form of capital gains preferable to equivalent amounts of taxable dividends and interest.

Although taxes on capital gains would normally be a concern to investors with low-cost-basis stock, this is not a major concern for the Muellers because they have a tax loss carryforward of $100,000. The Muellers can offset up to $100,000 in realized gains with the available tax loss carryforward without experiencing any cash outflow or any reduction in asset base.

> **For the Exam:** Your exam answer: "Capital gains preferred to ordinary gains. Can harvest the $100,000 loss to offset gains from selling concentrated position in company stock."

vi. *Unique circumstances.* The large holding of the low-basis stock in Andrea's company, a "technology company with a highly uncertain future," is a key factor to be included in the evaluation of the risk level of the Muellers' portfolio and the future management of their assets. In particular, the family should systematically reduce the size of the investment in this single stock. Because of the existence of the tax loss carryforward, the stock position can be reduced by at least 50% (perhaps more depending on the exact cost basis of the stock) without reducing the asset base to pay a tax obligation.

In addition, the trust distribution in ten years presents special circumstances for the Muellers, although they prefer to ignore these future assets in their current planning. The trust will provide significant assets to help meet their long-term return needs and objectives. Any long-term investment policy for the family must consider this circumstance, and any recommended investment strategy must be adjusted before the distribution takes place.

> **For the Exam:** Your exam answer: "1/3 of portfolio in company stock. $100,000 tax-loss carry forward; family trust in ten years."

B. *Personal portfolio.* Portfolio A is the most appropriate portfolio for the Muellers. Because their pension income will not cover their annual expenditures, the shortfall will not likely be met by the return on their investments, so the 10% cash reserve is appropriate. As the portfolio is depleted over time, it may be prudent to allocate more than 10% to cash equivalents. The income deficit will be met each year by a combination of investment return and capital invasion.

> **For the Exam:** This is a rare example of the client not wanting to preserve the principal. Note that this is specifically stated. Always preserve the principal unless, as in this case, specifically told otherwise.

Now that their daughter is financially independent, the Muellers' sole objective for their personal portfolio is to provide for their own living expenses. Their willingness and need to accept risk is fairly low. Clearly, there is no need to expose the Muellers to the possibility of a large loss. Also, their health situation has considerably shortened their time horizon. Therefore, a 70% allocation to intermediate-term high-grade fixed-income securities is warranted.

The income deficit will rise each year as the Muellers' expenses rise with inflation, but their pension income remains constant. The conservative 20% allocation to equities should provide diversification benefits and some protection against unanticipated inflation over the expected maximum 10-year time horizon.

Portfolio B, the second-best portfolio, has no cash reserves, so it could not meet the Muellers' liquidity needs. Also, although it has a higher expected return, Portfolio B's asset allocation results in a somewhat higher standard deviation of returns than Portfolio A.

Portfolios C and D offer higher expected returns but at markedly higher levels of risk and with relatively lower levels of current income. The Muellers' large income requirements and low risk tolerance preclude the use of Portfolios C and D.

C.

> *Professor's Note: The trust will pay taxes on gains, so there are no current or expected taxes for the Muellers. If they, or their beneficiaries, received income from the trust during the five years before the assets are turned over to the charity, this would be a charitable remainder trust. If the charity received income from the trust for a period with the balance going to beneficiaries, it would be a charitable leading trust. In either case, in the IPS you would state that legal counsel is recommended.*

Trust distribution portfolio. Portfolio B is the most appropriate for the trust assets. Portfolio B's expected return of 5.8% exceeds the required return of 5.4%, and the required return will actually decline if the surviving spouse lives longer than five years to a maximum of 10 years. The Muellers' sole objective for this money is to adequately fund the building addition. The portfolio's growth requirements are modest, and the Muellers have below-average willingness to accept risk. The portfolio would be unlikely to achieve its objective if large, even short-term losses were absorbed during the minimum five-year time horizon. Except for taxes, no principal or income disbursements are expected for at least five years; therefore, only a minimal or even zero cash reserve is required. Accordingly, an allocation of 40% to equities to provide some growth and a 60% to intermediate-term fixed-income to provide stability and capital preservation is appropriate.

There is no second-best portfolio. Portfolio A's cash level is higher than necessary, and the portfolio's expected return is insufficient to achieve the $2,600,000 value within the minimum value in five years. Portfolio C has a sufficient expected return, but it has a higher cash level than is necessary and, more importantly, a standard deviation of return that is too high given the Muellers' below-average risk tolerance. Portfolio D has a sufficient return and an appropriate cash level but a clearly excessive risk (standard deviation) level. Portfolios C and D share the flaw of having excessive equity allocations that fail to recognize the relatively short time horizon and that generate risk levels much higher than necessary or warranted.

Answer: Question 12, 2008 Level 3 Curriculum, Volume 2, page 204

12. **For the Exam:** Finding inconsistencies and other mistakes in an IPS for an individual used to be fairly common on the Level 3 exam, and it looks as though that might be returning after several years. In the following guideline answer, CFA Institute uses complete sentences. On the exam, you should always strive to say as little as possible and use bullet points and incomplete sentences. After each guideline answer below, I have inserted the way I would write the answer.

A. To prepare an appropriate IPS, a manager should address the Smiths' return objective, risk tolerance, and constraints. *Return objective.* To achieve its objectives, the Family Portfolio must provide for after-tax distributions equal to the difference between the Smiths' expenses and their fixed income payments. To maintain its real value, the portfolio must also grow at a rate that offsets inflation's impact on the Smiths' total expenses, including those currently covered by the fixed pension and Gift Fund payments.

A secondary objective is the gifting of $1 million to the Smiths' granddaughter. Because the Family Portfolio will be worth $1 million after the renovation of their house, the Smiths need no further capital growth to reach their nominal goal. To maintain its real value, the portfolio must have growth at least equal to the rate of inflation.

For the Exam:
- Meet living expense shortfall.
- Cover inflation.
- Leave $1 million to grandchild.

Risk tolerance. The Smiths are in a relatively late stage of the investor life cycle, and their comments suggest a conservative bias or below-average willingness to accept risk. In light of their long-term goals and current financial security, however, the Smiths have the ability to accommodate moderate portfolio volatility.

In the short term, the consequences of an adverse investment outcome are limited; the Smiths could use principal from the Family Portfolio to cover occasional performance shortfalls. They are thus able to accommodate some measure of short-term volatility in return for greater long-term expected returns. In extreme circumstances, the Smiths could modify or forgo their secondary objective of leaving $1 million to their granddaughter.

The consequences of an adverse portfolio outcome in the long term, however, could be serious. Depending on the length of their remaining lifetimes and the growth rate of their expenses, the Smiths could seriously deplete the corpus of the Family Portfolio and jeopardize their financial security.

The Smiths' comments imply that they have spent a lifetime saving and building a "safe" collection of income-oriented investments. Their desire to preserve market value and the WealthMax Financial Consultants (WFC) policy statement's emphasis on secure investments suggest that they may fall, at least partially, into the "cautious" category, a group with below-average risk tolerance.

> **For the Exam:***
> - Willingness: below average because of age, liquidity needs, and statements.
> - Ability: average because of long time horizon and ability to modify goals.
> - Overall: below average to honor willingness.
>
> * You will probably be asked to list a specific number of reasons for your conclusion for willingness, ability, and overall tolerance.

Time horizon. The Family Portfolio should have an intermediate to slightly longer-term investment horizon.

The Smiths' joint life expectancy, at 65 years of age, is still substantial. Because their objective of financial security is well provided for in the short term (see discussion of risk tolerance), the Smiths can afford to focus more on the long-term aspects of that objective.

To the extent that the Smiths emphasize the objective of leaving $1 million to their granddaughter in their planning, a longer-term time horizon would be warranted.

> **For the Exam:** Long-term (20–25 years) single-stage time horizon.

Professor's Note: There is nothing in the current Level 3 curriculum related to the "focus" of the investment policy, as is mentioned in the guideline answer. The Smiths clearly have a single-stage, long time horizon, since there are no expected changes in their needs or income that would warrant changing the IPS and/or the portfolio allocation. Had they had a two-stage horizon (e.g., retire in ten years), the "focus" of the objectives and constraints portion of the IPS would be those ten years. That is, you would calculate the return, determine risk tolerance, ate cetera, for those ten years. At retirement, the IPS would have to be rewritten, due to typical changes in most objectives and constraints.

Liquidity requirements. The Smiths' current annual living costs ($150,000 after taxes) are being met, which allows them to address longer-term growth objectives. The Smiths must plan for the upcoming expense of renovating their home. Their Family Portfolio should anticipate the renovation costs by holding a reserve of at least $200,000 in highly liquid, short-term funds.

> **For the Exam:**
> - $45,000 (150,000 – 65,000 – 40,000) in living expenses not met by pensions and Gift Fund.
> - The $200,000 needed for renovations should be put in T-bills and not considered part of the asset allocation.

Laws and regulations. No special legal or regulatory problems are apparent.

Tax concerns. The Smiths must pay a higher tax on dividends and interest than on capital gains. All else being equal, therefore, they prefer portfolio returns in the form of capital gains rather than equivalent amounts of taxable investment income.

> **For the Exam:** The Smiths are taxable investors, so the focus should be avoiding or at least minimizing taxes.

Unique circumstances. Establishment of the Gift Fund had increased the Smiths' dependence on fixed payments. As a consequence of this increased exposure to the eroding effects of inflation, the Smiths' long-term financial security is significantly reduced.

> **For the Exam:** No unique circumstances.

 Professor's Note: Being exposed to inflation is not a unique circumstance, and they have already established the Gift Fund, so they don't require legal counseling. If they were establishing the fund or a trust for the grandchild, you would mention that and suggest legal counsel.

Synopsis. The Smiths may not fully appreciate the impact of inflation and taxes on their financial security. The Family Portfolio can meet their immediate needs, but it is unlikely to grow at the same rate as disbursements. Depending on how long the Smiths live, the secondary objective of giving $1 million to their granddaughter may not be fully attainable, even in nominal terms.

> **For the Exam:** There isn't usually a synopsis like this. In the return portion, you could mention that the $1 million bequest to the grandchild is a secondary goal.

B. Rather than a true policy statement, the WFC statement is a compendium of opinions and assertions that may or may not be supportable by evidence and may or may not be appropriate to the Smiths' specific situation. WFC's statement fails to:
- Identify specific return requirements
- Consider inflation
- Consider the Smiths' willingness and ability to accept risk
- Consider the Smiths' investment time horizon
- Specify the Smiths' liquidity requirements
- Address the possibility of legal and regulatory constraints
- Consider tax concerns
- Consider possible unique circumstances

C.

i. Portfolio B is an appropriate recommendation based on three portfolio characteristics other than expected return and yield: diversification, efficiency (Sharpe ratio), and risk.
- Diversification across asset classes contributes to portfolio efficiency and is a desirable portfolio characteristic. Portfolio B appears to be the most broadly diversified.
- Efficiency, as measured by return for each unit of risk (Sharpe ratio), is a desirable portfolio characteristic. Portfolio B dominates the other portfolios on this criterion.
- Risk is an attribute that must be constrained to fit the Smiths' fiscal and psychological tolerance levels. The 85% allocation to equities and venture capital in Portfolio C entails relatively high risk. Portfolio B, which is more balanced

between fixed-income and equity markets, is better suited to the Smiths' below-average risk profile.

> **For the Exam:** You could more than likely eliminate Portfolio C, and particularly Portfolio D, based on their allocations to venture capital. With their below-average willingness to tolerate risk, it is highly unlikely they would accept either C or D. In addition, C has 75% allocated to equities, so it clearly is not appropriate. This leaves portfolios A and B, and A has no equities; it's 80% corporate bonds and 20% T-bills, so it's no good.

ii. Meeting the Smiths' return objectives in the first year will require an after-tax total return of 7.5% on the $1 million remaining in the Family Portfolio after their house renovation. The Family Portfolio must accommodate a disbursement of $45,000 and grow at a rate that offsets the impact of inflation.

> **For the Exam:** The request for you to calculate the required return is a little vague, and it's confusing because of the fixed pension receipts and growing expenses. This is why recent exam questions have asked for the required return over one specific year, such as the first year of retirement.

Expenses		($150,000)
Source of funds		
Pension (after tax)	65,000	
Gift Fund (after tax)	40,000	105,000
Family Portfolio disbursement (after tax)		45,000
		$150,000
Required return		
Disbursement	($45,000)	4.50%
Inflation		3.00%
Total		7.50%

Subsequent distribution from the Family Portfolio will increase at a rate substantially higher than inflation (to offset the lack of growth in $105,000 of fixed pension and Gift Fund payments):

	Year 1	Year 2	Change
Expenses (3% growth)	$150,000	$154,500	3%
Portfolio distribution	$45,000	$49,500	10%

Portfolios B and C both have expected returns that meet the Smiths' projected disbursements in Year 1. Portfolio C's expected return is closer to that necessary to meet their objective over a longer time frame. However, Portfolio C's level of risk is too high given the Smiths' risk tolerance. Although Portfolio C should allow the Smiths to both fund their lifetime real income needs and leave $1 million to their grandchild, the risk in Portfolio C may endanger both their income and the bequest.

The Smiths' advisor should select Portfolio B based on its appropriate risk level and conformity with the Smiths' constraints. As a consequence of Portfolio B's probable inability to meet the Smiths' long-term spending needs, however, principal invasion may be necessary, and the secondary objective of giving $1 million, even in nominal terms, to their granddaughter may be forfeited.

Answer: Question 13, Level 3 Curriculum, Volume 2, page 206

13. A.

    i.   The Maclins' overall risk objective must consider both willingness and ability to take risk:

        Willingness. The Maclins have a below-average willingness to take risk, based on their unhappiness with the portfolio volatility they have experienced in recent years and their desire not to experience a loss in portfolio value in excess of 12% in any one year.

> **For the Exam:** Starting at average willingness to tolerate risk, look for reasons to drop that a notch. The Maclins' statements about portfolio volatility and not wanting a loss greater than 12% indicate their focus on risk and their reduced (i.e., below average) willingness to tolerate risk.

        Ability. The Maclins have an average ability to take risk. Although their fairly large asset base and long time horizon in isolation would suggest an above-average ability to take risk, their living expenses of £74,000 are significantly higher than Christopher's after-tax salary of £80,000(1 − 0.40) = £48,000, causing them to be very dependent on projected portfolio returns to cover the difference and thereby reducing their ability to take risk.

> **For the Exam:** Starting at average ability to tolerate risk, we look for answers to increase or decrease. The size of their portfolio and their long time horizon increases their ability to tolerate risk to above average. The need for the portfolio to help meet living expenses, however, drops it back to average.

        Overall. The Maclins' overall risk tolerance is below average, as their below-average willingness to take risk dominates their average ability to take risk in determining their overall risk tolerance.

    ii.

> **For the Exam:** Again, this question is very broad. On the exam, you can expect a more precise question, such as, "Calculate the Maclins' required return for the coming year."

        The Maclins' return objective is to grow the portfolio to meet their educational and retirement needs as well as to provide for ongoing net expenses. The Maclins will require annual after-tax cash flows of £26,000 (calculated below) to cover ongoing net expenses and will need £2 million in 18 years to fund their children's education and their retirement. To meet this objective, the Maclins' pretax required return is 7.38%, which is determined below.

        The after-tax return required to accumulate £2 million in 18 years beginning with an investable asset base of £1,235,000 (calculated below) and with annual outflows of £26,000 is 4.427%, which when adjusted for the 40% tax rate, results in a 7.38% pretax return [4.427%/(1 − 0.40) = 7.38%].

Christopher's annual salary	£80,000
Less: Taxes (40%)	−32,000
Living expenses	−74,000
Net annual cash flow	−£26,000
Inheritance	900,000
Barnett Co. common stock	220,000
Stocks and bonds	160,000
Cash	5,000
Subtotal	£1,285,000
Less one-time needs:	
Down payment on home	−30,000
Charitable donation	−20,000
Investable asset base	£1,235,000

Note: No inflation adjustment is required in the return calculation because increases in living expenses will be offset by increases in Christopher's salary.

Professor's Note: This is a time value of money calculation. On your TI BAII Professional:

FV	=	*2,000,000*
PV	=	*−1,235,000*
PMT	=	*26,000*
n	=	*18*
CPT I/Y	=	*4.427*

B. The Maclins' investment policy statement should include the following constraints:

  i. *Time horizon.* The Maclins have a two-stage time horizon, because of their changing cash flow and resource needs. The first stage is the next 18 years. The second stage begins with their retirement and the university education years for their children.

  ii. *Liquidity requirements.* The Maclins have one-time immediate expenses totaling £50,000 that include the deposit on the house they are purchasing and the charitable donation in honor of Louise's father.

  iii. *Tax concerns.* A 40% tax rate applies to both ordinary income and capital gains.

  iv. *Unique circumstances.* The large holding of the Barnett Co. common stock represents almost 18% of the Maclins' investable asset base. The concentrated holding in Barnett Co. stock is a key risk factor of the Maclins' portfolio, and achieving better diversification will be a factor in the future management of the Maclins' assets.

  The Maclins' desire not to invest in alcohol and tobacco stocks is another constraint on investment.

Study Session 5

Question 4 (2006) Answer:

4. **Part A**

The ACLP's Investment Committee has adopted an investment objective to build a plan surplus by setting a return objective that is 200 basis points (2.0%) above the minimum required rate of return. Therefore, the ACLP's return objective is equal to the minimum required return of 5%* plus the 2% needed to build its surplus, for a total of 7%.

> **For the Exam:** The command word "formulate" does not typically imply calculations are necessary. If you see it on the exam, especially if it's associated with a return objective, assume you are to write out the objective, unless specifically told otherwise. For this answer, I would write a paraphrased version of the first paragraph. The other two paragraphs are there as explanation and would not be required on the exam.

*Since ACLP is 100% funded (i.e., the market value of its assets is equal to the present value of its liabilities), the minimum return requirement for the plan is the 5% discount rate used to calculate ACLP's Projected Benefit Obligation. If ACLP returns 5%, then its assets should be exactly sufficient to make its required pension payments to retired workers.

Note: The minimum 10% return mentioned by ACL's President Johnson is not an appropriate return objective for the ACLP. It is a return expectation, not a return objective, and there is no reason to believe 10% is attainable with an appropriate level of risk. The investment objectives for ACLP are set by its investment committee, not by ACL's President.

Part B

Risk factor	Indicate whether ACLP has a below-average, average, or above average ability to take risk compared with the average for the cruise industry with respect to *each* of the following risk factors (circle one)	Justify *each* response with *one* reason*
i. Sponsor financial status and profitability	**Above average**	ACL is [financially sound, with a lower debt/equity ratio and a higher return on equity than the averages for its industry.] ACL is therefore currently in a good position to make any needed contributions to ACLP (should the portfolio not perform as well as expected, for example). This gives ACLP an above average ability to take risk compared with the average for ACL's industry.
ii. Workforce age	**Above average**	With an average age of 33, ACL's [workforce is younger than the industry average] of 40 years old. Although 14% of the workforce is more than 50 years old, this is less than the 17% industry average. Overall, the relatively younger age of the employees increases the relative duration of ACLP's liabilities and gives ACLP an above-average ability to take risk compared to the average for ACL's industry.
iii. Retired employees	**Below average**	ACL has a [lower percentage of current employees (85%) and a higher percentage of retired employees] (15%) than the average for its industry (90% and 10%, respectively). This reduces the relative duration of the ACLP's liabilities and gives ACLP a below average ability to take risk compared to the average for ACL's industry.

*Brackets indicate the exam answer.

Part C

Factor	Indicate whether *each* of the following factors increases, leaves unchanged, or decreases ACLP's ability to take risk (circle one)	Justify *each* response with *one* reason*
i. Sponsor (ACL) and pension fund (ACLP) common risk exposures	Decreases	Currently, [10% of ACLP's assets are invested in leisure companies] (especially leisure companies with whom ACLP has a business relationship) [that are likely to be highly correlated with ACL's own business.] Unless Wilson can convince the Investment Committee to reduce ACLP's 10% exposure to these stocks, this factor reduces ACLP's ability to assume risk.
ii. Retirement plan features	Decreases	The ACLP has an [early retirement plan] with an annuity or lump-sum payout option. [14% of ACL's workforce is old enough to qualify for the early retirement feature.] Although few employees are currently planning to exercise the early retirement option, this could change. Cash requirements associated with the potential increase in annuity payments and lump sum payouts reduce ACLP's ability to assume risk.

*Brackets indicate the exam answer.

Part D

Constraint	Formulate *each* of the following constraints in ACLP's investment policy statement. Justify *each* response with *one* reason. Note: Your answer should specifically address ACLP's circumstances.

i. Liquidity requirement	• In the absence of any information to the contrary, the ACLP is likely to have low liquidity needs.
	  • The ACLP is fully funded.
	  • ACL has a relatively young and stable workforce. The plan is unlikely to need to make sizable payouts in the near future given the fifteen-year average duration of ACLP's liabilities.
	  • Few employees are currently planning to exercise the ACLP's early retirement feature. However, ACLP may want to set aside a reserve to deal with the possibility that changing conditions might cause the 14% of employees who are over age 50 to take advantage of ACLP's early retirement annuity and lump-sum payout features at some point in the future.

ii. Time horizon	• ACLP, as a going concern, has a long, single-stage time horizon.
	  • Although 14% of ACL's employees are more than 50 years old, the average age of its employees is 33.
	  • The workforce is stable.
	  • ACLP's liabilities have a duration of 15 years.

For the Exam: Notice the command word "formulate" and the text (i.e., non-computational) answers. For the liquidity requirement the following would suffice:

• Low liquidity needs –plus–
  • Young stable workforce –or–
  • Long duration liabilities –or–
  • May want to establish a reserve in case employees start taking early retirement

For the time horizon:

• Long-term, single stage –plus–
  • Young average age –or–
  • Liability duration 15 years

©2008 Schweser

Question 6 (2006) Answer

Statement	Determine whether you agree or disagree with *each* of the four statements made by Arnold (circle one)	If you disagree, support your opinion with *one* reason related to portfolio management Note: Supporting your opinion by simply reversing an incorrect statement will receive no credit.
"The sole return objective of both Vrieland and a defined benefit pension plan is to maintain purchasing power."	Disagree	• Neither foundations nor defined benefit pension plans have return objectives to exclusively maintain purchasing power. • Both have spending requirements, foundations to fund operations (annual disbursements and/or required distributions), and pension plans to fund required benefits. Therefore, both may require returns in excess of inflation. • Some pension plans do not need inflation protection depending on the nature of their liabilities. **For the Exam:** Your exam answer: "In addition to inflation, foundations and DB plans must earn enough to meet annual disbursements."
"Vrieland, unlike a defined benefit pension plan, does not need to consider the correlation between plan sponsor financial performance and the performance of the portfolio."	Agree	
"Like a defined benefit pension plan, the liquidity needs of Vrieland fluctuate over time."	Agree	

"The primary objective of both Vrieland and a defined benefit pension plan is to exist in perpetuity, resulting in an infinite investment time horizon."	Disagree	There are two portions of the statement for which the candidate may disagree. **Primary Objective:** The primary objective of Vrieland is not to exist, but rather to achieve its mission. The primary objective of a defined benefit pension plan is not to exist in perpetuity, but rather to provide funding to meet pension liabilities. **Infinite Time Horizon** Some foundations can be established with limited time horizons, with the intent of being "spent down" over a predetermined period of time. Pension funds however have a primary objective of meeting benefit obligations, therefore the time horizon will be based on the expected life of the plan. The expected life of the plan depends on: 1. Whether the plan sponsor is a going concern or plan termination is expected, and 2. The age of the workforce and the proportion of active lives. The plan's horizon will be longer if the workforce is young and the plan is open to new entrants.

For the Exam: Any one of the following would suffice:

- Some foundations have finite lives
- Foundation time horizon can be infinite or finite
- Pension plan time horizon depends on average age
- Pension plans established to provide retirement benefits, not just to exist
- Foundations established for various funding reason, not just to exist

Question 1 (2005) Answer:

Part A

BC Plc has below average risk tolerance, compared to the average FTSE 350 company pension plan, for any four of the following reasons:
- BC Plc's pension plan is more under-funded. The ratio of plan assets to plan liabilities at 0.83 is less than 1.0 and below the FTSE 350 average of 0.97.
- BC Plc's workforce has a higher average age.
- BC Plc's workforce has a higher ratio of retired lives to active lives.
- BC Plc's workforce has higher years of service.
- BC Plc has lower profitability.
- BC Plc has a higher debt ratio.

> **For the Exam:** Your exam answer:
>
> Below average risk tolerance –plus– any 4 of those listed.

Part B

Constraint	Characterize, for the BC Plc pension plan relative to the average FTSE 350 company pension plan, *each* of the two plan constraints of concern to the trustees (circle one)	Justify *each* of your responses with *two* reasons*
i. Liquidity requirement	**Higher**	1. [Older than average workforce] will lead to higher cash outflows sooner. 2. [Higher than average ratio of retired lives to active lives] requires higher cash outflows. 3. Plan is receiving [no contributions from/for new employees,] thereby increasing cash outflows required from the pension plan. 4. [Higher than average years of service] implies higher cash outflows sooner. 5. The [under-funded status of the plan] will increase liquidity requirements, because the workforce is older than average and therefore there is less time to reach a fully-funded status.

ii. Time horizon	**Shorter**	1. [Older than average workforce] will lead to more retirements sooner. 2. [Higher than average years of service] implies more retirements sooner. 3. [Plan is not accepting new members,] meaning that adverse trends (workforce age, years of service, etc.) will accelerate proportion of retired employees. 4. [Higher than average ratio of retired lives to active lives] shortens the time horizon due to greater number of current retirees.

*Brackets indicate the exam answer.

Part C

A change to 6% in the discount rate applied to the plan liabilities would cause the funded status of the BC Plc pension plan to deteriorate.

Reducing the discount rate (from 7% to 6%) applied to the plan liabilities would increase the present value of the plan's benefit obligations, while the value of plan assets would not change (the assumed long-term rate of return is unchanged at 8%). The widening in the difference between the value of the plan assets and the value of the plan's benefit obligations (due to increase in liabilities) would cause the plan's already underfunded status to deteriorate further. (PV assets − PV liabilities).

> **For the Exam:** Your exam answer:
>
> - Deteriorate
> - Reducing discount rate increases PV of liabilities. If asset remains constant, underfunding increases.

Answer: Question 2, 2008 Level 3 Curriculum, Volume 2, page 371

2. LightSpeed Connections

A. i. Concentrating LSC's pension assets as Donovan has done subjects the plan beneficiaries to an extraordinarily high level of risk because of the high correlation between the market values of the portfolio and LSC's business results.

ii. By concentrating the pension assets heavily in technology and Internet companies, Donovan has increased the company's risk as the pension plan's sponsor. LightSpeed now faces the prospect of having to provide additional funding to the pension plan at a time when the company's own cash flow and/or earnings position may be weakened. A more prudent approach would be to invest in assets expected to be less highly correlated with the company's market value, so in the event additional funding for the pension plan becomes necessary, it will be less likely to occur when LSC is in a weakened financial position.

B. i. The IPS drafted by Jeffries and the investment committee correctly identifies that the return requirement should be total return, with a need for inflation protection that is sufficient to fund the plan's long-term obligations. The IPS is weak in that it neglects to state a specific return requirement.

ii. The IPS fails to address the pension plan's risk tolerance, one of the two main objectives of a complete investment policy statement. Consequently, the IPS does not provide the guidance on risk tolerance that would highlight the potential risk to the beneficiaries and the company of LSC's current aggressive investment strategy.

iii. The IPS correctly address the time horizon constraint by stating that the assets are long-term in nature, both because of LSC's young workforce and the normal long-term nature of pension investing.

iv. The IPS fails to address the liquidity constraint; although liquidity is a minimal concern in this case, the IPS should nonetheless address that fact.

For the Exam: These questions are vague at best. CFA Institute has come a long way in specifying exactly what they want, so I would not expect questions structured like this on the exam this year. This is a good question to use for studying and review, however, as it discusses many of the concerns associated with managing pension plan assets.

Answer: Question 4, 2008 Level 3 Curriculum, Volume 2, page 373

4. **Food Processors, Inc. (FPI)**

   A. In the United States, every ERISA-qualified defined-benefit pension plan has a projected benefit obligation, which represents the discounted present value of the retirement benefits that the plan is obligated by law to make, given certain assumptions about future rates of pay and workforce factors. If the plan assets at fair market value excess the PBO, the plan is said to be overfunded. Conversely, if the value of the plan assets falls short of the PBO, the plan is said to be underfunded. Given that FPI's plan is underfunded by $200 million and its assets total $750 million, its PBO must be $950 million.

   B. FPI faces a dilemma. On the one hand, it needs to improve returns in order to "catch up" on its underfunding; this necessity implies that more risk should be taken. On the other hand, FPI cannot afford to have the underfunding become worse, which it would if FPI incurs more risk that does not produce higher returns in the short run. Alternatively, the company might be tempted, as the chair suggest, to raise the actuarial assumption of what future return levels will be, thereby making the asset base automatically more productive simply by declaring it to be so. Future returns, however, are generated not by actuaries or other individuals but by markets, by asset-class exposures within markets, and by long-term relationships between economic and market factors—all taking place in the context of funding, allocation, and payout decision unique to FPI's pension plan.

   Of primary importance is that the return expected must be consistent with the return the various alternative investment instruments available to the plan can reasonable offer in the long term.

   C. A U.S. pension plan's discount rate is the rate applied in determining the present value of its pension obligations. Because pension liabilities are typically long term, the discount rate should bear some rational relationship to the long-term interest rates in the marketplace at the time of the calculation. The usual model for the discount rate is the rate at which high-quality, long-term bonds such as the long Treasury bond are quoted, reflecting consensus expectations of long-run inflation plus a real rate of return. Thus, a manager may decide to reduce the discount rate based on capital market conditions reflecting a decline in long-term interest rates, as seen in Exhibit P-4. Based on the consensus forecasts for long-term Treasury bonds and inflation shown in Exhibit P-4, a discount rate of 6% to 7% would be reasonable. FPI is currently using an 8% discount rate, which is out of line with current capital market conditions. FPI should thus consider adopting a lower discount rate.

   D. Reducing the discount rate applied to FPI's PBO would have the effect of increasing the present value of FPI's pension benefit obligations. Because the market value of the assets available to liquidate this obligation remains unchanged, the underfunded situation would be made worse by a reduction in the discount rate. The size of the gap between the PBO and the value of the assets, now $200 million, would increase.

For the Exam: Note that once again the questions are not nearly as focused as you can expect on your exam. I would not waste my time trying to come up with an "exam answer" for these questions, if I were you. Instead, use them as a basis for discussing managing pension plan assets with fellow Level 3 candidates.

Answer: Question 5, 2008 Level 3 Curriculum, Volume 2, page 374

5. **Medical Research Foundation**

A. Key elements that should determine the foundation's grant-making (spending) policy are as follows:
   - Average expected inflation over a long horizon
   - Average expected nominal return on the endowment portfolio over the same long horizon
   - The 5% of asset value payout requirement imposed by the tax authorities as a condition for ongoing tax exemption.

   To preserve the real value of its assets and to maintain its spending in real terms, the foundation cannot pay out more, on average over time than the average real return it earns from its portfolio net of investment management expenses. The portion of the total return representing the inflation rate must be retained and reinvested if the foundation's principal is to grow with inflation. Because of the minimum 5% spending policy mandated by tax considerations, the real return of the portfolio will have to equal or exceed 5% plus the cost of earning investment returns in order to preserve the foundation's tax-exempt status and maintain its real value of principal and future payouts.

B. The new IPS should include the following components:
   - *Return objective.* A total return approach is recommended to meet the foundation's objective of maintaining real value after grants. The required annual return shall be the sum of the spending rate plus the expected inflation rate. [1]
   - *Risk tolerance.* The adoption of a clear-cut spending policy will permit cash flows to be planned with some precision, adding stability to annual budgeting and reducing the need for liquidity. Based on its long time horizon, low liquidity needs, and (now) amply assets, the foundation's risk tolerance is above average.
   - *Liquidity requirements.* Based on asset size and the predictable nature of cash payouts, liquidity needs are low.
   - *Time horizon.* The foundation, with an unlimited lifespan, has a very long time horizon.
   - *Tax considerations.* The foundation is tax-exempt under present U.S. law as long as the annual minimum payout of 5% is met.
   - *Legal and regulatory constraints.* The foundation is governed by the Uniform Management of Institutional Funds Act (UMIFA) as well as IRS regulations.
   - *Unique circumstances.* None apply, other than those previously discussed.

> **For the Exam:** As with most of the questions provided in the 2008 Level 3 curriculum, this is not a very good example of a real exam question. You'll notice the open-ended nature of the questions. On your exam, should there be a question dealing with a foundation, the questions will be much more focused. As you have seen with other curriculum questions, however, this question provides a sound basis for discussing foundations with fellow Level 3 candidates.

---

1. This additive return objective is easy to understand; as discussed in the reading, a multiplicative return objective would be more precise.

Answer: Question 6, 2008 Level 3 Curriculum, Volume 2, page 374

6. **James Children's Hospital**

A. The current spending request of $1,600,000 represents $1,600,000/$20,000,000 = 0.08 or 8% of the value of the endowment. This level of spending is high given the endowment's long-term expected total return of 8.6% per year (in nominal terms) and expected 4% inflation rate for medical equipment prices. If such spending is permitted, the current beneficiaries of the JCHE (for example, the patients of JCH) may receive benefits at the expense of future beneficiaries, because the endowment is unlikely to be able to maintain its value in inflation-adjusted terms.

B. JCHE has a perpetual time horizon; it can thus tolerate a higher risk level (in terms of volatility of returns) than a fund with a shorter time horizon. The higher risk tolerance results from the longer period available to make up for any market downturns. With a higher risk tolerance, JCHE can target a higher expected return.

C. JCHE's long-term spending policy should balance the needs of current and future beneficiaries. Its spending policy should balance income needs and the need to build the payout stream to preserve purchasing power. JCHE balances these conflicting objectives only when future beneficiaries receive the same inflation-adjusted distribution that current beneficiaries receive. With zero real growth, intergenerational neutrality exists. Because market returns are variable, JCHE should use a smoothing mechanism that will apply the spending rate to a moving average of market value:

Expected total return	8.6%
– Inflation	–4.0
Real expected return	4.6
– Spending rate	–4.6
Expected real growth	0.0%
Recommended spending rate	4.6%

For the Exam: This question presents some important concepts associated with endowments. Again, don't look for "exam answers;" use the questions and answers as more of a study tool. Intergenerational neutrality, mentioned in the answer to Part C, is a goal to which most endowments subscribe. To achieve this goal they usually employ spending rules to enable the fund to pay out as much to future generations as they pay out to the current (or past) generation (i.e., intergenerational neutrality).

Answer: Question 7, 2008 Level 3 Curriculum, Volume 2, page 375

7. **Donner Life Insurance**

Leighton made both incorrect and correct statements about life insurance and endowment portfolios:

1. *Both endowments and life insurance companies have aggressive return requirements* is an inaccurate statement. The return requirements of life insurance companies are first and foremost liability driven, matching assets with fixed obligations, and must be consistent with their conservative stance toward risk. Life insurance companies' return requirements also include, as an objective, the earning of a competitive return on the assets that fund surplus.

   The return requirements of endowments, although subject to a range of risk tolerances, are driven by the endowment's spending rate, the need to preserve purchasing power, and the need to provide a growing financial contribution to the endowed organization.

2. *Endowments are less willing to assume risk than life insurance companies because of donor concerns about volatility and loss of principal* is an inaccurate statement. Life insurance companies tend to have a lower tolerance for risk than endowments do. Confidence in a life insurance company's ability to pay its benefits (obligations) as they come due is a crucial element in the industry's financial viability. Life insurance companies thus are sensitive to the risk of any significant chance of principal loss or any significant interruption of investment income.

   Endowments, by contrast, tend to have a higher tolerance for risk. Their long-term time horizons and predictable cash flows, relative to their spending rate requirements, enable them to pursue more aggressive strategies than life companies can.

3. *Endowments are less able to assume risk than life insurance companies because of expectations that endowments should provide stable funding for charitable operations* is an inaccurate statement. Life insurance companies' ability to assume risk is circumscribed by their need to ensure the funding of liabilities to policyholders. The ALM focus of life insurance companies typically requires major holdings of bonds to offset the interest-sensitive nature of most life insurance liabilities. Regulations, including risk-based capital requirements, generally constrain the ability of life insurance companies to invest in higher risk assets.

   In contrast, the main risk facing an endowment is loss of purchasing power over time. Endowments have very long time horizons and are not focused on funding liabilities. Therefore, endowments should be able to accept higher volatility than life insurance companies in the short term to maximize long-term total returns.

4. *Endowments have lower liquidity requirements than life insurance companies because endowment spending needs are met through a combination of current income and capital appreciation* is an accurate statement. Life insurance companies face the need for liquidity as a key investment constraint, because life insurance products are promises to pay money depending on certain expected or unexpected events.

   Endowments typically have low liquidity needs, except to fund periodic distributions and to cover emergency needs. Distributions are usually foreseeable and can usually be met from a combination of investment income and the sale of readily marketable securities.

5. *Both endowments and life insurance companies are subject to stringent legal and regulatory oversight* is an inaccurate statement. Life insurance companies are subject to relatively rigorous legal and/or regulatory oversight with respect to their portfolio composition and investment strategies.

   In contrast, endowments are relatively unburdened with legal and/or regulatory restraints, at least at the federal level in the United States, although some states do have specific rules and regulations regarding management of endowment assets.

   For the Exam: This is a great question for comparing life insurance companies and endowments from a risk and return perspective. Again, don't look for "exam answers" as these questions are far more open-ended than what you will see, and you are not likely to see this type of comparison question.

Study Session 7

Question 5 (2006) Answer:

Part A

The most appropriate portfolio for ACLP is portfolio D.

Justification:
- Portfolio D has the minimum required cash equivalents to fund the expected lump sum payments ($200,000 per employee × 100 employees = $20 million or 10% cash requirement).
- Portfolio D meets the shortfall risk objective $(9.04 − (2 × 8.19) = −7.34\%)$
- Portfolio D has reduced exposure to the stocks of other companies in the cruise industry.

Because the plan sponsor (ACL) and cruise industry equities are highly correlated, minimizing exposure to other companies in the cruise industry is desirable to meet the policy objective.

For the Exam: Your exam answer:

- Portfolio D – plus any 2 –
  - Required cash for lump sum payments (10%)
  - Meets short fall objective: $9.04 − 2(8.19) = −7.34\%$
  - 0 exposure to cruise industry stocks.

Part B

Portfolio A is not most appropriate because
- Portfolio A does not match assets and liabilities, particularly in the short-term where there is insufficient cash.
- Portfolio A contains additional exposure to cruise industry equities.

Portfolio B is not most appropriate because
- Portfolio B does not meet the shortfall risk objective.

Portfolio C is not most appropriate because
- Portfolio C does not match assets and liabilities, particularly in the short-term where there is insufficient cash.

Portfolio E is not most appropriate because
- Portfolio E does not match assets and liabilities, particularly in the short-term where there is insufficient cash.
- Portfolio E does not meet the shortfall risk objective.

For the Exam: Your exam answer:

- Portfolio A: Insufficient cash or contains cruise stocks
- Portfolio B: Exceeds shortfall risk: $9.06 − 2(8.83) = −8.60$
- Portfolio C: Insufficient cash
- Portfolio E: Insufficient cash or exceeds shortfall risk: $9.07 − 2(8.57) = −8.07$

Question 7 (2006) Answer:

Part A

Corner portfolios 3 and 4 are the portfolios that will be used to interpolate the most appropriate strategic asset allocation.

For the Exam: When borrowing is prohibited, select the two corner portfolios whose returns bracket the required return.

Part B

Using the corner portfolio theorem and the expected returns for corner portfolio 3 of 10.3% and corner portfolio 4 of 9.1%.

$9.5 = 10.3w + 9.1(1-w)$

$w = 0.33$

The most appropriate strategic asset allocation will consist of 33% of corner portfolio 3 and 67% of corner portfolio 4.

Part C

The amount of U.S. equities that would be owned is calculated by multiplying the percentage of this asset held by each corner portfolio by the percentage of each portfolio and then summed.

U.S. equities weight = (0.33) (74.1%) + (0.67) (33.70%)

U.S. equities weight = 24.45% + 22.58%

U.S. equities weight = 47.03%

Level 3 Practice Exams
Old Question Review

Question 3 (2005) Answer:

3. Part A

i. Corner Portfolios 4 (expected return = 8.2%) and 5 (expected return = 8.0%) should be included in the optimal strategic asset allocation, given Lourie's return requirement of 8.1% (using an additive formulation of the return requirement; 8.145% using a compound formulation).

Not required but provided as basis for part ii:

Return requirement = 8.1% = (7.5% + 0.6%)

8.1 = 8.0w + 8.2(1 − w)

w = 0.50

1 − w = 0.50. The two corner portfolios are equally weighted.

Return target = 8.145% = (1 + 0.075)(1 + 0.006%) − 1

8.145 = 8.0w + 8.2(1 − w)

w = 0.275

1 − w = 0.725

(weights become 0.25 and 0.75 if return requirement is rounded to 8.15%)

In addition to achieving the return requirement, the appropriate combination of Corner Portfolios 4 and 5:
- has the highest Sharpe ratio among the efficient portfolios that meet Lourie's requirements
- is consistent with Lourie's specified risk tolerance (less than 15% standard deviation)
- is efficient (lies on efficient frontier)

ii. The most appropriate strategic asset allocation for the Lourie Foundation should be determined as follows:

Asset Class	Weight (%), return requirement = 8.1%	Weight (%), return requirement = 8.145%	Weight (%), return requirement = 8.15%
U.K. Equities	54.4 = (53.2 + 55.6)/2	54.94 = (53.2)(0.275) + (55.6)(0.725)	55.0 = (53.2)(0.25) + (55.6)(0.75)
U.K. Intermediate Term Bonds	6.7 = (13.3 + 0.0)/2	3.66 = (13.3)(0.275) + (0.0)(0.725)	3.3 = (13.3)(0.25) + (0.0)(0.75)

©2008 Schweser
Page 101

Note: The weights are given for an additive formulation of the return requirement (8.1%) and for a compound formulation (8.145% or 8.15%, depending on rounding).

> **For the Exam:** Again you are asked to combine two corner portfolios, so select the two whose returns bracket the required return. The second part of the question is important. Be able to perform those calculations on the exam.

Part B

Corner Portfolio 5 and the risk-free portfolio should be included in the new strategic asset allocation, because some combination of the two portfolios will be mean-variance superior to any other combination of different portfolios that also satisfy the director's revised return requirement and risk tolerance. The Corner 5 portfolio is the tangency portfolio (the highest-Sharpe-ratio efficient portfolio at 0.284). Combinations of the tangency portfolio (expected return = 8.00%) and the risk-free portfolio (expected return = 4.00%) that place at least a 50% weight on the tangency portfolio will satisfy the dire tor's return requirement [(8% × 0.50) + (4% × 0.50) = 6%] and will lie on the Capital Allocation Line (CAL). Portfolios on the CAL provide the lowest level of risk for a given level of expected return (or highest expected return for a given level of risk). Among the portfolios satisfying the director's return requirement, some—including the 50/50 portfolio mix of Corner Portfolio 5 and the risk-free portfolio—will also be consistent with the director's specified risk tolerance. (For example, the standard deviation of the 50/50 portfolio is 7.05% = (0.5)(14.1), well below the new constraint of 12%). Lourie would choose from among these latter portfolios for the new strategic asset allocation.

Professor's Note: Although the question may be a little vague, combining the corner portfolio with the highest Sharpe Ratio with the risk-free asset will always produce a portfolio that dominates any others on the efficient frontier. This concept is analogous to combining the market portfolio with the risk-free asset to form either the SML or CML. In those cases, the market portfolio is the portfolio on the efficient frontier with the highest Sharpe Ratio.

PRACTICE EXAM 1
SCORE SHEET

MORNING SESSION		
Topic	Question	Points
Portfolio Management	1A	4
Portfolio Management	1B	4
Portfolio Management	2	8
Portfolio Management	3A	13
Portfolio Management	3B	6
Portfolio Management	4A	9
Portfolio Management	4B	9
Portfolio Management	5A	9
Portfolio Management	5B	6
Asset Valuation	6A	6
Asset Valuation	6B	4
Asset Valuation	6C	6
Asset Valuation	6D	9
Asset Valuation	7A	4
Asset Valuation	7B	4
Portfolio Management	8A	15
Portfolio Management	8B	10
Portfolio Management	8C	6
Asset Valuation	9A	6
Asset Valuation	9B	6
Asset Valuation	9C	2
Asset Valuation	10A	6
Asset Valuation	10B	6
Portfolio Management	11A	9
Portfolio Management	11B	3
Asset Valuation	12A	3
Asset Valuation	12B	4
Asset Valuation	12C	3
Total		180

AFTERNOON SESSION		
Topic	Question	Points
Ethical and Professional Standards	13	18
Ethical and Professional Standards	14	18
Portfolio Management	15	18
Asset Valuation	16	18
Asset Valuation	17	18
Asset Valuation	18	18
Portfolio Management	19	18
Asset Valuation	20	18
Portfolio Management	21	18
Portfolio Management	22	18
Total		180

Practice Exam 1
Score Sheet

MORNING SESSION		
Question	Maximum Points	Your Approximate Score
1A	4	
1B	4	
2	8	
3A	13	
3B	6	
4A	9	
4B	9	
5A	9	
5B	6	
6A	6	
6B	4	
6C	6	
6D	9	
7A	4	
7B	4	
8A	15	
8B	10	
8C	6	
9A	6	
9B	6	
9C	2	
10A	6	
10B	6	
11A	9	
11B	3	
12A	3	
12B, C	4, 3	
Total	180	

AFTERNOON SESSION		
Question	Maximum Points	Your Approximate Score
13	18	
14	18	
15	18	
16	18	
17	18	
18	18	
19	18	
20	18	
21	18	
22	18	
Total	180	

Certain Passing Score: 252 of 360 (70%)
Probable Passing Score: 234

Please note that we write these exams to be as challenging and representative as possible. However, due to the relaxed conditions that most candidates apply when they "take" these tests (i.e., "I'm getting a little tired, I think I'll go to the refrigerator and get a snack"), you should adjust your score downward by 10–15% to get a more accurate measure of the score you would have actually received on exam day. Also, you must be honest with yourself for your score on this exam to have any meaning. Don't assume, for example, that if your answer is close, the graders will be generous with points.

PRACTICE EXAM 1
MORNING SESSION

Questions 1, 2, and 3 relate to Terry Malloy. A total of 30 minutes is allocated to these questions. *Candidates should answer these questions in the order presented.*

Terry Malloy, 52, is an executive for a marketing firm in New York City. Malloy is married and has one child, a daughter who has just started law school. All of the Malloys are in excellent health. Malloy and his wife both work and have a combined pre-tax annual income of $300,000. Malloy's wife, 54, plans to retire three years from now. Her retirement will reduce the couple's annual income by $90,000, and her employer does not offer any retirement benefits. The Malloys are contributing $65,000 for each of the remaining three years of their daughter's law school. Malloy estimates his annual living expenses (excluding the expenditures for his daughter) at $180,000.

The Malloys own a vacation home valued at $500,000. The vacation home can be rented out, and the after-tax annual income on renting the home is $40,000. Malloy would like to keep the vacation home, and upon his retirement sell his New York condominium and move to the vacation home as his primary residence. Malloy expects the after-tax proceeds of his New York condominium to be $1.0 million, and that his annual living expenses (excluding income tax) would decline to $150,000 after his retirement. Malloy has expressed a concern that he does not want to "outlive his assets" and become a financial burden on his daughter.

Malloy himself plans to retire eight years from now, when he reaches the age of 60. Malloy has a defined contribution plan with his employer. The balance in that account is currently $800,000. His employer offers the four different investment options shown in Exhibit 1, and Malloy has his funds evenly divided amongst the available funds. He rebalances at the end of each year to keep the balances equal.

Figure 1: Malloy Retirement Account Investment Options

Asset	Description	Expected Return
Bond fund	Invests primarily in intermediate to long-term debt instruments rated BBB or better (investment grade securities only).	4.0%
Balanced fund	Assets split 60/40 between investment-grade bonds and large capitalization domestic equities.	5.6%
Core fund	Invests primarily in large capitalization domestic securities.	8.0%
Growth fund	Invests primarily in small- to mid-capitalization equities with above-average growth prospects.	10.0%

Malloy has come to you for investment advice because of a recent inheritance. A family member has died, leaving to Malloy an after-tax estate containing two assets: $750,000 of cash and an interest in a venture capital limited partnership currently valued at $400,000.

Malloy would like to sell the venture capital partnership interest, but unfortunately the interest is restricted and cannot be sold (or borrowed against) for the next three years. Malloy hopes that in three years the partnership interest will appreciate from its current value, but he wants to use the current value for all planning purposes.

Malloy's current tax rate is 30%, which he expects to remain stable for several years, even after his retirement. Malloy prefers that all projections exclude inflation as he anticipates similar inflationary effects on both expenses and income. The Malloys have no significant assets or liabilities beyond those previously discussed.

QUESTION 1 HAS TWO PARTS FOR A TOTAL OF 8 MINUTES

A. **Identify** and **discuss** *two* weaknesses commonly found in defined-contribution retirement plans that are evident in Malloy's current asset allocation of his retirement account.

(4 minutes)

B. **Identify** and **comment** on the effect of the following two factors on Malloy's discretionary wealth to total assets ratio.

i. Inheritance from family member.

ii. Desire to avoid "outliving his assets."

Answer Question 1B in the template provided.

(4 minutes)

Template for Question 1B

Factor	Effect on discretionary wealth to total assets ratio	Comments
Inheritance from family member	Increase Decrease	
Desire to avoid "outliving his assets"	Increase Decrease	

　　　　　　　　　　　　©2008 Schweser

QUESTION 2 HAS ONE PART FOR A TOTAL OF 8 MINUTES

Critique Malloy's current asset allocation within his retirement account by suggesting whether his allocation to each asset class should be higher or lower, based only on his situation prior to his inheritance. **Justify** your responses.

Answer Question 2 in the template provided.

(8 minutes)

Template for Question 2

Asset	Allocation SHOULD be: (circle one)	Justification
Bond fund	Higher Lower	
Balanced fund	Higher Lower	
Core fund	Higher Lower	
Growth fund	Higher Lower	

QUESTION 3 HAS TWO PARTS FOR A TOTAL OF 19 MINUTES

Malloy has specified that upon his retirement in four years, he would like be able to make a 5% annual withdrawal to cover his living expenses without invading his portfolio's principal. Beyond this requirement, Malloy would like to achieve the maximum possible capital appreciation in his portfolio to allow for more financial flexibility later in his retirement.

A.   **Formulate** the risk and return objectives of an investment policy statement for the Malloys. Your response should include a calculation of the portfolio balance required at retirement in order to meet Malloy's objectives, as well as the return required on Malloy's current portfolio in order to achieve that balance.

Answer Question 3A in the template provided.

(13 minutes)

B.   **Formulate** the constraints portion of an investment policy statement for the Malloys, addressing *each* of the following:

i. Time horizon.

ii. Liquidity requirements.

Answer Question 3B in the template provided.

(6 minutes)

Template for Question 3A

Note: Your response should include appropriate content for each objective based on Malloy's overall situation.

Objectives	Comments
Risk	
Return	

Template for Question 3B

Note: Your response should include appropriate content for each constraint based on Malloy's overall situation.

Constraints	Comments
Time horizon	
Liquidity	

QUESTION 4 HAS TWO PARTS FOR A TOTAL OF 18 MINUTES

Lawrence Engles works for HiLo Investments (HiLo), a hedge fund. HiLo does not believe that investors are rational decision makers, or that all available information is fully reflected in the pricing of securities. Instead, HiLo develops decision making models that do not assume perfect rationality by investors. In other words, HiLo's strategy is based on taking advantage of mispriced opportunities provided by the stock market. For example, Engles' analysis of the oilfield service sector uncovered several interesting investment opportunities. Engles identified the best investment opportunity as Offshore, Inc., based on his calculation of future discounted cash flows. To hedge his bet, Engles shorted Coastal, Inc., a competitor of Offshore. Coastal has a similar cash flow profile to Offshore under all future scenarios developed by Engles. In addition, Engles conducted a regression of the returns of Offshore compared to those of Coastal, which yielded an R^2 of 50%. Engles believes this arbitrage will benefit HiLo as Offshore's mispricing is corrected, while reducing the risk exposure for HiLo.

A. **List** and **describe** *two* different investment risks and *one* cost that can be associated with HiLo's arbitrage strategy.

(9 minutes)

B.   **Identify** and **discuss** the limiting factors to a "best (perfect) substitute" arbitrage.

(9 minutes)

QUESTION 5 HAS TWO PARTS FOR A TOTAL OF 15 MINUTES

Jacque Claude is an analyst for Lafayette Portfolio Managers, a French firm. Lafayette provides investment advice regarding stocks and bonds for wealthy individuals. Claude is discussing the characteristics of international investments before a group of clients, during which he makes the following comments:

- "Although withholding taxes are frequently assessed by foreign governments on dividends and interest, the presence of domestic tax credits means that they are no longer a significant obstacle to international investing."
- "I would recommend that the return on a stock be compared to global sector benchmarks because industry factors have increased in importance for explaining stock returns. In fact, I believe that diversifying across borders is no longer necessary as long as the investor has adequate industry representation."
- "Differing governmental monetary and fiscal policies cause bond market correlations to be low, often lower than that between equity markets. As a result, adding global bonds to global equity portfolios can improve the performance of a global efficient frontier, especially for lower risk portfolios."

A.   **State** whether or not *each* of these comments is correct. If incorrect, **explain** why.

Answer Question 5A in the template provided.

(9 minutes)

Claude is examining the risk and returns for an investment in a Japanese stock and has collected the following statistics.

- The return on the stock in yen terms was 12%.
- The yen has appreciated by 5%, relative to the euro.
- The standard deviation of stock returns was 29% and the standard deviation of the yen-euro exchange rate was 14%.
- The correlation between the stock returns and the yen-euro exchange rate is 0.30.

B.   **Calculate** the return on the stock in euro terms and the contribution of currency risk.

(6 minutes)

Template for Question 5A

Comment	Correct or incorrect? (circle one)	Explanation, if incorrect
"Although withholding taxes are frequently assessed by foreign governments on dividends and interest, the presence of domestic tax credits means that they are no longer a significant obstacle to international investing."	Correct Incorrect	
"I would recommend that the return on a stock be compared to global sector benchmarks because industry factors have increased in importance for explaining stock returns. In fact, I believe that diversifying across borders is no longer necessary as long as the investor has adequate industry representation."	Correct Incorrect	
"Differing governmental monetary and fiscal policies cause bond market correlations to be low, often lower than that between equity markets. As a result, adding global bonds to global equity portfolios can improve the performance of a global efficient frontier, especially for lower risk portfolios."	Correct Incorrect	

QUESTION 6 HAS FOUR PARTS FOR A TOTAL OF 25 MINUTES

In 1955, David Peebles, founder of the successful California-based Peebles Winery, set up the Tokay Endowment. The Tokay Endowment was established to attract talented individuals to the wine industry and to encourage research designed to produce California grapes that would be competitive with those produced in France. The initial $1 million contribution has grown to $75 million. Peebles' grandson was recently given responsibility for management of the endowment. He believes the endowment's asset mix needs to be updated to reflect the alternative investments of hedge funds, managed futures, and private equity. The private equity investment will be an indirect investment using middle-market buyout funds (labeled "buyout funds" in the exhibits below). The endowment currently has 60% invested in equities and 40% in bonds. The endowment must maintain a 50% equity weighting and the grandson wants to invest 20% of total assets in the alternative investment category.

Exhibit 1: Returns and Standard Deviation for the Most Recent 10-year Period

	Annualized Return	Standard Deviation
Tokay equities	9.8%	14.9%
Tokay bonds	6.9%	4.3%
Buyout funds	13.9%	15.2%
Hedge funds	14.6%	7.1%
Managed futures	12.5%	11.9%

Exhibit 2: Correlations for the Most Recent 10-year Period

	Tokay Equities	Tokay Bonds	Buyout Funds	Hedge Funds	Managed Futures
Tokay equities	1.00				
Tokay bonds	0.37	1.00			
Buyout funds	0.86	0.28	1.00		
Hedge funds	0.70	0.01	0.45	1.00	
Managed futures	0.02	0.10	−0.04	−0.14	1.00

A trusted financial advisor recommended investing in hedge funds rather than managed futures because hedge funds offer a better risk/return profile.

A.   **Discuss** *six* major due diligence criteria that Tokay Endowment should use
     to select an active manager for its alternative investments.

(6 minutes)

Answer Question 6A in the template provided.

B.   **Evaluate** the financial advisor's statement recommending hedge funds
     rather than managed futures (refer to Exhibits 1 and 2).

(4 minutes)

C.   **Discuss** *two* reasons managed futures should be added to Tokay's
     Endowment portfolio.

(6 minutes)

D.	**Discuss** the criteria Tokay Endowment should consider when evaluating a potential investment in middle-market buyout funds. Specifically, **comment** on the following:

- Benchmarks.
- Investment characteristics.
- Impact on the overall portfolio's risk/return profile.

(9 minutes)

Answer Question 6D in the template provided.

Template for 6A

Due diligence discussion
1.
2.
3.
4.
5.
6.

Template for 6D

1. Benchmarks	
2. Investment characteristics	
3. Impact on the overall portfolio's risk/return profile	

QUESTION 7 HAS TWO PARTS FOR A TOTAL OF 8 MINUTES

Angus Company is a major beef processor. In the course of its normal operations, Angus will from time to time enter into forward contracts to secure additional beef supplies to maintain its operations. The rising public concern of potential health risks associated with eating red meat has caused consumption to decline. The industry has been slow to respond and consequently fewer cattle have been slaughtered. The industry trade association has developed an advertising program to fight the negative public perception. The trade association hopes the new promotion emphasizing a leaner beef product will generate higher future revenues.

DVE Ranch, which supplies Angus Company with cattle, plans to hedge the expected price of its spring born feeder cattle that it will deliver in the fall. DVE Ranch has 150 calves weighing on average 600 pounds apiece. DVE Ranch wants to lock in the current cattle price, but delivery of the cattle will not occur until the fall. DVE Ranch intends on using the feeder cattle futures contract which covers 50,000 pounds.

A.   **Indicate** whether the forward cattle price curve is best described as contango or backwardation and support your conclusion.

(4 minutes)

Answer Question 7A in the template provided.

B.   **Discuss** the potential basis risk associated with locking in the current cattle price using the feeder cattle futures contract.

(4 minutes)

Template for Question 7A

Circle one	Support your conclusion
Contango or Backwardation	

QUESTION 8 HAS THREE PARTS FOR A TOTAL OF 31 MINUTES

First National Bank is a regional bank with most of its offices in rural areas. The bank has $5 billion in assets. During the most recent year, First National Bank earned $27 million, or $1.80 per share. The bank's loan portfolio can be characterized as higher risk, with many small- to medium-sized company loans, a substantial portion of which are to the farming community. Rick Black, First National's CFO, manages the bank's $2 billion investment portfolio. Black has neither the time nor the resources to effectively manage the portfolio, so he relies on the advice of a major brokerage house. Black simply buys and holds the invested securities, with an objective of earning the highest current income possible to support the bank's operations. The table below highlights First National's securities investment portfolio:

First National Security Portfolio	Interest Rate	(in millions)
Short-term tax exempt securities	1.5%	$200
Intermediate tax exempt securities	3.0%	200
Long-term tax exempt securities	4.5%	400
BBB rated 15-year corporate securities	8.0%	150
BB+ rated 20-year corporate securities	10.0%	150
BBB- rated CMO with a duration of 20	7.0%	400
20-year Treasury bonds	5.5%	500
Total portfolio		$2,000

The bank uses an economic consultant to provide all needed economic forecasts. The economist is currently projecting that interest rates will increase by 75 to 150 basis points during the next year. All of First National's operational planning is based on the economist's forecast. A major drought in First National's geographic area is impacting the entire farming community. The bank is attempting to increase the percentage earned from fee income. To date, the effort has had mixed results.

A. **Identify** and **discuss** the *five* most important objectives of the security portfolio for a commercial bank. **Comment** on First National's current security portfolio relative to these objectives.

Answer Question 8A in the template provided.

(15 minutes)

B.   **Identify** and **discuss** *five* constraints to be considered in developing an investment policy statement for a commercial bank and **comment** on how each constraint might be applied to First National Bank.

Answer Question 8B in the template provided.

(10 minutes)

C.   **Identify** and **discuss** *three* potential negatives with First National Bank's current investment portfolio.

(6 minutes)

Template for Question 8A

Commercial Bank Objectives	Discussion
1.	
2.	
3.	
4.	
5.	

Template for Question 8B

Commercial Bank Constraints	Comments
1.	
2.	
3.	
4.	
5.	

QUESTION 9 HAS THREE PARTS FOR A TOTAL OF 14 MINUTES

Helen Baker, CFA, invests in distressed securities. Specifically, she creates an arbitrage by shorting the underlying company equity and purchasing a long position in the company's distressed debt. Baker concentrates on sound companies that have significantly exceeded their debt capacity. Baker's strategy is to capitalize on her knowledge of, and patience for, particular situations. To this end, she takes advantage of creditors that want to liquidate securities of companies that are in bankruptcy or near bankruptcy. In addition, Baker exploits the fact that distressed companies lack adequate research coverage. Baker buys the distressed debt for 50 cents or less on the dollar.

A.   Assuming the distressed company's prospects improve, **explain** how Baker's arbitrage would perform.

(6 minutes)

B.   **Describe** the following three sources of risk in distressed debt investing, and **comment** on the relative importance of each.

   i.   Event risk.

   ii. Market liquidity risk.

   iii. Market risk.

(6 minutes)

C.   **Describe** J factor risk as it relates to distressed debt.

(2 minutes)

QUESTION 10 HAS TWO PARTS FOR A TOTAL OF 12 MINUTES

Stewart Davis, CFA, manages the $3 billion internal equity portfolio for Gemsbok Insurance utilizing an enhanced index strategy. Gemsbok's Chairman has a low equity risk tolerance and Davis believes the high degree of risk control offered by an enhanced index strategy provides the greatest degree of downside protection. Davis uses a quantitative model to replicate the risk profile of the S&P 500 index. Based on the model, only 300 of the 500 stocks in the index are required to meet his objectives. To enhance returns, Davis overweights the ten most attractive stocks based on their 200-day moving average returns. Gemsbok's Chairman believes Davis should fully replicate the S&P 500 index. Two portfolios are created. The Gemsbok 300 uses Davis' previously described strategy while the Gemsbok 500 pursues a full replication strategy based on the S&P 500 index. Exhibit 1 provides data on the Gemsbok 300, S&P 500 index, and Gemsbok 500.

Exhibit 1: Quarterly Data for the Gemsbok 300, S&P 500, and Gemsbok 500

	Gemsbok 300	S&P 500	Gemsbok 500
Quarter 1 return	5.0%	6.5%	6.0%
Quarter 2 return	−0.5%	−1.5%	−1.3%
Quarter 3 return	8.8%	8.1%	8.4%
Quarter 4 return	3.2%	3.5%	3.4%
Tracking error	1.4%		0.7%
Information coefficient	0.075		0.053

A. Based on Exhibit 1, **calculate** the quarterly alpha and information ratio for the Gemsbok 300 portfolio.

(6 minutes)

B.   Based on Exhibit 1, **recommend** which of the Gemsbok portfolios the company's Chairman should select. **Justify** the recommendation using the Fundamental Law of Active Management.

(6 minutes)

QUESTION 11 HAS TWO PARTS FOR A TOTAL OF 12 MINUTES

Nick Richards is a pension consultant and is asked to evaluate the following portfolios:

- Portfolio 1 is highly concentrated, with five stocks representing 75% of the total portfolio.
- Portfolio 2 is highly diversified with over 400 stocks, none of which represent more than 1% of the total portfolio.
- Portfolio 3 is a diversified portfolio of 70 stocks, with the top 10 names representing 30% of the total portfolio.

The following investment results were recorded during 2007:

	Portfolio 1	Portfolio 2	Portfolio 3	S&P 500
Return	42.0%	25.0%	16.0%	20.0%
Standard deviation	1.2	0.4	0.2	0.5
Beta	1.8	1.2	0.5	1.0

Risk-free rate: 6%

A.   **Compute** the Sharpe, Treynor, and Jensen measures for each portfolio.

Answer Question 11A in the template provided.

(9 minutes)

B.   **Identify** which portfolio had the best risk-adjusted performance in 2007. **Justify** your selection with *two* supporting arguments.

(3 minutes)

Template for Question 11A

Performance Measure	Portfolio	Calculation	Value
Sharpe	1		
	2		
	3		
Treynor	1		
	2		
	3		
Jensen	1		
	2		
	3		

QUESTION 12 HAS THREE PARTS FOR A TOTAL OF 10 MINUTES

Otis Burg, CFA, is a consultant currently advising the investment committee of the Luther Manufacturing, Inc. pension plan. Burg has recommended to the committee that they consider adding an investment in real estate to their current portfolio. Currently, the Luther Pension portfolio, with $60 million in assets, is invested 65% in stocks and 35% in fixed income securities. Burg has presented a model to the committee comparing their current portfolio with his proposed portfolio (Exhibit 1 below). The proposed portfolio changes the asset allocation to 55% stocks, 30% bonds, and 15% real estate. The risk free rate is 4%.

Exhibit 1: Burg Model

	Current Portfolio	Proposed Portfolio
E(R)	7.1%	8.0%
Std Dev of return	12.1%	12.4%

Burg suggests that the Luther pension plan make direct investments in real estate as opposed to real investment trusts (REITs). His projections are based on his expectations for returns on the National Council of Real Estate Investment (NCREIF) unsmoothed index.

A. **State** whether the investment committee should accept Burg's proposal, and **justify** your response with *one* supporting reason.

(3 minutes)

Answer Question 12A in the template provided.

B. Burg's preference for direct investment in real estate as opposed to REITs is based on his interpretation of the relative advantages of direct investment. For each issue below, **identify** whether that issue is an advantage or disadvantage of direct investment in real estate relative to using REITs, and **justify** your answer.

   i. Portfolio diversification benefit.
   ii. Liquidity.

(4 minutes)

Answer Question 12B in the template provided.

C. **Indicate** whether the smoothed or unsmoothed NCREIF index is a better proxy for the Luther pension plan to use for a direct investment in real estate, and **justify** your response with *one* supporting reason.

(3 minutes)

Answer Question 12C in the template provided.

Template for Question 12A

Burg's Proposal	Justification
Accept Reject	

Template for Question 12B

Issue	Direct Investment vs. REITs	Explanation
Portfolio diversification	Advantage Disadvantage	
Liquidity	Advantage Disadvantage	

Template for Question 12C

NCREIF Index	Justification
Smoothed Unsmoothed	

END OF MORNING SESSION

PRACTICE EXAM 1
AFTERNOON SESSION

Questions 13.1–13.6 relate to Dynamic Investment Services.

Dynamic Investment Services (DIS) is a global full service investment advisory firm based in the United States. Although the firm provides numerous investment services, DIS specializes in portfolio management for individual and institutional clients and only deals in publicly traded debt, equity, and derivative instruments. Walter Fried, CFA, is a portfolio manager and the director of DIS's offices in Austria. For several years, Fried has maintained a relationship with a local tax consultant. The consultant provides a DIS marketing brochure with Fried's contact information to his clients seeking investment advisory services, and in return, Fried manages the consultant's personal portfolio and informs the consultant of potential tax issues in the referred clients' portfolios as they occur. Because he cannot personally manage all of the inquiring clients' assets, Fried generally passes the client information along to one of his employees but never discloses the relationship with the tax accountant. Fried recently forwarded information on the prospective Jones Family Trust account to Beverly Ulster, CFA, one of his newly hired portfolio managers.

Upon receiving the information, Ulster immediately set up a meeting with Terrence Phillips, the trustee of the Jones Family Trust. Ulster began the meeting by explaining DIS's investment services as detailed in the firm's approved marketing and public relations literature. Ulster also had Phillips complete a very detailed questionnaire regarding the risk and return objectives, investment constraints, and other information related to the trust beneficiaries, which Phillips is not. While reading the questionnaire, Ulster learned that Phillips heard about DIS's services through a referral from his tax consultant. Upon further investigation, Ulster discovered the agreement set up between Fried and the tax consultant, which is legal according to Austrian law but was not disclosed by either party. Ulster took a break from the meeting to get more details from Fried, which she then disclosed to the client. Before the meeting with Phillips concluded, Ulster began formalizing the investment policy statement (IPS) for the Jones Family Trust and agreed to Phillips' request that the IPS should explicitly forbid derivative positions in the Trust portfolio.

A few hours after meeting with the Jones Family Trust representative, Ulster accepted another new referral client, Steven West, from Fried. Following DIS policy, Ulster met with West to address his investment objectives and constraints and explain the firm's services. During the meeting, Ulster informed West that DIS offers three levels of account status, each with an increasing fee based on the account's asset value. The first level has the lowest account fees but receives oversubscribed domestic IPO allocations only after the other two levels receive IPO allocations. The second-level clients have the same priority as third-level clients with respect to oversubscribed domestic IPO allocations and receive research with significantly greater detail than first-level clients. Clients who subscribe to the third level of DIS services receive the most detailed research reports and are allowed to participate in both domestic and international IPOs. All clients receive research and recommendations at approximately the same time. West decided to engage DIS's services as a second-level client. While signing the enrollment papers, West told Ulster, "If you can give me the kind of performance I am looking for, I may move the rest of my assets to DIS." When Ulster inquired about the other accounts, West would not specify how much or what type of assets he held in other accounts. West also noted that a portion of the existing assets to be transferred to Ulster's control were private equity investments in small start-up companies, which DIS would need to manage. Ulster assured him that DIS would have no problem managing the private equity investments.

After her meeting with West, Ulster attended a weekly strategy session held by DIS. All managers were required to attend this particular meeting since the focus was on a new strategy designed to reduce portfolio volatility while slightly enhancing return using a combination of futures and options on various asset classes. Intrigued by the idea, Ulster implemented the strategy for all of her clients and achieved positive results for all portfolios. Ulster's average performance results after one year of using the new strategy are presented in Figure 1. For comparative purposes, performance figures without the new strategy are also presented.

Figure 1

	Average Sharpe Ratio	
	Without Strategy	*With Strategy*
Individual portfolios	0.80	0.89
Institutional portfolios	0.63	0.71

At the latest strategy meeting, DIS economists were extremely pessimistic about emerging market economies and suggested that the firm's portfolio managers consider selling emerging market securities out of their portfolios and avoid these investments for the next 12 to 15 months. Fried placed a limit order to sell his personal holdings of an emerging market fund at a price 5% higher than the market price at the time. He then began selling his clients' (all of whom have discretionary accounts with DIS) holdings of the same emerging market fund using market orders. All of his clients' trade orders were completed just before the price of the fund declined sharply by 13%, causing Fried's order to remain unfilled.

13.1. Did Ulster violate CFA Institute Standards of Professional Conduct by accepting either Phillips or West as new clients?

Phillips	West
A. No	No
B. Yes	Yes
C. No	Yes
D. Yes	No

13.2. Does the referral agreement between Fried and the tax consultant violate any CFA Institute Standards of Professional Conduct?
   A. No.
   B. Yes, because client confidentiality is being undermined by the arrangement.
   C. Yes, because it involves non-monetary compensation with no observable cost.
   D. Yes, because referral arrangements are not permitted under any circumstances.

13.3. During her initial meeting with West, did Ulster violate any CFA Institute Standards of Professional Conduct?
   A. Yes.
   B. No, because she developed a detailed investment policy to ensure the suitability of investment choices for the client's account.
   C. No, because she ensured that all conflicts of interest were disclosed to the client before the investment policy statement was created.
   D. No, because she acted with loyalty, prudence, and care by determining applicable fiduciary duty owed to West in the management of his portfolio.

13.4. According to CFA Institute Standards of Professional Conduct, which of the following statements regarding Ulster's meeting with West is **TRUE**? Ulster may:
   A. offer the different service levels and may accept the account without full knowledge of West's other accounts.
   B. not offer the different service levels but may accept the account without full knowledge of West's other accounts.
   C. offer the different service levels but may not accept the account without full knowledge of West's other accounts.
   D. not offer the different service levels and may not accept the account without full knowledge of West's other accounts.

13.5. By utilizing the futures and options strategy as suggested by DIS's economists, did Ulster violate any CFA Institute Standards of Professional Conduct?
   A. Yes.
   B. No, because she acted in her clients' best interest by reducing portfolio risk while increasing portfolio return.
   C. No, because she treated all clients fairly by applying the strategy to both individual and institutional clients.
   D. No, because she fulfilled her duty to her employer by utilizing accepted methodologies to manage her portfolios.

13.6. According to CFA Institute Standards of Professional Conduct, should Fried have taken a different course of action with respect to the limit order on the emerging market fund?
   A. No.
   B. Yes, Fried should not have sold any shares of the emerging market fund.
   C. Yes, Fried should have waited to place the limit order until after the market orders were filled.
   D. Yes, Fried should have placed limit orders for his clients after he placed the original limit order.

Questions 14.1–14.6 relate to Crane & Associates.

Shirley Schmidt, CFA, has just been promoted, from vice president of trading to chief investment officer (CIO) at Crane & Associates, LLC (CA), a large investment management firm. Schmidt has been with CA for eight years, but she has much to learn as she assumes her new duties as CIO. Schmidt has decided to hire Denny Kirk, CFA, as the new compliance officer for CA. Schmidt and Kirk have been reviewing procedures and policies throughout the firm and have discovered several potential issues.

Communications with Clients

Portfolio managers are encouraged to communicate with clients on a regular basis. At a minimum, managers are expected to contact clients on a quarterly basis to review portfolio performance. Each client must have an investment policy statement (IPS), created when their account is opened, and specifying the objectives and constraints for their portfolio. IPSs are reviewed at client request at any time. Any time market conditions dictate a change in the investment style or strategy of a client portfolio, the client is notified immediately by phone or e-mail.

Employee Incentive Program

CA offers several incentive programs to employees. One of the most popular of these programs is the CA IPO program. Whenever CA is involved in an initial public offering (IPO), portfolio managers are allowed to participate. The structure is simple—for every 100 shares purchased on behalf of a client, the manager is awarded five shares for his own account. The manager is thus rewarded for getting an IPO sold and at the same time is able to share in the results of the IPO. Any time shares are remaining 72 hours before the IPO goes public, other employees are allowed to participate on a first-come, first-serve basis. Employees seem to appreciate this opportunity, but CA does not have exact numbers on employee participation in the program.

Private Equity Fund

CA has a private equity fund that is internally managed. This fund is made available only to clients with more than $5 million in assets managed by CA, a policy that is fully disclosed in CA's marketing materials. Roughly one-third of the fund's assets are invested in companies that are either very small capitalization or thinly traded (or both). The pricing of these securities for monthly account statements is often difficult. CA support staff get information from different sources—sometimes using third party services, sometimes using CA valuation models. In some instances, a manager of the private equity fund will enter an order during the last trading hour of the month to purchase 100 shares of one of these small securities at a modest premium to the last trade price. If the trade gets executed, that price can then be used on the account statements. The small size of these trades does not significantly affect the fund's overall position in any particular company holding, which is typically several thousand shares.

Soft Dollar Usage

Several different managers at CA use independent research in developing investment ideas. One of the more popular research services among CA managers is "Beneath the Numbers (BTN)," which focuses on potential accounting abuses at prominent companies. This service often provides early warnings of problems with a stock, allowing CA managers the opportunity to sell their positions before a negative surprise lowers the price. Stocks covered by BTN are typically widely held in CA client accounts. Managers at CA have been so happy with BTN that they have also subscribed to a new research product provided by the same authors—"Beneath the Radar (BTR)." BTR recommends small capitalization securities that are not large enough to attract much attention from large institutional investors. The results of BTR's recommendations are mixed thus far, but CA managers are willing to be patient.

As they discuss these issues, Schmidt informs Kirk that she is determined to bring CA into full compliance with the CFA Institute's "Asset Manager Code of Professional Conduct." The following questions should be answered with this Asset Manager Code as a guide.

14.1.   Indicate whether CA's policies related to investment policy statement (IPS) reviews and notification of changes in investment style/strategy are consistent with the Asset Manager Code of Professional Conduct.

IPS review	Changes in style/strategy
A. Yes	Yes
B. Yes	No
C. No	Yes
D. No	No

14.2.   Indicate whether CA's policies related to its IPO program, specifically allowing portfolio manager participation and employee participation, are consistent with the Asset Manager Code of Professional Conduct.

Portfolio managers	Employees
A. Yes	Yes
B. Yes	No
C. No	Yes
D. No	No

14.3.   Participation in CA's private equity fund is limited to clients with $5 million under management. This policy:
   A. does not violate the Asset Manager Code of Professional Conduct.
   B. would be acceptable so long as a similar investment vehicle was made available to all clients.
   C. would be acceptable so long as the minimum asset level was $1 million.
   D. is not consistent with the Asset Manager Code of Professional Conduct.

14.4.   In discussing the pricing of thinly traded securities in the private equity fund, Schmidt suggested that CA should choose one pricing method and apply it consistently, thus avoiding the need to disclose specific pricing methods to clients. Kirk responded that using third party sources or internal valuation models was acceptable, so long as the pricing sources are fully disclosed to clients. Indicate whether Schmidt's comment or Kirk's response are *correct* or *incorrect*.

	Schmidt	Kirk
A.	Correct	Correct
B.	Correct	Incorrect
C.	Incorrect	Correct
D.	Incorrect	Incorrect

14.5.   Trading stocks during the last trading hour of a month to establish a fair market price:
   A. does not violate the Asset Manager Code of Professional Conduct.
   B. is acceptable so long as the trade is not material relative to the overall CA position in the security.
   C. is acceptable so long as the trade is a sale and not a purchase.
   D. is not consistent with the Asset Manager Code of Professional Conduct.

14.6.   Kirk has verified that CA has adequate disclosures of its soft dollar usage. Given that full disclosure is made to clients, indicate whether CA's use of soft dollars for BTN and BTR are consistent with the Asset Manager Code of Professional Conduct.

	BTN	BTR
A.	Yes	Yes
B.	Yes	No
C.	No	Yes
D.	No	No

Questions 15.1–15.6 relate to Travis Smith.

Travis Smith, CFA, is chief economic strategist and market analyst for Nashville Capital Management. He is developing a forecast of the S&P 500 and utilizing different approaches.

Using microeconomic analysis, Smith wants to value the S&P using a dividend discount model (DDM) valuation approach. The trailing recent 52-week dividend estimate is $19. Used as a proxy for the nominal risk-free rate, Treasury rates are as follows:

- 3-month T-bill rate: 3.5%
- 30-year T-bond rate: 5.0%

Smith has determined that two different levels of risk premium need to be considered: 4% (low) and 7% (high). His estimate for the long-term outlook for ROE is 11%, and the long-run dividend retention rate is estimated at 60%.

Smith also is forecasting the market trends using varied macroeconomic techniques. He believes that security prices reflect expectations about the general economy. During his monitoring and forecasting of the overall economy, Smith is evaluating cyclical indicators and the business cycle. Smith has focused his analysis on three indicators:

1. Index of industrial production.
2. Interest rate spread between 10-year T-bonds and the fed funds rate.
3. Stock prices.

Smith is particularly interested in using stock market trends to predict economic turning points.

In conducting his research, Smith has found that the business cycle appears to be in the slowdown phase. Two factors which affect the business cycle are monetary and fiscal policy. In his capital markets forecasting activities, Smith looks at government policy, and attempts to predict business and consumer activity, along with foreign trade. Smith has determined that government policy has a high influence on the business cycle, and he is trying to predict changes in government policy, specifically monetary policy of the Federal Reserve. Smith has estimated the following variables:

- Short-term interest rate, neutral value: 3.5%
- GDP growth rate trend: 4.25%
- Inflation target: 2.25%

Smith assumes that inflation is forecasted to increase to 3.0%, and GDP is expected to grow at a 1.5% rate.

15.1. In determining the S&P market valuation using the reduced form DDM, what is the estimate of D_1, assuming that the investor's holding period is long term?
A. $20.25.
B. $19.84.
C. $19.95.
D. $21.09.

15.2. Again using the reduced form DDM, what would be Smith's two estimates for S&P market valuation, given the "low" and the "high" risk premium(s)?

	S&P value – low risk premium	S&P value – high risk premium
A.	791.67	351.85
B.	431.30	261.05
C.	843.75	375.00
D.	2,250.00	519.23

15.3. Indicate the proper classification, according to the National Bureau of Economic Research's (NBER) analysis of economic indicators, for the Index of industrial production and the interest rate spread between 10-year T-bonds and the fed funds rate.

	Index of industrial production	Interest rate spread
A.	Leading	Leading
B.	Leading	Coincident
C.	Coincident	Leading
D.	Coincident	Coincident

15.4. According to the NBER, leading indicators of the business cycle include various economic series that generally reach peaks/troughs before correlative peaks/troughs in overall combined economic activity. Given Smith's focus on stock market trends, the typical lead time for stock market activity to indicate an economic turning point is *closest* to:
A. 6 months.
B. 4 months.
C. 18 months.
D. 1 month.

15.5. Assuming Smith's conclusion, that the business cycle is currently in the slowdown phase, is correct, indicate which of the following *best* describes the effects on the capital markets.
A. Short-term rates low or declining, with stocks rising rapidly.
B. Short-term rates topping out, with stocks declining.
C. Short-term rates rising, with stocks topping out, volatile.
D. Short-term rates declining, with stocks at a trough, starting to increase.

15.6. In order to assess the Fed's position and forecast changes in short-term interest rates, using the Taylor Rule, what is the optimal short-term interest rate, based on Smith's assumed values for interest rates, inflation, and growth?
    A. 1.5%.
    B. 3.5%.
    C. 5.75%.
    D. 2.5%.

Questions 16.1–16.6 relate to Garrison Investments.

Garrison Investments is a money management firm focusing on endowment management for small colleges and universities. Over the past 20 years, the firm has primarily invested in U.S. securities with small allocations to high quality long-term foreign government bonds. Garrison's largest account, Point University, has a market value of $800 million and an asset allocation as detailed in Figure 1.

Figure 1: Point University Asset Allocation

Asset Class	Allocation	Dividend/Coupon	Beta
Large cap equities	40%	2.0%	1.0
Mid cap equities	25%	1.2%	1.3
Small cap equities	15%	0.9%	1.5
U.S. Bonds	10%	5.0%	0
U.K. Bonds	5%	4.7%	0
German Bonds	5%	4.0%	0
European Index	0%	1.8%	1.2

*Bond coupon payments are all semiannual.

Managers at Garrison are concerned that expectations for a strengthening U.S. dollar relative to the British pound could negatively impact returns to Point University's U.K. bond allocation. Therefore, managers have collected information on swap and exchange rates. Currently, the swap rates in the United States and the United Kingdom are 4.9% and 5.3%, respectively. The spot exchange rate is 0.45 GBP/USD. The U.K. bonds are currently trading at face value.

Garrison recently convinced the board of trustees at Point University that the endowment should allocate a portion of the portfolio into international equities, specifically European equities. The board has agreed to the plan but wants the allocation to international equities to be a short-term tactical move. Managers at Garrison have put together the following proposal for the reallocation:

> To minimize trading costs while gaining exposure to international equities, the portfolio can use futures contracts on the 12 month mid-cap equity index and on the 12-month European equity index. This strategy will temporarily exchange $80 million of U.S. mid-cap exposure for European equity index exposure. Relevant data on the futures contracts are provided in Figure 2.

Figure 2: Mid-cap Index and European Index Futures Data

Futures Contract	Price	Beta	Multiplier
Mid-cap Index	$908	1.10	250
European Index	$2,351	1.05	50

Three months after proposing the international diversification plan, Garrison was able to persuade Point University to make a direct short-term investment of $2 million in Haikuza Incorporated (HI), a Japanese electronics firm. HI exports its products primarily to the United States and Europe, selling only 30% of its production in Japan. In order to control the costs of its production inputs, HI uses currency futures to mitigate exchange rate fluctuations associated with contractual gold purchases from Australia. In its current contract, HI has one remaining purchase of Australian gold that will occur in nine months. The company has hedged the purchase with a long 12-month futures contract on the Australian dollar (AUD).

Managers at Garrison are expecting to sell the HI position in one year, but have become nervous about the impact of an expected depreciation in the value of the Yen relative to the U.S. dollar. Thus, they have decided to use a currency futures hedge. Analysts at Garrison have determined that the covariance between the local currency returns on HI and changes in the USD/Yen spot rate is equal to 0.184 and that the variance of changes in the USD/Yen spot rate is equal to 0.92.

16.1. Which of the following is *closest* to the notional principal on a swap that would allow Point University to hedge the currency risk of the interest payments from their U.K. bond holdings?
A. GBP 16,000,000.
B. USD 38,000,000.
C. GBP 18,000,000.
D. USD 40,000,000.

16.2. With regard to Garrison's proposal to generate temporary exposure to European equities in the Point University portfolio, determine the appropriate position in the mid-cap equity index futures.
A. Buy 298 contracts.
B. Buy 416 contracts.
C. Sell 298 contracts.
D. Sell 416 contracts.

16.3. With regard to Garrison's proposal to generate temporary exposure to European equities in the Point University portfolio, determine the appropriate position in the European equity index futures.
A. Buy 595 contracts.
B. Buy 778 contracts.
C. Sell 595 contracts.
D. Sell 778 contracts.

16.4. Which of the following types of exchange rate risk exposure has Haikuza hedged using currency futures?
A. Political exposure.
B. Economic exposure.
C. Translation exposure.
D. Transaction exposure.

16.5. Which of the following *best* describes the risks and costs associated with Haikuza's currency hedging strategy?
A. Haikuza's strategy is subject to basis risk and will have lower transaction costs than a short-term contract strategy.
B. Haikuza's strategy is subject to basis risk and will have higher transaction costs than a short-term contract strategy.
C. Haikuza's strategy is not subject to basis risk and will have lower transaction costs than a short-term contract strategy.
D. Haikuza's strategy is not subject to basis risk and will have higher transaction costs than a short-term contract strategy.

16.6. Which of the following *best* describes the minimum variance hedge ratio for Garrison's currency futures hedge on the Haikuza investment?
A. For every futures contract sold to hedge translation risk, 0.8 futures contracts must be sold to hedge economic risk.
B. For every futures contract sold to hedge translation risk, 0.2 futures contracts must be sold to hedge economic risk.
C. For every futures contract sold to hedge translation risk, 1.2 futures contracts must be sold to hedge economic risk.
D. For every futures contract sold to hedge translation risk, 0.2 futures contracts must be purchased to hedge economic risk.

Questions 17.1–17.6 relate to Fred Warner.

Fred Warner is a fixed income portfolio manager with Avoyelles Capital Management. On June 1, 2008, Warner evaluates bonds to add to his portfolio. Warner is considering one AA/Aa1 rated bond issued by Boyd Manufacturing. The Boyd bonds mature on June 1, 2013, and are currently priced to yield 6.48%. U.S. Treasury bonds maturing in five years are currently priced to yield 5.80%. The 5-year swap spread is 46 basis points (bp) above the 5-year Treasury yield. The Boyd bonds have had an average spread over Treasuries of 68 bp over the past two years, with a standard deviation of 10 bp.

Warner is also considering two other bond issues: Collins Corp and Natalie Clothing. Both of these bonds also mature in five years. The Collins Corp bond is a BBB–/Baa3 rated bond currently priced to yield 6.82%. Over the past two years, the average spread over U.S. Treasuries has been 65 bp with a standard deviation of 20 bp. The Natalie Clothing bonds, rated BB+/Ba1 are priced to yield 7.16%. The 2-year average spread over Treasuries has been 110 bp with a standard deviation of 25 bp.

Warner has been discussing his analysis with other portfolio managers at Avoyelles and has heard the following comments from his colleagues:

Comment 1:   If you expect higher interest rates and lower interest rate volatility, you should use structure trades to shift from bullet maturities to callable bonds.

Comment 2:   Don't fall into the trap of trading for an extra 20 basis points in yield. You should focus on total return.

17.1.   Warner has decided to evaluate the Boyd bonds based on a swap spread analysis. Assume that a fixed-rate payer would receive LIBOR in exchange for the 5-year Treasury yield plus the swap spread. What would Warner earn if he bought the Boyd bonds and simultaneously entered into a 5-year swap as the fixed rate payer?
A. 8.48% – LIBOR.
B. LIBOR + 22 bp.
C. 8.26% – LIBOR.
D. LIBOR + 146 bp.

17.2. Which of the following is *least likely* to explain the growing acceptance of the swap spread methodology? The:
   A. popularity of the swap spread technique in European and Asian credit markets.
   B. problems with using nominal spreads when certain U.S. Treasury market sectors experience unusual transaction volumes.
   C. ease of application of the swap spread technique to a wide spectrum of credit risk levels, including speculative securities.
   D. the growing importance of various types of agency and asset-backed securities within the U.S. bond market.

17.3. Warner believes that mean-reversion analysis will help him choose between the bonds he has been analyzing. Based on mean-reversion analysis, which of the following statements would be *most accurate*?
   A. The low standard deviation of the spread on the Boyd bonds indicates that they are the most undervalued.
   B. Mean-reversion analysis would suggest that the Natalie Clothing and Collins Corp bonds are both overvalued.
   C. The Natalie Clothing bonds appear undervalued relative to the Collins Corp bonds.
   D. The Collins Corp bonds have the most potential for price appreciation based on mean reversion.

17.4. Evaluate the comments of Warner's colleagues. The comments concerning structure trades and reliance on total return instead of yield were:

	Comment 1	Comment 2
A.	Correct	Correct
B.	Correct	Incorrect
C.	Incorrect	Correct
D.	Incorrect	Incorrect

17.5. Warner has closely analyzed the financial statements of all three companies, and he has concluded that all three bonds have a reasonable probability of ratings upgrades. If Warner were to make his investment decision on the basis of a credit upside trade, he would be *most likely* to:
   A. buy the Boyd bonds due to their low risk relative to the return.
   B. buy the Collins Corp bonds due to the more favorable impact of an upgrade on their pricing.
   C. buy the Natalie Clothing bonds due to the more favorable impact of an upgrade on their pricing.
   D. be indifferent between the three bonds since their pricing seems to reasonably reflect their upgrade potential.

17.6.   Warner plans to use the new bonds in his portfolio as part of a credit barbell strategy. In combination with the bonds described previously, he could create the credit barbell by purchasing:
   A.   high duration U.S. government securities.
   B.   default rated securities with a duration similar to the 5-year bonds.
   C.   U.S. Treasury bills.
   D.   short-term corporate bonds rated AA/Aa or above.

Questions 18.1–18.6 relate to Andre Hickock.

Andre Hickock, CFA, is a newly hired fixed income portfolio manager for Deadwood Investments, LLC. Hickock is reviewing the portfolios of several pension clients that have been assigned to him to manage. The first portfolio, Montana Hardware, Inc., has the characteristics shown in Figure 1.

Figure 1

Sector	% of	Duration
U.S. Treasury	14.6%	7.54
U.S. agencies	23.7%	9.02
U.S. corporates	31.8%	4.52
U.S. mortgages (MBS)	11.4%	1.33
Non-U.S. governments	18.5%	3.22
	100.0%	

Hickock is attempting to assess the risk of the Montana Hardware portfolio. The benchmark bond index that Deadwood uses for pension accounts similar to Montana Hardware has an effective duration of 5.25. His supervisor, Carla Mity, has discussed bond risk measurement with Hickock. Mity is most familiar with equity risk measures, and is not convinced of the validity of duration as a portfolio risk measure. Mity told Hickock, "I have always believed that standard deviation is the best measure of bond portfolio risk. You want to know the volatility, and standard deviation is the most direct measure of volatility."

Hickock is also reviewing the bond portfolio of Buffalo Sports, Inc., which is comprised of the following assets shown in Figure 2.

Figure 2

Sector	% of	Duration
U.S. Treasury	10.1%	6.15
U.S. agencies	14.5%	7.20
U.S. corporates	20.9%	5.80
U.S. mortgages	33.7%	4.65
U.S. ABS	8.2%	3.67
Non-U.S.	12.6%	2.50
	100.0%	

The trustees of the Buffalo Sports pension plan have requested that Deadwood explore alternatives to reduce the risk of the MBS sector of their bond portfolio. Hickock responded to their request as follows:

"I believe that the current option-adjusted spread (OAS) on the MBS sector is quite high. In order to reduce your risk, I would suggest that we hedge the interest rate risk using a combination of 2-year and 10-year Treasury security futures. I would further suggest that we do not take any steps to hedge spread risk at this time."

18.1   Mity's comment regarding the use of standard deviation instead of duration to measure bond portfolio risk is:
A. incorrect because standard deviation does not address interest rate risk.
B. incorrect because historical variance measures for specific bonds are not meaningful predictors of future volatility.
C. correct because calculating an accurate portfolio duration measure requires an unwieldy amount of data.
D. correct because duration does not directly address volatility.

18.2.   Calculate the duration of the Montana Hardware pension portfolio and assess the interest rate risk of the portfolio versus Hickock's benchmark index:

Duration	Interest rate risk
A. 5.13	Greater than benchmark
B. 5.13	Less than benchmark
C. 5.42	Greater than benchmark
D. 5.42	Less than benchmark

18.3.   Hickock is reviewing other risk measures for the Montana Hardware portfolio. He has estimated the static spread duration for the portfolio to be 6.25. Which of the following statements regarding the Montana Hardware pension bond portfolio is **TRUE**?
A. The portfolio has higher sensitivity to changes in interest rate levels than to changes in the spread over Treasury securities.
B. The portfolio spread duration could be decreased by adding Treasury securities to the portfolio.
C. A 50 basis point change in the zero volatility spread would lead to an approximately 6.25% change in the value of the portfolio.
D. The spread duration calculation would be more accurate if the international bonds were excluded from the calculation.

18.4.   Evaluate Hickock's comments concerning the *appropriate* strategy for hedging interest rate risk and his suggestion **NOT** to hedge spread risk:

Interest rate hedge	No hedge of spread risk
A. Correct	Correct
B. Correct	Incorrect
C. Incorrect	Correct
D. Incorrect	Incorrect

18.5. In assessing the risk of a portfolio containing both bullet maturity corporate bonds and MBS, Hickock should always consider that:
   A. the duration of MBS securities will increase as the level of interest rates declines.
   B. MBS values will benefit from higher convexity as interest rates decline.
   C. the duration of MBS securities will remain stable even for relatively large changes in interest rates.
   D. MBS values will be more sensitive to changes in the shape of the yield curve than bullet maturity corporate bonds.

18.6. Under most circumstances, the *most* effective means of hedging the risk of a portfolio of MBS is to take an offsetting position in a:
   A. single Treasury security with a duration similar to the average duration of the MBS portfolio.
   B. single Treasury security with a duration similar to the longest duration security in the MBS portfolio.
   C. portfolio consisting of a 2-year Treasury security and a 10-year Treasury security.
   D. portfolio consisting of a T-bill and a 30-year Treasury security.

Questions 19.1–19.6 relate to Kim Simpson and Janet Long

Kim Simpson, CFA manages a $75 million multi-cap growth portfolio. Simpson utilizes a growth at a reasonable price (GARP) investment strategy and her investment universe consists of small, medium and large capitalization stocks. She turns the entire portfolio over once each year. Simpson is concerned about the amount of trading costs she has generated through the implementation of her investment strategy. Simpson decides to conduct a trade cost analysis with the cooperation of her trader, Janet Long, CFA. Simpson believes the results of the trading analysis can be used to improve trading performance and help to refine her investment strategy. The first trade they examine is a purchase of 2000 shares of Technology Company that was completed using a market order. Simpson remembers adding to her Technology Company position based on her analyst's recommendation that the company was going to generate earnings significantly above the consensus estimate in a soon to be released earnings report. The order was split into two trades as shown in Figure 1.

Figure 1 – Technology Company buy order for 2000 shares

Shares Purchased	Purchase Price	Ask Size	Ask Price	Bid Size	Bid Price
700	$79.25	700	$79.25	900	$79.00
1,300	$80.00	800	$80.10	1,100	$79.75

In conducting a comprehensive analysis of the trading markets, Simpson states that she is most concerned about market liquidity. Simpson defines a market with good liquidity as one with diversity of opinion, many buyers/sellers and relatively wide bid-ask spreads. In addition to reviewing market liquidity, Simpson believes that, in order to assess market quality, both the ease with which investors can obtain accurate information and the certainty that a trade will be completed must be evaluated.

Simpson and Long review their trade of Nano Corporation, a small biotechnology company. Simpson used a limit order because her analyst had established a specific buy target and she wanted to hold down transaction costs. To handle both explicit and implicit trading costs, Simpson measures execution costs using implementation shortfall. The buy order for 100,000 shares of Nano stock has the following timeline:

- Nano stock price closes at $35.00 per share.
- *Day one:* Simpson places a limit order for 100,000 shares of Nano stock at $34.75 per share or better at the opening of trading. However, Nano's stock never falls below $35.00 per share and closes at $36.50 per share.
- *Day two:* Simpson adjusts her limit order price to $37.00 per share or better. Long is able to fill 50,000 shares of the order at $36.75 per share. Nano's stock climbs to $38.00 per share during the day and Simpson moves the limit price to $40.00 per share or better. Long completes the purchase of the remaining

50,000 shares of Nano at $40.00 per share, which is also the closing price of Nano's stock.
* The commission for each block trade is $2,500.

Long suggests implementing the Best Execution concept as established by the CFA Institute in its Trade Management Guidelines. Long states best execution would accept a high portfolio turnover strategy provided the overall portfolio value is greater after trading costs. Long adds that her professional relationships are integral to best execution.

19.1. The buy order for the Technology Company shares has an average effective spread *closest* to:
   A. $0.05.
   B. $0.10.
   C. $0.15.
   D. $0.20.

19.2. Simpson discusses both the definition of market liquidity and how to assess market quality. Are her statements correct?

	Market liquidity	Market quality
A.	No	No
B.	No	Yes
C.	Yes	No
D.	Yes	Yes

19.3. The explicit cost component of the total implementation shortfall for the Nano Corporation trade is *closest* to:
   A. 0.15%.
   B. 0.25%.
   C. 0.35%.
   D. 0.55%.

19.4. The total implementation shortfall for the Nano Corporation trade is *closest to*:
   A. 1%.
   B. 4%.
   C. 7%.
   D. 10%.

19.5. Evaluate the Technology Company and Nano Corporation trades and indicate which type of trader *best* describes each trade's motivation.

	Technology Company	Nano Corporation
A.	Information-motivated	Information-motivated
B.	Value-motivated	Information-motivated
C.	Information-motivated	Value-motivated
D.	Value-motivated	Value-motivated

19.6.   Long states that her professional relationships are a key component in achieving best execution. Long also states best execution would accept a high portfolio turnover strategy provided that the portfolio value is greater after trading costs. Are these statements consistent with the CFA Institute Trade Management Guidelines?

	Professional relationships	High portfolio turnover
A.	No	No
B.	No	Yes
C.	Yes	No
D.	Yes	Yes

Questions 20.1–20.6 relate to Donaghy Management Company.

Donaghy Management Company (DMC) manages several funds only available to high net worth individuals. In preparation for an upcoming meeting, the firm has circulated among its managers the information in Figure 1 on objectives and market expectations relevant to each of three funds.

Figure 1: Fund Strategies and Market Expectations

	Fund A	Fund B	Fund C
Objectives	Predict and profit from volatility in the equity market using options on a broad equity index.	Market neutral fund with offsetting long and short equity positions. The fund utilizes leverage to enhance returns.	Long only international equity fund. Individual securities may be delta hedged using call options to reduce exposure to the position without selling it.
Market Expectations	Volatility in the equity market is expected to increase in the near future. However, the direction of the volatility is not known.	Credit markets are expected to tighten in the near future. Increased interest rates are expected across all credit qualities.	International equity markets are forecasted to rise in general. Certain securities are forecast to decline in value temporarily.

The manager of Fund A has collected data on put and call options on the broad market index underlying his strategy. The option data is presented in Figure 2. All options presented have the same expiration date.

Figure 2: Option Data for the Broad Market Index

Call Price	Strike Price	Put Price
35.40	1,475	6.80
18.10	1,500	17.00
7.90	1,515	24.60

During the meeting, the manager of Fund B states that in order to enhance returns for the fund, he intends to implement a box-spread strategy. The manager justifies the strategy with the following comments:

Comment 1:   Using a box-spread strategy is relatively simple since it does not require an assumption of an underlying option pricing model. However, assumptions must still be made about the volatility of the asset underlying the options used in the strategy.

Comment 2:   The ending price of the asset underlying the box-spread strategy has no impact on the payoff of the strategy. Thus, if the market price of the strategy implies a rate of return greater than the risk-free rate, an arbitrage opportunity exists.

Also during the meeting, DMC's president questioned the manager of Fund C about the mechanics of his hedging strategy. The manager explained the strategy with the following comments:

Comment 1:   The hedge position is established to reduce the exposure to certain equity positions by writing call options on the equity positions. The necessary number of short option positions per share of stock held is calculated as the inverse of the option delta.

Comment 2:   The hedge position only requires adjusting in the event of a price or volatility change in the underlying and is effective for small changes in the price of the underlying security.

20.1.   Which of the following option strategies would be *most* beneficial in terms of potential payoff for Fund A given its objectives and market expectations?
   A. Long straddle.
   B. Long bull spread.
   C. Short bear spread.
   D. Short butterfly spread.

20.2.   Using the data in Figure 2, determine which of the following is *closest* to the maximum profit from a long butterfly spread strategy if the price of the broad market index is currently 1,502.
   A. 7.1.
   B. 13.0.
   C. 17.9.
   D. 27.6.

20.3. In 110 days, the manager of Fund B expects to borrow $50,000,000 for 180 days at a rate of 180-day LIBOR plus 150 bp to pursue a leveraged strategy. LIBOR is currently 6.5%. The manager purchases an interest rate call on 180-day LIBOR that expires in 110 days with a premium of $120,000 and exercise rate of 6%. If LIBOR at the option expiration is 7.3%, calculate the effective annual rate on the loan.
   A. 6.71%.
   B. 7.30%.
   C. 8.29%.
   D. 8.80%.

20.4. Determine whether the comments made by the manager of Fund B with respect to the assumptions and arbitrage opportunities of the box-spread strategy are correct.

	Assumptions	Arbitrage opportunities
A.	No	No
B.	No	Yes
C.	Yes	No
D.	Yes	Yes

20.5. Determine whether the comments made by the manager of Fund C with respect to determining the hedge position and adjusting the hedge position are correct.

	Determining hedge position	Adjusting hedge position
A.	No	No
B.	No	Yes
C.	Yes	No
D.	Yes	Yes

20.6. Under which of the following scenarios will Fund C be *most* exposed to the gamma effect resulting from delta hedged equity positions? When the option used to delta hedge is:
   A. at-the-money and close to expiration.
   B. at-the-money and not close to expiration.
   C. deep in-the-money and close to expiration.
   D. deep in-the-money and not close to expiration.

Questions 21.1–21.6 relate to Joan Nicholson and Kim Fluellen.

Joan Nicholson, CFA, and Kim Fluellen, CFA, sit on the risk management committee for Thomasville Asset Management, located in the southeastern United States. Nicholson is the chair of the committee and chief executive officer of the firm. Fluellen was added as a committee member two years ago and is chief investment officer of the firm.

Although Thomasville manages the majority of its investable assets, it also utilizes outside firms for special situations such as market neutral and convertible arbitrage strategies. Thomasville has hired a hedge fund, Boston Advisors, for both of these strategies. The managers for the Boston Advisors funds are Frank Amato, CFA, and Joseph Garvin. Amato uses a market neutral strategy and has generated a return of $20 million this year on the $100 million Thomasville has invested with him. Garvin uses a convertible arbitrage strategy and has lost $15 million this year on the $200 million Thomasville has invested with him, with most of the loss coming in the last quarter of the year. Thomasville pays each outside manager an incentive fee of 20% on profits. Nicholson and Fluellen evaluate the characteristics of their arrangement with Boston Advisors during the risk management committee meeting. Nicholson states that the asymmetric nature of Thomasville's contract with Boston Advisors creates adverse consequences for Thomasville's net profits. Fluellen adds that the compensation contract resembles a put option for Boston Advisors.

Nicholson asks Fluellen to provide an assessment of risk for the firm's large cap growth portfolio using a monthly dollar VAR. To do so, Fluellen obtains the following statistics from the fund manager. The value of the fund is $80 million and has an annual expected return of 14.4%. The annual standard deviation of returns is 21.50%. Assuming a standard normal distribution, 5% of the potential portfolio values are 1.65 standard deviations below the expected return.

Thomasville periodically engages in options trading for hedging purposes or when they believe that they are mispriced. One of their positions is a long position in the call option for the Moffett Corporation. The option is a European option with a 3-month maturity. The underlying stock price is $27 and the strike price of the option is $25. The option sells for $2.86. Thomasville has also sold a put on the stock of the McNeill Corporation. The option is an American option with a 2-month maturity. The underlying stock price is $52 and the strike price of the option is $55. The option sells for $3.82. Fluellen assesses the credit risk of these options to Thomasville and states that the current credit risk of Moffett option is $2.86 and the current credit risk of the McNeill option is $3.82.

Thomasville also uses options quite heavily in their Special Strategies Portfolio. This portfolio seeks to exploit mispriced assets using the leverage provided by options contracts. Although this fund has achieved some spectacular returns, it has also produced some rather large losses on days of high market volatility. Nicholson has calculated a 5% VAR for the fund at $13.9 million. In most years, the fund has produced losses exceeding $13.9 million in 13 of the 250 trading days in a year, on average. Nicholson is concerned about the accuracy of the estimated VAR because when the losses exceed $13.9 million, they are typically much greater than $13.9 million.

In addition to using options, Thomasville also uses swap contracts for hedging interest rate risk and currency exposures. Fluellen has been assigned the task of evaluating the credit risk of these contracts. The characteristics of the swap contracts Thomasville uses are shown in Figure 1.

Figure 1: Thomasville Swap Contracts

	Contract A	*Contract B*	*Contract C*	*Contract D*
Type of Contract	Interest Rate Swap	Currency Swap	Interest Rate Swap	Currency Swap
Original maturity	5 years	3 years	4 years	4 years
Terms of swap	Plain vanilla	Yen-dollar	Plain vanilla	Euro-dollar
Time Remaining to Maturity	0.25 years	2.5 years	3.75 years	1.0 years

Nicholson and Fluellen later discuss credit risk in general. Nicholson states that cross-default-provisions generally protect a creditor because they prevent a debtor from declaring immediate default on the obligation owed to the creditor when they default on other obligations. Fluellen states that credit risk and credit VAR can be quickly calculated because bond rating firms provide extensive data on the defaults for investment grade and junk grade corporate debt at reasonable prices.

21.1. Regarding Thomasville's compensation contract with Boston Advisors, are Nicholson and Fluellen correct?

	Nicholson	Fluellen
A.	No	No
B.	No	Yes
C.	Yes	No
D.	Yes	Yes

21.2. Which of the following is *closest* to the monthly VAR Fluellen will calculate for the large cap growth portfolio?
   A. $4.0 million.
   B. $7.2 million.
   C. $16.9 million.
   D. $18.0 million.

21.3. Regarding Fluellen's comments on the credit risk of the Moffett and McNeill options, is she correct?

	Moffett option	McNeill option
A.	No	No
B.	No	Yes
C.	Yes	No
D.	Yes	Yes

21.4. Which of the following *best* describes the accuracy of the VAR measure calculated for the Special Strategies Portfolio?
   A. It is accurate but should be supplemented with scenario analysis.
   B. It is accurate and provides a complete measure of the fund's risk.
   C. It is inaccurate and should be calculated using Monte Carlo analysis.
   D. It is inaccurate and should be supplemented with comprehensive stress testing.

21.5. Which of the following swap contracts *likely* has the highest credit risk?
   A. Contract A.
   B. Contract B.
   C. Contract C.
   D. Contract D.

21.6. Regarding Nicholson's and Fluellen's comments on credit risk in general, are they correct?

	Nicholson	Fluellen
A.	No	No
B.	No	Yes
C.	Yes	No
D.	Yes	Yes

Questions 22.1–22.6 relate to Tri-mar Investment Advisors.

Tri-mar Investment Advisors is a worldwide firm with an excellent global reputation. The firm is headquartered in Durham, North Carolina. Pam Dubar, CFA, has recently been hired as compliance director.

One of Dubar's first duties is to carefully examine all of Tri-mar's marketing materials and presentations of past investment performance. Dubar believes that CFA Institute has created GIPS in order to set forth an ethical framework for the calculation and presentation of the investment performance history of an investment firm. However, she is troubled by some of the confusing details on how Tri-mar should properly present its investment results.

22.1. Dubar has been reviewing the proper calculation methodology. She is aware that performance must be calculated after the deduction of all trading expenses. Examining this requirement in more detail, which of the following statements is *least accurate*?
   A. If all trading expenses are not yet available, an estimate may be made based on historical data.
   B. Trading expenses are typically brokerage commissions or spreads from internal or external brokers.
   C. Custody fees are not to be included in direct transaction costs.
   D. Trading costs are to be included because these are costs that have to be paid in order for the firm to implement the investment strategy.

22.2. Which of the following would **NOT** be a required disclosure in a GIPS-compliant performance presentation?
   A. If the firm has a minimum asset level.
   B. Whether or not performance results are calculated gross or net of fees, along with other fees paid by clients to the firm or its affiliates.
   C. Cumulative composite and benchmark returns for all periods are to be presented.
   D. Whether or not the firm has included any non-fee-paying portfolios in composites, along with percentage of composite assets which are non-fee-paying.

22.3. Tri-mar typically makes the asset allocation decisions for its clients. However, the cash allocation in client accounts is held in a money market fund managed by the custodian of the client assets. Since Tri-mar does not manage the cash, it does not include the cash assets in the Tri-mar total return calculation. This practice is:
   A. consistent with GIPS requirements.
   B. acceptable under GIPS so long as the cash return is disclosed in the footnotes of the performance report.
   C. in violation of GIPS because Tri-mar must still include the return on the cash assets in its total return calculation.
   D. in violation of GIPS because Tri-mar cannot delegate the management of cash assets without written client authorization.

22.4. Dubar is carefully reviewing all of the extensive rules regarding composite construction. Which of the following is only a recommendation, as opposed to a firm requirement, regarding composite construction?
A. Carve-out returns must not be included in single asset class composite returns unless the carve-outs are actually managed separately with their own cash balance.
B. Composites must include only assets under management, and they may not link model portfolios with actual performance.
C. Composites must include new portfolios on a timely, consistent basis after the portfolio comes under management.
D. Convertible securities must be treated consistently across time and also within composites.

22.5. Dubar is researching a specific GIPS requirement relating to presentation and reporting. How much time does a compliant firm that acquires or is acquired by a noncompliant firm have to bring the noncompliant firm's assets into compliance?
A. 6 months.
B. 2 years.
C. 90 days.
D. 1 year.

22.6. Tri-mar manages a number of smaller accounts for individuals, particularly IRA accounts and personal trusts. Dubar knows that there has been an ongoing internal debate about how to handle the performance reporting on these small accounts. A year ago, Tri-mar decided to exclude all portfolios valued under
$1 million from its composites. Dubar was in a meeting last week where this policy was questioned. The strong performance by many of the small accounts was re-igniting the debate over an appropriate minimum asset size. Tri-mar is thinking of lowering the minimum back to $500,000. Which of the following statements is **NOT** consistent with GIPS requirements concerning minimum asset levels?
A. The minimum asset size must be disclosed in performance presentations.
B. Any changes to a composite-specific minimum asset level are permitted to be applied retroactively.
C. The minimum asset level can be used to exclude portfolios that are too small to be representative of the intended strategy.
D. Changes in the minimum asset level should not occur frequently.

END OF AFTERNOON SESSION

PRACTICE EXAM 2
SCORE SHEET

MORNING SESSION		
Topic	Question	Points
Portfolio Management	1A	4
Portfolio Management	1B	6
Portfolio Management	1C	5
Portfolio Management	2A	6
Portfolio Management	2B	6
Portfolio Management	3A	17
Portfolio Management	3B	12
Asset Valuation	4	6
Portfolio Management	5	6
Asset Valuation	6	12
Asset Valuation	7A	4
Asset Valuation	7B	3
Asset Valuation	7C	5
Asset Valuation	7D	4
Asset Valuation	8A	4
Asset Valuation	8B	4
Portfolio Management	9A	12
Portfolio Management	9B	6
Portfolio Management	9C	6
Portfolio Management	10	4
Portfolio Management	11A	9
Portfolio Management	11B	3
Portfolio Management	12A	15
Portfolio Management	12B	9
Asset Valuation	13	12
Total		180

AFTERNOON SESSION		
Topic	Question	Points
Ethical and Professional Standards	14	18
Ethical and Professional Standards	15	18
Asset Valuation	16	18
Asset Valuation	17	18
Portfolio Management	18	18
Asset Valuation	19	18
Asset Valuation	20	18
Asset Valuation	21	18
Asset Valuation	22	18
Portfolio Management	23	18
Total		180

PRACTICE EXAM 2
SCORE SHEET

MORNING SESSION		
Question	Maximum Points	Your Approximate Score
1A	4	
1B	6	
1C	5	
2A	6	
2B	6	
3A	17	
3B	12	
4	6	
5	6	
6	12	
7A	4	
7B	3	
7C	5	
7D	4	
8A	4	
8B	4	
9A	12	
9B	6	
9C	6	
10	4	
11A	9	
11B	3	
12A	15	
12B	9	
13	12	
Total	180	

AFTERNOON SESSION		
Question	Maximum Points	Your Approximate Score
14	18	
15	18	
16	18	
17	18	
18	18	
19	18	
20	18	
21	18	
22	18	
23	18	
Total	180	

Certain Passing Score: 252 of 360 (70%)
Probable Passing Score: 234

Please note that we write these exams to be as challenging and representative as possible. However, due to the relaxed conditions that most candidates apply when they "take" these tests (i.e., "I'm getting a little tired, I think I'll go to the refrigerator and get a snack"), you should adjust your score downward by 10–15% to get a more accurate measure of the score you would have actually received on exam day. Also, you must be honest with yourself for your score on this exam to have any meaning. Don't assume, for example, that if your answer is close, the graders will be generous with points.

PRACTICE EXAM 2
MORNING SESSION

QUESTION 1 HAS THREE PARTS FOR A TOTAL OF 15 MINUTES

Lauren Shoemaker, CFA, is the director of equity trading for a large mutual fund group. Shoemaker oversees the execution of roughly 5 million shares of daily trading volume. Over the past several years, it has become more difficult to efficiently handle the mutual fund group's large trade volume because the average trade size on the New York Stock Exchange has fallen so dramatically. Based on a recent conference attended by Shoemaker, she believes the solution to the mutual fund group's problem is algorithmic trading. Her hope is that the trading algorithms deliver as advertised by automatically breaking up large orders into smaller sizes and blending them into the normal trade flow. Shoemaker has a major concern that, in the future, traders will become irrelevant and the job of the trader will be eliminated. Figure 1 provides a partial trade blotter for Shoemaker's mutual fund group.

Figure 1: Trade blotter

Stock	Trade	Size (shares)	Avg. Daily Volume	Last Price	Bid Price	Ask Price	Urgency
Star	Sell	1,150,000	11,500,000	$39.75	$39.74	$39.76	High
Moon	Buy	500,000	2,200,000	$150.00	$149.62	$150.37	Low
Sun	Buy	500,000	6,000,000	$80.00	$79.98	$80.02	Low

A.   **Discuss** the rationale behind algorithmic trading.

(4 minutes)

B.   **State** the appropriate algorithmic trading strategy for each stock listed in the trade blotter and **justify** your selection. (Refer to Exhibit 1)

(6 minutes)

Answer Question 1B in the template provided.

C.   **State** whether Shoemaker's concern about the future of the traders is accurate or inaccurate and **defend** your selection.

(5 minutes)

Answer Question 1C in the template provided.

Template for 1B

Stock	Appropriate algorithmic trading strategy	Justification
1. Star		
2. Moon		
3. Sun		

Template for 1C

Circle one	Defend your selection
Accurate Inaccurate	

QUESTION 2 HAS TWO PARTS FOR A TOTAL OF 12 MINUTES

Dennis Richardson is the chief investment officer for Delray Portfolio Managers. Delray provides investment management services for institutions and wealthy individuals. Richardson is discussing the requirements for compliance with the Global Investment Performance Standards (GIPS®) and makes the following comments:

- "We have not reported the performance for our real estate composite because we only have eight portfolios in it, which is less than the minimum number of portfolios required to form a composite. Once we have the required ten portfolios necessary for composite creation, we will begin reporting performance for the real estate composite."
- "We have different policies for when portfolios are added to a composite. The time period for inclusion of new portfolios is longer for the private equity composite than it is for the small cap equity composite."

A.   **State** whether or not *each* of these comments is consistent with the GIPS standards. If inconsistent, **recommend** the change necessary to bring the firm into compliance with the GIPS standards.

Answer Question 2A in the template provided.

(6 minutes)

Delray has a real estate portfolio that invests in apartment buildings. Richardson is using the following data to calculate and report quarterly returns to current and prospective investors. The capital contribution in the table came 43% of the way into the quarter and the capital disbursement came 87% of the way into the quarter.

Total capital as of	January 1	$15,000,000
Capital contribution on	February 9	$800,000
Capital disbursement on	March 19	$620,000
Capital expenditure		$510,000
Property taxes paid		$148,000
Property sales		$930,000
Total non-recoverable expenses		$125,000
Interest paid on borrowed funds		$78,000
Accrued investment income		$546,000
Market value—beg. of quarter	January 1	$16,300,000
Market value—end of quarter	March 31	$17,100,000

B. **Calculate** the capital return and income return for the real estate portfolio.

(6 minutes)

Template for Question 2A

Comment	Is the comment consistent with the requirements of GIPS? (circle one)	If not, recommend the change that will bring the firm into GIPS compliance
"We have not reported the performance for our real estate composite because we only have eight portfolios in it, which is less than the minimum number of portfolios required to form a composite. Once we have the required ten portfolios necessary for composite creation, we will begin reporting performance for the real estate composite."	Yes No	
"We have different policies for when portfolios are added to a composite. The time period for inclusion of new portfolios is longer for the private equity composite than it is for the small cap equity composite."	Yes No	

Questions 3 and 4 relate to the following scenario. A total of 35 minutes is allocated to these questions. *Candidates should answer questions in the order presented.*

Karen Brown is a trustee of Shailor College, a 4-year liberal arts college with an enrollment of around 2,500 students. Brown chairs the investment committee of the college's board of trustees, which oversees the school's endowment. The endowment fund totals $80 million and is currently split between fixed-income (70% of assets) and equity securities (30% of assets). The fund is required to make annual distributions, adjusted for inflation, to supplement the school's operating budget. This year's distribution has been set at $3.6 million.

Currently, the equity portion of the fund is invested in an S&P 500 Index fund. The fixed-income portion of the fund is indexed to replicate the returns on an established index of investment grade (A) corporate bonds. The by-laws of Shailor College require that the endowment invest only in U.S. domiciled securities. The college has recently completed a new library and conference facility and has no plans for additional major capital expenditures for the next three years. The long-range planning committee has proposed substantial renovations to the school's athletic facilities beginning four years from now. These renovations are expected to cost $25 million, but the planning committee believes that $15 million of that amount can be raised from alumni and local donors. The remaining $10 million will be taken from the endowment fund.

Brown believes that the endowment fund is not adequately diversified. The policy governing the endowment has not been updated for many years. Brown would like to bring the policy up to date. Brown is particularly concerned about the fund's stated return objectives, which she believes are overly simplistic. The return objective specified in the endowment policy is:

"The portfolio will be managed so as to generate adequate revenues to enable the Shailor endowment to distribute 4.5% of its assets annually to the Shailor College general operating fund."

QUESTION 3 HAS TWO PARTS FOR A TOTAL OF 29 MINUTES

Brown would like to update the return objective of the Shailor College endowment so that the return includes a long-term adjustment for inflation and for the costs associated with managing the endowment. Brown believes that inflation will average 4% over the next several years. The endowment's investment management fees have averaged 0.35% of assets over the past five years. Brown would also like to generate a revised asset allocation reflecting more diversification across asset classes.

A. **Prepare** an investment policy statement using the objectives and constraints format for Shailor College's endowment portfolio. **Calculate** the compound long-term return requirement of the fund in order to meet Brown's requirements, and include this number in the investment policy statement.

Answer Question 3A in the template provided.

(17 minutes)

B. Brown has developed the asset allocation provided in Figure 1 for the Shailor College endowment. **Suggest** *six* changes to Brown's allocation that would make the portfolio more consistent with the stated investment objectives.

(12 minutes)

Figure 1: Proposed Asset Allocation

Asset	Yield	Return	Weight
T-bills	4.00%	4.00%	5.0%
U.S. Treasury notes	5.25%	5.25%	10.0%
Corporate bonds	7.00%	7.00%	25.0%
Large-cap stocks	2.00%	10.00%	10.0%
Small-cap stocks	0.50%	12.00%	20.0%
Hedge fund	0.00%	22.00%	5.0%
REIT	6.00%	11.00%	10.0%
Venture capital fund	0.00%	18.00%	15.0%
			100%
Expected annual total return (%)			10.78
Expected annual yield (%)			3.38

Template for Question 3A

Objectives	Comments
1.	
2.	

Constraints	Comments
1.	
2.	
3.	
4.	
5.	

Note: Your response should include appropriate content for each objective and constraint based on Shailor College's current situation.

QUESTION 4 HAS ONE PART FOR A TOTAL OF 6 MINUTES

Jeff Stone, another trustee of the Shailor College endowment, has questioned Brown's recommendation to employ an active management strategy for the entire equity portion of the endowment portfolio. Specifically, Stone made the following three statements:

Statement 1:   Active management is appropriate for large-cap stocks, where managers can take big enough positions to capitalize on pockets of inefficiency.

Statement 2:   An S&P 500 Index fund does not make sense because the fund will increase the relative weightings of stocks that perform well, increasing our exposure to potentially overvalued securities.

Statement 3:   The Shailor College endowment should employ a passive index vehicle, such as a Russell 2000 index fund, for our small-cap stock portfolio, because the market for small-cap stocks tends to be more efficient than the market for large-cap stocks, thus reducing the potential benefits of active investing.

Critique Stone's comments regarding active and passive strategies for large- and small-cap investing. Your answer should respond only to Stone's comments.

(6 minutes)

QUESTION 5 HAS ONE PART FOR A TOTAL OF 6 MINUTES

James Underwood is interviewing a potential client with a net worth of $10 million. During the interview process, Underwood learned that the person:

- Is very skeptical about investment advice.
- Wants to be invested in the best-performing stocks at all times.
- Believes an investor must rely on instinct to best perform in the stock market.
- Believes that to be a successful investor, a high turnover of the portfolio may be required.
- In the past has experienced below-average results, which he attributes to bad investment advice.

Based on the facts outlined above, **identify** which personality the potential client represents. **Discuss** how this information will improve the portfolio management process.

(6 minutes)

QUESTION 6 HAS ONE PART FOR A TOTAL OF 12 MINUTES

Stan Morgan manages a global commodity stock hedge fund with assets totaling $4 billion. The Fund owns equities in any developed or emerging country that produces commodities. Lynn Merrill has been asked to construct a global benchmark to evaluate Morgan's portfolio. Merrill has made the following suggestions:

i.   To determine the benchmark index value, each company's weighting should be calculated using both the market value of debt and equity. Merrill explains that the represented commodity companies are heavily leveraged.

ii. The benchmark index should include all commodity stocks with a market capitalization plus market value of debt greater than $50 million dollars.

iii. The benchmark index should add all companies whose market value grows to exceed $50 million and drop all companies that fall below $50 million.

iv. The benchmark index should follow a rigid set of rules that determine which companies are to be added and subtracted from the index when a merger and/ or acquisition occurs.

Indicate whether Stan should accept or reject Lynn's proposals, and **discuss** your reasoning.

Answer Question 6 in the template provided.

(12 minutes)

Template for Question 6

Accept or Reject (circle one)	Discussion
i. Accept Reject	
ii. Accept Reject	
iii. Accept Reject	
iv. Accept Reject	

©2008 Schweser

QUESTION 7 HAS FOUR PARTS FOR A TOTAL OF 16 MINUTES

Sid Mulder, CFA, manages an $250 million fixed income portfolio. Currently, the weighted average duration for his portfolio is 6.8. Mulder is concerned about rising interest rates and has decided that he should adjust the duration of his portfolio to reduce the impact of rising interest rates. Mulder plans to use futures contracts to achieve his target duration of 5.0. The duration of the cheapest-to-deliver (CTD) bond is 6.5, and its price is $100,000. The conversion factor for this bond is 1.3.

Mulder is also concerned about credit risk in his portfolio. Specifically, he is worried that there is significant risk of a spread widening for $10 million in Blum Development bonds. Currently, the Blum bonds trade at a spread of 250 basis points (bp) over comparable maturity U.S. Treasury securities. Mulder is considering a derivative to protect against this risk, a credit forward in the amount of $10 million at a contract spread of 250bp, with a risk factor of 3.0.

Aledo Corp. bonds are an additional holding in Mulder's portfolio that he believes are a significant credit risk. Mulder is considering entering into a credit default swap as the protection buyer to control this risk. Mulder is concerned, however, that since Aledo Corp. is a private placement, he will be unable to hedge his risk.

A. **Describe** the futures transaction Mulder should execute in order to achieve his target duration. Your response should include the number of contracts and whether these contracts should be bought or sold.

(4 minutes)

B. Mulder has chosen to modify his portfolio duration using futures, as opposed to buying/selling additional securities. **Identify** one advantage of using futures in this situation, and **describe** how basis risk might affect Mulder's strategy.

(3 minutes)

C.   For the credit derivative Mulder is considering, **determine** the following:

      i.   The maximum potential loss to Mulder on the credit forward.

      ii.   The payoff if the spread widens to 300bp at the maturity of the derivative.

      iii.   The payoff if the spread narrows to 200bp at the maturity of the derivative.

(5 minutes)

Answer Question 7C in the template provided.

D.   A credit derivatives dealer has offered to sell Mulder protection against any default by Aledo Corp, in the form of a credit default swap. **Comment** on the flexibility available to protection buyers in credit default swaps, and **describe** how the protection seller is able to leverage credit risk exposure through such a transaction.

(4 minutes)

Template for Question 7C

	Credit forward at a contract spread of 250bp
i. The maximum potential loss to Mulder on the credit forward.	
ii. The payoff if the spread widens to 300bp at the maturity of the derivative.	
iii. The payoff if the spread narrows to 200bp at the maturity of the derivative.	

QUESTION 8 HAS TWO PARTS FOR A TOTAL OF 8 MINUTES

Free Range, Inc. (FRI) is a communications technology company based in the United States. The company was formed through a merger between Freedom, Inc., a traditional wired network technology company, and North Range Technologies, a wireless technology company. Managers at the firm are compensated largely through stock options. Over the past several years, the communications technology industry has been rapidly moving towards inventing and improving wireless communications technologies, generally seen as the future of the network communication industry. FRI has been a true innovator in this area, on average introducing a new patented wireless technology product once every nine months. However, the firm has not been free from difficulties. Concerned that the firm may not have met its potential, FRI's board of directors has hired an outside consultant to assess its operations. The consultant's report included the following comments:

- "One of the top executives at FRI, James Baltus, is a former executive from Freedom, Inc. Because he has obtained the approval for several investment initiatives related to traditional wired network technologies, Baltus has managed to shift the majority of FRI investments away from wireless communications technology to the detriment of shareholders."
- "In addition, another top executive, Uri Korkov, a former executive with North Range Technologies, has convinced FRI's investment committee to invest in several media production ventures. The media companies FRI has invested in generally require long investment periods and have high levels of risk, making them relatively expensive capital projects that divert attention away from FRI's core operations."
- "I recommend increasing the level of short-term debt financing in the capital structure of FRI in order to impose discipline on the firm's management and better align the interests of the firm's management with its shareholders."

A. **Determine** which *two* types of moral hazard are described by the consultant's comments related to the executives at FRI, and **state** how, other than using debt, the managers' incentives could be changed to better coincide with shareholders' best interests. **Suggest** a different change for each manager.

(4 minutes)

Answer Question 8A in the template provided.

B.   **Explain** *two* ways in which debt would provide incentives for management at FRI to act in the best interest of the firm's shareholders, and **explain** *two* limitations to the use of debt to motivate FRI's management.

(4 minutes)

Template for Question 8A

Comment	Type of moral hazard	Change in management's incentives
"Because he has obtained the approval of several investment initiatives related to traditional wired network technologies, Baltus has managed to shift the majority of FRI investments away from wireless communications technology to the detriment of shareholders."		
"Korkov … has convinced FRI's investment committee to invest in several media production ventures. The media companies FRI has invested in generally require long investment periods and have high levels of risk, making them relatively expensive capital projects that divert attention away from FRI's core operations."		

Questions 9 through 11 relate to John Diamond. A total of 40 minutes is allocated to these questions. *Candidates should answer these questions in the order presented.*

QUESTION 9 HAS THREE PARTS FOR A TOTAL OF 24 MINUTES

John Diamond, age 34, is a mid-level marketing executive for Rome Corp., a fast-growing company in the mortgage lending business. Rome has also become the nation's largest trader of interest rate derivative contracts to hedge its portfolio of loans. Additionally, the company takes very significant derivative positions when it develops a strong opinion on the direction of future interest rate changes. Diamond's current annual salary is $150,000, but he usually gets a year-end bonus equal to one-third of his annual salary. Diamond's assets are as follows:

- Stock options on 100,000 shares of Rome, strike price $40, not exercisable for five years, expire in 20 years (Rome stock has a current market price of $45 and pays no dividend).
- In Rome's 401k plan, Diamond owns 12,500 shares of Rome stock.
- Owns another 10,000 shares of Rome stock outside of the retirement plan (cost $50,000).
- Owns $200,000 (cost $400,000) of the Financial Services Growth Mutual Fund.
- Owns $500,000 of 3-month Treasury bills yielding 3%.

Diamond recently bought a new home for $1,000,000 with a 5% down payment and an 8%, 30-year mortgage. Long-term government bonds yield 7%. Diamond's annual living expenses excluding his mortgage payment are $100,000. Diamond is in a 30% income tax bracket.

A.   **Prepare** an investment policy statement using the objectives and constraints format for John Diamond.

Answer Question 9A in the template provided.

(12 minutes)

B.   **Suggest** *three* specific changes in his current asset allocation.

Answer Question 9B in the template provided.

(6 minutes)

C.   **Describe** how Diamond could create an equity collar on the 10,000 shares of Rome that he owns outside of the retirement plan, without having the transaction treated as a "constructive sale" for income taxes.

(6 minutes)

Template for Question 9A

Note: Your response should include appropriate content for each objective and constraint based on John Diamond's current situation.

Objectives	Comments
1.	
2.	

Constraints	Comments
1.	
2.	
3.	
4.	
5.	

Template for Question 9B

Suggested changes to Diamond's current asset allocation
1.
2.
3.

QUESTION 10 HAS ONE PART FOR A TOTAL OF 4 MINUTES

One year later, John Diamond decides to marry Sarah Gullen, who has five children aged 12 to 18. Diamond has agreed to pay college expenses for all of Sarah's children (assume four years of college, with costs of $20,000 per year per child). Strong performance of trading activities in interest rate derivative contracts has caused Rome stock to go to $80/share.

Discuss *two* changes to Diamond's asset allocation that would be appropriate under the new circumstances.

(4 minutes)

QUESTION 11 HAS TWO PARTS FOR A TOTAL OF 12 MINUTES

John Diamond, now 55 years old, has been promoted to President and Chief Executive Officer of Rome Corp. His stepchildren have all graduated from college. Diamond's salary has increased to $1 million per year plus bonus. Diamond and his wife have a combined retirement plan worth $5 million. Diamond's sister died of cancer one year ago and he has become active in raising funds to find a cure for cancer. Diamond would like to contribute a part of his wealth to cancer research. Rome Corp. has prospered over the last 20 years and the company's stock has experienced similar growth. By virtue of his advancement, Diamond currently owns 750,000 shares of Rome stock with a cost basis of $10 per share. The company's stock trades for $75 per share. The loan on the house purchased 20 years ago has been fully repaid. In addition, Diamond has $3 million in money market funds and an additional $3 million in stock and bond mutual funds.

A.   **Evaluate** *three* wealth planning options—personal accounts, tax-deferred pension vehicles, and charitable trusts—that Diamond should consider. Your response should address *five* evaluation criteria: term, access, control, valuation, and tax efficiency.

(9 minutes)

Answer Question 11A in the template provided.

B.   **Describe** the tax consequences to Diamond if he makes a charitable bequest of his Rome holdings.

(3 minutes)

Template for Question 11A

Wealth planning options	Evaluation
Personal accounts	
Tax-deferred pension vehicles	
Charitable trust	

QUESTION 12 HAS TWO PARTS FOR A TOTAL OF 24 MINUTES

Ned Anthony is the Chief Investment Officer of ALL Life Insurance Company (ALL). Anthony oversees a total portfolio of $5 billion. The investment committee of ALL's board of directors recently completed a thorough review of the investment policy statement, which was last revised 11 years ago.

The committee has proposed the following revised investment policy statement of ALL's investment portfolio for board approval.

Portfolio Objectives

- A real return objective of 4% per annum to fund corporate obligations.
- Preserve the long term corpus of the fund.
- Maximize total return within prudent risk parameters.

Portfolio Constraints

- Liquidity requirements must address the issues of disintermediation, asset-liability mismatch, and asset marketability risk.
- Investment holding periods can be as long as 20 years. However, asset-liability management practices tend to shorten the overall time horizon.
- Assets may be held in commingled funds and/or privately managed separate accounts. Exposure through commingled funds shall be evaluated on a case-specific basis through analysis of the fund's "offering document."
- Since a portion of ALL's business is conducted offshore, the investment portfolio regulations of the foreign countries supersede that of the varying states in which ALL conducts business.
- ALL is a highly taxed company and performance should be looked at from an after-tax point of view.
- No investment or action pursuant to an investment may be taken unless expressly permitted by this policy.

Asset Allocation

The following four factors should be used to determine the optimum mix of asset classes:

1. The expected rate of return for each asset classification.
2. The estimated risk of each asset classification (expressed as the standard deviation of the rate of return).
3. The correlation between the rates of return of the asset classifications.
4. The investment objectives and risk constraints of the fund.

Based on these four factors, the Portfolio's policy mix is as follows:

Asset class	Percent of Total Portfolio
Fixed income	50%
Domestic equities	25%
International equities	25%

A more detailed proposed asset allocation is as follows:

Strategy Mix	% of Total Portfolio
50% of fixed income managed passively by internal staff in a portfolio consisting of long-duration bonds.	25%
20% of fixed income managed passively/semi-passively by one or more managers in a portfolio consisting of mortgage- and asset-backed securities with tight risk controls relative to the Lehman Mortgage (67%) and the Lehman Asset-Backed Indices (33%).	10%
20% of fixed income managed by internal staff in a portfolio consisting of high quality, intermediate-duration corporate bonds.	10%
10% of fixed income managed passively/semi-passively by one or more manager(s) investing in a commodity overlay program with the intent of providing a return comparable to the Goldman Sachs Commodity Index.	5%
60% of the domestic equity portfolio managed passively/semi-passively in an S&P 500 Index-like portfolio.	15%
40% of the domestic equity portfolio managed actively by one or more hedge fund managers.	10%
60% of the international equity portfolio managed actively in developed countries by one or more managers.	15%
40% of the international equity portfolio managed passively/semi passively in developed and emerging countries by one or more managers with tight risk control relative to a composite benchmark comprised of the MSCI EAFE and EMF benchmark.	10%

The Asset Allocation Policy Benchmarks are:

Policy Benchmarks	Percentage of Total Benchmark
Fixed income composites	50%
Russell 2000	25%
MSCI EAFE & EMF	25%

The following investment vehicles may be used:

Fixed Income Investment Vehicles:	**Equity Investment Vehicles:**
• Treasury and agency debt • Corporate debt • Convertible stocks and convertible bonds • Mortgage-backed and asset-backed securities • Cash and cash-equivalent securities • Money market funds • Bank short-term investment funds (STIFs) • Commodity index products • Inflation indexed (real) bonds • Private placement mortgages • Equity real estate • Commingled real estate funds	• Common stocks • Preferred stocks • Convertible stocks and convertible bonds • Private equity • American Depository Receipts (ADRs) • Real Estate Investment Trusts (REITs) • Hedge funds

A. **Identify** and **discuss** *five* corrections needed to the Investment Committee's proposal to the board concerning ALL Life Insurance's investment policy statement.

Answer Question 12A in the template provided.

(15 minutes)

B.   ALL's Investment Committee has also been discussing periodic rebalancing of their portfolio. They are concerned about increasing volatility in the market in recent months, and they have debated rebalancing the portfolio in response to changing capital market conditions.

Describe the following *three* reallocation strategies. For *each* strategy, **comment** on *both* the suitability of the strategy for different investor risk tolerances and the market conditions under which that strategy would offer superior relative performance.

i.   Constant mix.

ii. Constant proportion portfolio insurance (CPPI).

iii. Buy and hold.

(9 minutes)

Template for Question 12A

Corrections	Discussion
1.	
2.	
3.	
4.	
5.	

QUESTION 13 HAS ONE PART FOR A TOTAL OF 12 MINUTES

Harold Spare, CFA, is the chief financial officer (CFO) of Neptune Company. Neptune manufactures auto parts. In addition to his responsibilities as CFO, Spare oversees the company's defined benefit pension plan. The pension plan has assets of $3.5 billion. However, the plan is currently underfunded by $700 million. Spare is unhappy with the investment performance of the plan and believes the current asset allocation needs to be altered. To assist him in making a decision, Spare has hired an outside consultant.

The consultant recommends changing the asset mix from the current 60% stocks and 40% bonds (60/40) allocation to a 60% stocks 30% bonds and 10% hedge fund (60/30/10) allocation. The consultant justifies the recommendation by highlighting the fact that hedge funds would generate equity-like returns while reducing the portfolio's overall risk level. Thus, the 60/30/10 asset mix would produce higher returns with a risk level comparable to or less than the old asset mix. The consultant provides Figures 1 and 2 containing return, risk and correlation measures of four hedge fund strategies – event-driven, equity hedge, distressed securities, and global macro for Spare's consideration.

Figure 1: Performance of Hedge Fund Strategies

Strategy or Index	Annual Return	Annual Standard Deviation	Sharpe Ratio
Event-driven	13.46%	5.59%	1.64
Equity hedge	15.90%	9.34%	1.24
Distressed securities	15.28%	6.07%	1.81
Global macro	16.98%	8.38%	1.51

Figure 2: Correlations Between Hedge Fund Strategies and Stocks and Bonds

	Stocks	Bonds	Event-Driven	Equity Hedge	Distressed Securities	Global Macro
Stocks	1.00					
Bonds	0.13	1.00				
Event-driven	0.59	0.07	1.00			
Equity hedge	0.64	0.09	0.70	1.00		
Distressed securities	0.42	0.04	0.87	0.56	1.00	
Global macro	0.26	0.34	0.33	0.46	0.29	1.00

After reviewing the consultant's proposal, Spare is skeptical that hedge funds will provide the desired results.

List and **discuss** *four* concerns related to hedge fund performance evaluation that Spare should review with his consultant before committing to the new asset mix.

(12 minutes)

END OF MORNING SESSION

PRACTICE EXAM 2
AFTERNOON SESSION

Questions 14.1–14.6 relate to John Green and Federal Securities.

John Green, CFA, is a sell-side technology analyst at Federal Securities, a large global investment banking and investment advisory firm. In many of his recent conversations with executives at the firms he researches, Green has heard disturbing news. Most of these firms are lowering sales estimates for the coming year. However, the stock prices have been stable despite management's widely disseminated sales warnings. Green is preparing his quarterly industry analysis and decides to seek further input. He calls Alan Volk, CFA, a close friend who runs the Initial Public Offering section of the investment banking department of Federal Securities.

Volk tells Green he has seen no slowing of demand for technology IPOs. "We've got three new issues due out next week, and two of them are well oversubscribed." Green knows that Volk's department handled over 200 IPOs last year, so he is confident that Volk's opinion is reliable. Green prepares his industry report, which is favorable. Among other conclusions, the report states that "the future is still bright, based on the fact that 67% of technology IPOs are oversubscribed." Privately, Green recommends to Federal portfolio managers that they begin selling all existing technology issues, which have "stagnated," and buy the IPOs in their place.

After carefully evaluating Federal's largest institutional client's portfolio, Green contacts the client and recommends selling all of his existing technology stocks and buying two of the upcoming IPOs, similar to the recommendation given to Federal's portfolio managers. Green's research has allowed him to conclude that only these two IPOs would be appropriate for this particular client's portfolio. Investing in these IPOs and selling the current technology holdings would, according to Green, "double the returns that your portfolio experienced last year."

Federal Securities has recently hired Dirks Bentley, a CFA candidate who has passed Level 2 and is currently preparing to take the Level 3 CFA® exam, to reorganize Federal's compliance department. Bentley tells Green that he may be subject to CFA Institute sanctions due to inappropriate contact between analysts and investment bankers within Federal Securities. Bentley has recommended that Green implement a firewall to rectify the situation and has outlined the key characteristics for such a system. Bentley's suggestions are as follows:

1. Any communication between the departments of Federal Securities must be channeled through the compliance department for review and eventual delivery.

2. The firm must create and maintain watch, restricted, and rumor lists to be used in the review of employee trading.

3. All beneficial ownership, whether direct or indirect, of recommended securities must be disclosed in writing.

4. The firm must increase the level of review or restriction of proprietary trading activities during periods in which the firm has knowledge of information that is both material and nonpublic.

Bentley has identified two of Green's analysts, neither of whom have non-compete contracts, who are preparing to leave Federal Securities and go into competition. The first employee, James Ybarra, CFA, has agreed to take a position with one of Federal's direct competitors. Ybarra has contacted existing Federal clients using a client list he created with public records. None of the contacted clients have agreed to move their accounts as Ybarra has requested. The second employee, Martha Cliff, CFA, has registered the name Cliff Investment Consulting (CIC), which she plans to use for her independent consulting business. For the new business venture, Cliff has developed and professionally printed marketing literature that compares the new firm's services to that of Federal Securities and highlights the significant cost savings that will be realized by switching to CIC. After she leaves Federal, Cliff plans to target many of the same prospects that Federal Securities is targeting, using an address list she purchased from a third-party vendor. Bentley decides to call a meeting with Green to discuss his findings.

After discussing the departing analysts, Green asks Bentley how to best handle the disclosure of the following items: (1) although not currently a board member, Green has served in the past on the board of directors of a company he researches and expects that he will do so again in the near future; and (2) Green recently inherited put options on a company for which he has an outstanding buy recommendation. Bentley replies by telling Green that Item 1 must be disclosed to clients, prospects, and Federal Securities but that Item 2 only needs to be disclosed to Federal Securities.

14.1.   According to Standard II(A) Material Nonpublic Information, when Green contacted Volk, he:
   A. violated CFA Institute Standards.
   B. violated CFA Institute Standards unless the contact occurred away from the workplace.
   C. violated of CFA Institute Standards unless the contact was disclosed to his clients.
   D. did not violate CFA Institute Standards since he was conducting a legitimate research activity.

14.2.   According to CFA Institute Standards of Professional Conduct, which of the following statements regarding Green's recommendation to Federal Securities' clients is **TRUE**?
   A. Green violated the Standards by making a material misrepresentation in his report to Federal Securities' clients.
   B. Green violated the Standards by failing to preserve the confidentiality of Federal Securities' investment banking clients.
   C. Green did not violate the Standards since he made a suitable recommendation in the best interest of Federal Securities' clients.
   D. Green violated the Standards by disclosing material nonpublic information to Federal Securities clients so that they may trade on such information.

14.3.   According to CFA Institute Standards of Professional Conduct, which of the following statements related to Green's investment recommendation to the large institutional client is **TRUE**?
   A. Green has misrepresented the expected performance of the IPOs and has dealt fairly with clients.
   B. Green has misrepresented the expected performance of the IPOs and has not dealt fairly with clients.
   C. Green has not misrepresented the expected performance of the IPOs and has dealt fairly with clients.
   D. Green has not misrepresented the expected performance of the IPOs and has not dealt fairly with clients.

14.4.   Which of Bentley's recommendations regarding the key characteristics of a firewall are inconsistent with those recommended by CFA Institute Standards of Professional Conduct?
   A. Characteristic 1.
   B. Characteristic 2.
   C. Characteristic 3.
   D. Characteristic 4.

14.5.   With respect to their plans to go into competition with Federal Securities, have Ybarra or Cliff violated any CFA Institute Standards of Professional Conduct?

	Ybarra	Cliff
A.	Yes	No
B.	No	Yes
C.	Yes	Yes
D.	No	No

14.6.   Assess whether, in light of CFA Institute Standards of Professional
        Conduct, Bentley's disclosure recommendations are correct or incorrect
        with respect to the two items noted by Green.

	Item 1	Item 2
A.	Incorrect	Correct
B.	Correct	Incorrect
C.	Correct	Correct
D.	Incorrect	Incorrect

Questions 15.1–15.6 relate to CMT Investments.

Robert Keith, CFA, has begun a new job at CMT Investments as Head of Compliance. Keith has just completed a review of all of CMT's operations, and has interviewed all the firm's portfolio managers. Many are CFA charterholders, but some are not. Keith intends to use the CFA Institute Code and Standards, as well as the Asset Manager Code of Professional Conduct, as ethical guidelines for CMT to follow.

In the course of Keith's review of the firm's overall practices, he has noted a few situations which potentially need to be addressed.

Situation 1:

CMT Investments' policy regarding acceptance of gifts and entertainment is not entirely clear.   There is general confusion within the firm regarding what is and is not acceptable practice regarding gifts, entertainment and additional compensation.

Situation 2:

Keith sees inconsistency regarding fee disclosures to clients. In some cases, information related to fees paid to investment managers for investment services provided are properly disclosed. However, a few of the periodic costs, which will affect investment return, are not disclosed to the clients. Most managers are providing clients with investment returns net of fees, but a few are just providing the gross returns. One of the managers stated "providing gross returns is acceptable, as long as I show the fees such that the client can make their own simple calculation of the returns net of fees."

Situation 3:

Keith has noticed a few gaps in CMT's procedure regarding use of soft dollars. There have been cases where "directed brokerage" has resulted in less than prompt execution of trades. He also found a few cases where a manager paid a higher commission than normal, in order to obtain goods or services. Keith is considering adding two statements to CMT's policy and procedures manual specifically addressing the primary issues he noted.

Statement 1: "Commissions paid, and any corresponding benefits received, are the property of the client. The benefit(s) must directly benefit the client. If a manager's client directs the manager to purchase goods or services that do not provide research services that benefit the client, this violates the duty of loyalty to the client."

Statement 2: "In cases of "directed brokerage", if there is concern that the client is not receiving the best execution, it is acceptable to utilize a less than ideal broker, but it must be disclosed to the client that they may not be obtaining the best execution."

Situation 4:

Keith is still evaluating his data, but it appears that there may be situations where proxies were not voted. After completing his analysis of proxy voting procedures at CMT, Keith wants to insert the proper language into the procedures manual to address proxy voting.

Situation 5:

Keith is putting into place a "disaster recovery plan," in order to ensure business continuity in the event of a localized disaster, and also to protect against any type of disruption in the financial markets. This plan includes the following provisions:

- Procedures for communicating with clients, especially in the event of extended disruption of services provided.
- Alternate arrangement for monitoring and analyzing investments in the event that primary systems become unavailable.
- Plans for internal communication and coverage of crucial business functions in the event of disruption at the primary place of business, or a communications breakdown.

Keith is considering adding the following provisions to the disaster recovery plan in order to properly comply with the CFA Institute Asset Manager Code of Professional Conduct:

Provision 1: "A provision needs to be added incorporating off-site backup for all pertinent account information."

Provision 2: "A provision mandating testing of the plan on a company-wide basis, at periodical intervals, should be added."

Situation 6:

Keith is spending an incredible amount of time on detailed procedures and company policies that are in compliance with the CFA Institute Code and Standards, and also in compliance with the CFA Institute Asset Manager Code of Professional Conduct. As part of this process, he has had several meetings with

CMT senior management, and is second-guessing the process. One of the senior managers is indicating that it might be a better idea to just formally adopt both the Code and Standards and the Asset Manager Code of Conduct, which would make a detailed policy and procedure manual redundant.

15.1. In response to Situation 1, Keith is redrafting the language outlining acceptable behavior regarding gifts and entertainment. Which statement would be the most accurate, or comply best with CFA Institute Code and Standards, and the Asset Manager Code of Professional Conduct?

   A. Managers must refuse to accept any gifts from those that provide a service to the firm, business partners, or prospective investment targets. Gifts with a value less than $1,000 US from clients are acceptable, as long as consent from CMT is received.

   B. Any gifts with a value under U.S. $100 are acceptable. All gifts and / or entertainment with a value in excess of U.S. $100 are to be accepted only after receipt of written consent from all parties involved.

   C. Managers must refuse to accept any gifts, other than those of minimal value, from those that provide a service to the firm, business partners, or prospective investment targets. Gifts from clients are acceptable, as long as consent from CMT is received.

   D. Gifts of reasonable value from clients and prospective investment targets are permitted. Managers must refuse to accept any gifts, other than those with a token value, from any parties who provide a service to the firm.

15.2. Which of the following statements *most accurately* describes the obligations of investment managers related to disclosure of fees under the CFA Institute Asset Manager Code of Professional Conduct?

   A. A general statement concerning certain fees and costs is acceptable, as long as the majority of the fees paid to the firm are disclosed to the client. Both gross- and net-of-fees returns must be disclosed.

   B. All fees must be disclosed to the client, including any periodic account costs. Both gross- and net-of-fees returns must be disclosed.

   C. Periodic expenses are difficult to predict, and do not have to be itemized. Only net-of-fees returns need to be reported.

   D. All fees, including periodic costs, must be reported to the client. Either gross- or net-of-fees results are acceptable, as long as the client can make the simple "net" calculation from the information provided.

15.3. Indicate whether Keith's statements in Situation 3 involving soft dollars / client brokerage are correct or incorrect.

	Statement 1	Statement 2
A.	Correct	Correct
B.	Correct	Incorrect
C.	Incorrect	Correct
D.	Incorrect	Incorrect

15.4. Which of the following statements *most accurately* describes the obligations of investment managers related to the voting of proxies under the CFA Institute Asset Manager Code of Professional Conduct?

A. Proxies, since they have economic value to the client, must always be voted on, whether on routine or non-routine issues.

B. Managers may exercise discretion, and especially in the case of index funds, they do not have to vote proxies.

C. Proxy issues that are not routine will require more analysis. Also, there may be cases in which all proxies do not have to be voted, if a cost-benefit analysis determines that the client would be better served to let some proxies go.

D. It is critical that proxies that are non-routine in nature, addressing issues such as takeover, management compensation, change in the firm's capitalization, etc. be voted. All other proxies are to be voted according to the manager's discretion.

15.5. Indicate whether Keith's suggested additional provisions to the disaster recovery plan are correct or incorrect.

	Provision 1	Provision 2
A.	Correct	Correct
B.	Correct	Incorrect
C.	Incorrect	Correct
D.	Incorrect	Incorrect

15.6. Keith wants to assure CMT's compliance with the requirements of the CFA Institute Code and Standards of Professional Conduct. Which of the following statements *most accurately* describes CMT's responsibilities in order to assure compliance?

A. CMT must adopt the Asset Manager Code of Conduct, as required by the CFA Institute Code and Standards. The policy manual is acceptable, but not necessary.

B. Although adoption of the CFA Institute Asset Manager Code of Conduct is not a requirement, the Standards of Practice encourage firms to adopt this Code. CMT must adopt supplemental policies and procedures as part of a policy manual in order to properly implement the CFA Institute guidelines.

C. Because some managers are not CFA charterholders, the Standards of Professional Conduct require the adoption of the CFA Institute Asset Manager Code of Conduct as well as the creation of a detailed policy and procedures manual.

D. The Standards of Practice do not require CMT to adopt the Asset Manager Code of Conduct, nor is there a requirement to publish a detailed procedural manual. Disclosure of policies is required, and any changes or updates to policies must be immediately disseminated.

Questions 16.1 – 16.6 relate to Eagle Fixed Income Advisors.

Jean Sims, CFA and Ellie Hayes, CFA are advisors for Eagle Fixed Income Investors. Eagle makes recommendations on bonds, mortgages, and other fixed income investments for wealthy individuals and institutions.

Eagle has a client, Parker Portfolio Managers, which has a large holding of mortgages. Due to a projected decline in the housing market in the United States, the yields on mortgages are expected to increase over the next year. The largest mortgage position for Parker is currently priced at 98.80. Given the projected increase in yields, Sims has calculated an expected price of the mortgage of 95.50 in one year. For the same magnitude of yield change, she projects a price of 101.20 if yields actually fall. Hayes states that Parker should hedge the mortgage by shorting a 10-year Treasury bond futures contract.

Discussing the performance of mortgages in general with Parker officers, Hayes states that they are market directional investments. Hayes's reasoning is that mortgages tend to follow the general direction of the fixed income market, where mortgages should be avoided when interest rates are expected to rise and favored when they are expected to fall.

Commenting on hedging mortgages in general at Parker headquarters, Sims states that a two Treasury bond futures hedge is usually more effective than a single Treasury bond futures hedge. Furthermore, she states, a mortgage can be hedged dynamically by adjusting the hedge through time, or by buying interest rate options. An option hedge would be used when its implied volatility is low, she states.

Examining the Parker portfolio in more detail, Sims gathers the following details on the mortgages they hold.

	Type	Amount	Average Prepayment Penalty
Mortgage A	Regular amortizing	$145 million	None
Mortgage B	Regular amortizing	$150 million	1%
Mortgage C	Interest only, principal due at maturity	$160 million	None
Mortgage D	Interest only, principal due at maturity	$155 million	2%

Later that day Sims and Hayes discuss the appropriate hedging of mortgages and make the following statements:

- Sims: "To hedge the duration exposure of a mortgage and maintain a constant duration, the investor should sell Treasury bond futures when interest rates fall and buy Treasury bond futures when interest rates rise."
- Hayes: "Mortgage investors face model risk where using a poor model increases the investor's risk. For example, if prepayments increase faster than expected, the investor faces greater risk. Unfortunately, there is no easy way to hedge model risk."

Examining the properties of principal only (PO) and interest only (IO) strips, Sims determines that the key rate durations for a client's PO strip are negative before year 8 but turn positive thereafter. The client's IO strip has key rate durations that are positive up until year 10 but turn negative thereafter. Overall, the duration is positive for the PO strip and negative for the IO strip. Sims is examining the effect of a yield curve change on the mortgages. Her assumption is that the short end of the yield curve increases while the long end of the curve is unchanged.

16.1. Regarding the Parker mortgage, what type of convexity does it possess when rates decline and will the hedge suggested by Hayes be effective?

Parker mortgage convexity	Hayes's suggested hedge
A. Positive	Effective
B. Positive	Ineffective
C. Negative	Effective
D. Negative	Ineffective

16.2. Are Hayes's statements to the Parker officers regarding the performance of mortgages correct?
A. Yes they are correct.
B. No, investors will avoid mortgages when rates fall.
C. No, market directional refers to the direction of credit spreads.
D. No, market directional refers to the direction of the stock market.

16.3. Are Sims's statements at Parker headquarters regarding hedging mortgages correct?
A. Yes, they are correct.
B. No, the investor would want to sell an interest rate option.
C. No, dynamic hedging is preferred when option implied volatility is low.
D. No, a two Treasury bond futures hedge is no more effective than a single Treasury bond futures hedge.

16.4.   Of the mortgages in Parker's portfolio, which of the following would be
         most appropriately hedged with a duration based strategy?
         A. Mortgage A.
         B. Mortgage B.
         C. Mortgage C.
         D. Mortgage D.

16.5.   Regarding comments of Sims and Hayes on hedging mortgages and model
         risk, are the comments correct?

	Sims: hedging mortgages	Hayes: model risk
A.	No	No
B.	No	Yes
C.	Yes	No
D.	Yes	Yes

16.6.   Based on Sims' assumed shift in the yield curve, what is the *most likely*
         effect on the prices of the PO and IO strips that Sims is examining?

	PO strip price will	IO strip price will
A.	Increase	Increase
B.	Increase	Decrease
C.	Decrease	Increase
D.	Decrease	Decrease

Questions 17.1–17.6 relate to Geneva Management, Marcus Reinhart and Jamison Kiley.

Geneva Management (GenM) selects long-only and long-short portfolio managers to develop asset allocation recommendations for their institutional clients.

GenM Advisor Marcus Reinhart recently examined the holdings of one of GenM's long-only portfolios managed by Jamison Kiley. Reinhart compiled the holdings for two consecutive non-overlapping five year periods. The Morningstar Style Boxes for the two periods for Kiley's portfolio are provided below:

Figure 1: Morningstar Style Box: Long-Only Manager for Five-Year Period 1

	Value	Blend	Growth
Large-cap	20	30	40
Mid-cap	2	3	5
Small-cap	0	0	0

Figure 2: Morningstar Style Box: Long-Only Manager for Five-Year Period 2

	Value	Blend	Growth
Large-cap	40	30	25
Mid-cap	1	2	2
Small-cap	0	0	0

Reinhart contends that the holdings-based analysis might be flawed because Kiley's portfolio holdings are known only as of the end of each quarter. Large changes in the portfolio holdings at the end of the reporting period might misrepresent the portfolio's average composition. To compliment his holdings-based analysis, Reinhart also conducts a returns-based style analysis on Kiley's portfolio. Reinhart selects four benchmarks:

1. SCV: a small-cap value index.

2. SCG: a small-cap growth index.

3. LCV: a large-cap value index.

4. LCG: a large-cap growth index.

Using the benchmarks, Reinhart obtains the following regression results:

Five Year Period 1: $R_p = 0.02 + 0.01(SCV) + 0.02(SCG) + 0.36(LCV) + 0.61(LCG)$

Five Year Period 2: $R_p = 0.02 + 0.01(SCV) + 0.02(SCG) + 0.60(LCV) + 0.38(LCG)$

Kiley's long-only portfolio is benchmarked against the S&P 500 Index which currently is characterized by the following sector allocations.

Figure 3: S&P 500 Index Sector Allocations

Sector	Percent Allocation
Energy	12
Materials	3
Industrials	11
Consumer Discretionary	9
Consumer Staples	10
Health Care	12
Financials	19
Information Technology	17
Telecommunications	4
Utilities	3

GenM strives to select managers whose correlation between forecast alphas and realized alphas has been fairly high, and to allocate funds across managers in order to achieve alpha and beta separation. GenM gives Reinhart a mandate to pursue a core-satellite strategy with a small number of satellites each focusing on a relatively small number of securities.

In response to the core-satellite mandate, Reinhart explains that a Completeness Fund approach offers two advantages:

Advantage 1:   The Completeness Fund approach is designed to maintain the active return of the portfolio while minimizing active risk.

Advantage 2:   The Completeness Fund approach is designed to maintain the active return of the portfolio while minimizing misfit risk.

17.1.   Comparing GenM's long-only and long-short portfolios, which one is more likely to involve pair trades, and which one has better ability to reduce systematic risk?

Pair trades	Reduced systematic risk
A. Long-only	Long-only
B. Long-only	Long-short
C. Long-short	Long-only
D. Long-short	Long-short

17.2. Indicate if Kiley's portfolio is characterized by style drift using the portfolio holdings approach and the returns-based style approach.

Holdings-based style approach	Returns-based style approach
A. No	No
B. No	Yes
C. Yes	No
D. Yes	Yes

17.3. Assuming Kiley feels that the Utilities Sector is overvalued now, the largest active weight that Kiley can apply to the Utilities sector equals:
A. −3%.
B. 0%.
C. 3%.
D. 100%.

17.4. Reinhart is more likely to satisfy the GenM alpha and beta separation objective by:
A. allocating funds to his long-only active managers and to his passive market index fund manager.
B. allocating funds to his market-neutral long-short managers and to his passive market index fund manager.
C. allocating funds solely to his market-neutral long-short managers.
D. allocating funds solely to his long-only managers.

17.5. Assuming no material change in the forecasting ability of GenM's managers and considering the core-satellite mandate faced by Reinhart, the GenM information coefficient and investor breadth are likely to be:

Information coefficient	Investor breadth
A. Relatively high	Relatively high
B. Relatively high	Relatively low
C. Relatively low	Relatively high
D. Relatively low	Relatively low

17.6. Determine whether the two advantages to the Completeness Fund approach explained by Reinhart are correct.

Advantage 1	Advantage 2
A. Correct	Correct
B. Correct	Incorrect
C. Incorrect	Correct
D. Incorrect	Incorrect

Questions 18.1–18.6 relate to Pace Insurance.

Pace Insurance is a large, multi-line insurance company that also owns several proprietary mutual funds. The funds are managed individually, but Pace has an investment committee that oversees all of the funds. This committee is responsible for evaluating the performance of the funds relative to appropriate benchmarks and relative to the stated investment objectives of each individual fund. Chuck Howie is both the CEO of Pace Insurance and Chairman of the investment committee. Howie exerts substantial influence on committee matters. Howie's first job out of college was as a stock broker in 1972. After experiencing the 1973 to 1974 stock market crash, Howie has remained convinced that another severe bear market is imminent. During a recent investment committee meeting, the poor performance of Pace's equity mutual funds was discussed. In particular, the inability of the portfolio managers to outperform their benchmarks was highlighted. Several members recommended dramatic restructuring of all of the equity funds with an emphasis on reviewing their long-term investment strategies. These members felt that there was significant evidence that active management was not producing favorable results and that the funds' strategies should be adjusted so that performance would be more in line with the benchmarks appropriate to each fund.

Still, the majority of the committee members believed that the long-term investment strategies were reasonable, and that the poor recent performance should be addressed through personnel actions. In short, these members believed that new portfolio managers were needed. The net conclusion of the committee was to review the performance of the manager responsible for each fund and dismiss those managers whose performance had lagged substantially behind the appropriate benchmark.

The fund with the worst relative performance is the Pace Mid-Cap Fund, which invests in stocks with a capitalization between $40 billion and $80 billion. A review of the operations of the fund found the following:

- The turnover of the fund was almost double that of other similar style mutual funds.
- The fund's portfolio manager solicited input from her entire staff prior to making any decision to sell an existing holding.
- The beta of the Pace Mid-Cap Fund's portfolio was 60% higher than the beta of other similar style mutual funds.
- No stock is considered for purchase in the Mid-Cap Fund unless the portfolio manager has 15 years of financial information on that company, plus independent research reports from at least three different analysts.
- The portfolio manager refuses to increase her technology sector weighting because of past losses the fund incurred in the sector.
- The portfolio manager sold all the fund's energy stocks as the price per barrel of oil rose above $40. She expects oil prices to fall back to the $20 to $25 per barrel range.

A committee member made the following two comments:

Comment 1: The reason for the poor recent performance of the Mid-Cap Mutual Fund is that the portfolio lacks recognizable companies. I believe that good companies always make good investments.

Comment 2: The underperformance of the Mid-Cap Mutual Fund can be directly traced to its low weighting in the energy sector. It was obvious to any investor that energy prices were going up.

The supervisor of the Mid-Cap Mutual Fund portfolio manager made the following statements:

Statement 1: The portfolio manager of the Mid-Cap Mutual Fund has engaged in quarter-end window dressing to make her portfolio look better to investors. The portfolio manager's action is a behavioral trait known as overreaction.

Statement 2: Each time the portfolio manager of the Mid-Cap Mutual fund trades a stock, she executes the trade by buying or selling one-third of the position at a time, with the trades spread over three months. The portfolio manager's action is a behavioral trait known as anchoring.

18.1. The impact of the 1973 to 1974 stock market crash on Howie's investment decision making can *best* be described as:
A. Overconfidence.
B. Regret.
C. Loss aversion.
D. Aversion to ambiguity.

18.2. A committee member suggested that the portfolio manager of the Mid-Cap Fund may be overconfident about her abilities. Which of the following facts from the review of the Mid-Cap fund is *least likely* to suggest that the manager is overconfident?
A. The high turnover of the Mid-Cap Fund relative to similar style mutual funds.
B. The reliance of the manager on staff input before selling an existing holding.
C. The high beta of the Mid-Cap fund relative to similar style mutual funds.
D. Consideration only of stocks with 15 years of financial data and three independent research reports.

18.3. Indicate whether the committee member's Comment 1 is an example of mental accounting or representative judgment, and indicate whether Comment 2 is an example of hindsight bias or loss aversion.

Comment 1	Comment 2
A. Mental accounting	Hindsight bias
B. Representative judgment	Hindsight bias
C. Mental accounting	Loss aversion
D. Representative judgment	Loss aversion

18.4. State whether the under-weighting of the technology sector by the Pace portfolio manager is an example of money illusion or regret aversion and state whether the portfolio manager's sale of all the energy stocks is an example of anchoring or gambler's fallacy.

Technology stocks	Energy stocks
A. Money illusion	Anchoring
B. Regret aversion	Anchoring
C. Money illusion	Gambler's fallacy
D. Regret aversion	Gambler's fallacy

18.5. Indicate whether Statement 1 and Statement 2 made by the supervisor *correctly* describe the behavioral traits exhibited by the portfolio manager's actions.

Statement 1	Statement 2
A. Incorrect	Incorrect
B. Correct	Incorrect
C. Incorrect	Correct
D. Correct	Correct

18.6. The investment committee believes that the portfolio managers use rules of thumb to process information, while their supervisor is adamant that they use statistical tools to process information. Which of the following statements comparing traditional finance and behavioral finance is *least likely* to be **TRUE**?
   A. Traditional finance assumes framing is transparent; that is, investors have the decision problem described in all different ways. Behavioral finance assumes the decision problem is opaque, or based on a particular frame used.
   B. Traditional finance assumes investors make decisions using statistical tools, while behavioral finance assumes investors base their decision making on rules of thumb.
   C. Traditional finance believes investors are rational, while behavioral finance believes investors are irrational.
   D. Traditional finance believes that any market anomalies are a result of misspecified systematic risk, while behavioral finance believes that security market prices can deviate from fundamental value as a result of a heuristic driven bias.

Questions 19.1–19.6 relate to Integrated Analytics.

Jack Higgins, CFA, and Tim Tyler, CFA, are analysts for Integrated Analytics, a U.S.-based investment analysis firm. Integrated provides bond analysis for both individual and institutional portfolio managers throughout the world. The firm specializes in the valuation of international bonds, with consideration of currency risk. Integrated typically uses forward contracts to hedge currency risk.

Higgins and Tyler are considering the purchase of a bond issued by a Norwegian petroleum products firm, Bergen Petroleum. They have concerns, however, regarding the strength of the Norwegian krone currency (NKr) in the near term, and they want to investigate the potential return from hedged strategies. Higgins suggests that they consider forward contracts with the same maturity as the investment holding period, which is estimated at one year. He states that if Integrated expects that the Norwegian NKr will depreciate and that the Swedish krona (Sk) will appreciate, then Integrated should enter into a hedge where they sell Norwegian NKr and buy Swedish Sk via a one-year forward contract. The Swedish Sk could then be converted to dollars at the spot rate in one year.

Tyler states that if an investor cannot obtain a forward contract denominated in Norwegian NKr and if the Norwegian NKr and euro are positively correlated, then a forward contract should be entered into where euros will be exchanged for dollars in one year. Tyler then provides Higgins the following data on risk-free rates and spot rates in Norway and the U.S., as well as the expected return on the Bergen Petroleum bond.

Return on Bergen Petroleum bond in Norwegian NKr terms	7.00%
Risk-free rate in Norway	4.80%
Expected change in the NKr relative to the U.S. dollar	–0.40%
Risk-free rate in United States	2.50%

Higgins and Tyler discuss the relationship between spot rates and forward rates and comment as follows.

* Higgins: "The relationship between spot rates and forward rates is referred to as interest rate parity, where higher forward rates imply that a country's spot rate will appreciate in the future."
* Tyler: "Interest rate parity depends on covered interest arbitrage which works as follows. Suppose the 1-year U.K. interest rate is 5.5%, the 1-year Japanese interest rate is 2.3%, the Japanese yen is at a one-year forward premium of 4.1%, and transactions costs are minimal. In this case, the international trader should borrow yen, invest in pound denominated bonds, and use a yen-pound forward contract to pay back the yen loan."

The following day, Higgins and Tyler discuss various emerging market bond strategies and make the following statements.

- Higgins: "Over time, the quality in emerging market sovereign bonds has declined, due in part to the contagion and the competitive devaluations that often accompany crises in emerging markets. When one country devalues their currency, others often quickly follow and as a result the countries default on their external debt, which is usually denominated in a hard currency."
- Tyler: "Investing outside the index can provide excess returns. Because the most common emerging market bond index is concentrated in Latin America, the portfolio manager can earn an alpha by investing in emerging country bonds outside of this region."

Turning their attention to specific issues of bonds, Higgins and Tyler examine the characteristics of three bonds: a 10-year maturity bond issued by the Roanoke Corporation; a six-year maturity bond issued by the Midlothian Corporation; and a twelve-year maturity bond issued by the Horgen Corporation. The Roanoke and Midlothian bonds are U.S. issues and the Horgen bond was issued by a firm based in Switzerland. The characteristics of each bond are shown in the table below. Higgins and Tyler discuss the relative attractiveness of each bond and, using a total return approach, which bond should be invested in, assuming a 1-year time horizon.

	Currency of Denomination	One year Risk-Free Rate in Country of Bond Issuance	Annualized Bond Yield	Bond Modified Duration	Semiannual Coupon Payment
Roanoke Bond	U.S. Dollars	2.50%	6.00%	7.44	$3.00
Midlothian Bond	U.S. Dollars	2.50%	8.00%	4.69	$4.00
Horgen Bond	Swiss franc	4.75%	9.00%	7.25	$4.50

19.1. What are the currency hedge strategies for the Bergen Petroleum bond that Higgins and Tyler are referring to?

	Higgins	Tyler
A.	Cross-hedge	Proxy-hedge
B.	Cross-hedge	Correlation-hedge
C.	Indirect-hedge	Proxy-hedge
D.	Indirect-hedge	Correlation-hedge

19.2. On the basis of expected return, should the Bergen Petroleum bond be hedged against currency risk? What is the hedged return?

Should the bond be hedged?	Hedged return
A. No	4.70%
B. No	6.60%
C. Yes	4.70%
D. Yes	6.60%

19.3. Regarding their statements concerning the relationship between spot rates and forward rates, are Higgins and Tyler correct?

	Higgins	Tyler
A.	No	No
B.	No	Yes
C.	Yes	No
D.	Yes	Yes

19.4. Regarding their statements concerning the emerging market bond investments, are Higgins and Tyler correct?

	Higgins	Tyler
A.	No	No
B.	No	Yes
C.	Yes	No
D.	Yes	Yes

19.5. Assume that both the Roanoke and Midlothian bonds are being considered for purchase and that the yield for the Roanoke bond will remain constant over the investment holding period. Which of the following statements provides the *best* description of the appropriate strategy using breakeven spread analysis? If the yield for the Midlothian bond:
   A. declines by 2.00% or more, invest in the Roanoke bond.
   B. increases by more than 2.00%, invest in the Midlothian bond.
   C. increases by more than 0.43%, invest in the Midlothian bond.
   D. does not increase by more than 0.43%, invest in the Midlothian bond.

19.6. Assume that both the Roanoke and Horgen bonds are being considered for purchase and that the yield for the Roanoke bond will remain constant over the investment holding period. Which of the following statements provides the *best* description of the appropriate strategy using breakeven spread analysis? If the yield for the Horgen bond:
   A. increases by more than 3.00%, invest in the Roanoke bond.
   B. declines by more than 3.00%, invest in the Roanoke bond.
   C. does not increase by more than 0.10%, invest in the Horgen bond.
   D. does not increase by more than 0.31%, invest in the Horgen bond.

Questions 20.1–20.6 relate to United Global Group.

United Global Group (UGG) is a major property and casualty insurance company. UGG has a total investment portfolio of $25 billion. The portfolio is divided into $22 billion worth of bonds and $3 billion worth of equities. UGG's equity strategy employs enhanced indexing with the S&P 500 Index as the benchmark. UGG adjusts its equity portfolio by employing the 200-day moving average technical indicator. When more than 80% of the stocks are trading above their 200-day moving average, this indicator considers the equity market overbought—a bearish signal. In contrast, if less than 20% of the stocks are trading above their 200-day moving average, the market is considered oversold—a bullish signal that means investors should expect a positive correction. UGG management uses this indicator to move in and out of equities. Rather than actually selling their equities, UGG uses futures to create a synthetic cash position to execute any bearish trigger. Relevant data is shown in Figure 1.

Figure 1: Selected Data

S&P 500 Index futures contract	1058
S&P 500 Index dividend yield	1.60%
Time to expiration	5 months
Risk free rate (annual)	3.00%
UGG equity portfolio beta	1.00
S&P 500 Index futures contract beta	1.00
UGG bond portfolio modified duration	5.90
Treasury bond futures contract price	$150,000
Treasury bond futures modified duration	5.10
Cash equivalents modified duration	0.20
S&P 500 Index futures contract multiplier	$250

20.1. The 200-day moving average is sending a bearish signal, so UGG management has decided to immediately neutralize its equity position. The number of futures contracts sold to create a synthetic cash position should be between:

  A. 5,000 and 7,000 contracts.
  B. 7,001 and 9,000 contracts.
  C. 9,001 and 11,000 contracts.
  D. 11,001 and 13,000 contracts.

20.2. Assume the S&P 500 Index is at 1,125 when the futures contract expires. The payoff of the futures contract would be a:

  A. loss of less than $1 million.
  B. loss between $1 million and $100 million.
  C. loss greater than $100 million.
  D. gain greater than $1 million.

20.3. Based on UGG's models, management intends to adjust its current asset allocation to 75% bonds and 25% stocks. Using the information provided in Figure 1, the strategy to adjust to the new bond and stock allocation is to buy:
A. 12,300 stock futures contracts and sell 24,200 bond futures contracts.
B. 13,800 stock futures contracts and sell 21,700 bond futures contracts.
C. 15,300 stock futures contracts and sell 20,900 bond futures contracts.
D. 16,800 stock futures contracts and sell 19,200 bond futures contracts.

UGG's management applied its technical indicator to the Japanese market and discovered that it is in an oversold situation. Based on this factor, management allocated half of UGG's equity portfolio, or 162,225,000,000 yen, to the Japanese market. The relevant data is shown in Figure 2.

Figure 2: Selected Data

Nikkei 225 index futures contract	10,337
Nikkei 225 index dividend yield	1.00%
Time to expiration	6 months
Japanese risk-free rate (annual)	2.00%
Multiplier	$5.00
Nikkei 225 index futures contract beta	1.00
UGG's Japanese portfolio beta	0.90
Exchange rate	108.15 yen to $1

20.4. UGG would like to fully hedge against a possible decline in the Japanese market. Using the data in Figure 2, the number of (short) contracts needed to hedge the yen-denominated portion of the equity portfolio is between:
A. 24,001 and 25,000 contracts.
B. 25,001 and 26,000 contracts.
C. 26,001 and 27,000 contracts.
D. 27,001 and 28,000 contracts.

20.5. Which of the following statements is **TRUE**?
A. UGG can hedge their foreign currency payment risk by selling a forward currency contract.
B. UGG can use futures contracts to solve all of their liquidity issues.
C. UGG can replicate a long stock position by buying futures on stock and a risk-free bond.
D. UGG can use yield beta to adjust their exposure to equities.

20.6. UGG is exposed to the U.S. bond market and both the U.S. and Japanese equity markets. Given these exposures, which of the following statements is correct?

A. UGG is likely to use a mixture of corporate and Treasury bond futures to hedge their U.S. bond portfolio.

B. UGG is likely to manage exchange rate risk using forward contracts on the yen/USD exchange rate for liquidity reasons.

C. UGG is likely to manage interest rate risk on the bond portfolio using forwards since this method is cheaper than using futures.

D. UGG can lock in the Japanese risk-free rate by using futures to hedge the equity portfolio and using a forward to hedge yen/USD currency risk.

Questions 21.1–21.6 relate to Director Securities.

Walter Skinner, CFA, manages a bond portfolio for Director Securities. The bond portfolio is part of a pension plan trust set up to benefit retirees of Thomas Steel Inc. As part of the investment policy governing the plan and the bond portfolio, no foreign securities are to be held in the portfolio at any time and no bonds with a credit rating below investment grade are allowable for the bond portfolio. In addition, the bond portfolio must remain unleveraged. The bond portfolio is currently valued at $800 million, and has a duration of 6.50. Skinner believes that interest rates are going to be increasing, and he wants to lower his portfolio's duration to 4.50. He has decided to achieve the reduction in duration by using swap contracts. He has two possible swaps to choose from:

1. Swap A, a 4-year swap with quarterly payments.

2. Swap B, a 5-year swap with semiannual payments.

Skinner plans to be the fixed-rate payer in the swap, receiving a floating-rate payment in exchange. Assume that the duration of a fixed rate bond is 75% of its term to maturity.

Several years ago, Skinner decided to circumvent the policy restrictions on foreign securities by purchasing a dual currency bond issued by an American holding company with significant operations in Japan. The bond makes semiannual fixed interest payments in Japanese yen but will make the final principal payment in U.S. dollars five years from now. Skinner originally purchased the bond to take advantage of the strengthening relative position of the yen. The result was an above average return for the bond portfolio for several years. Now, however, he is concerned that the yen is going to begin a weakening trend, as inflation in the Japanese economy is forecasted to accelerate over the next few years. Knowing Skinner's situation, one of his colleagues, Bill Michaels, suggests the following strategy:

"You need to offset your exposure to the Japanese yen by establishing a short position in a synthetic dual currency bond that matches the terms of the dual currency bond you purchased for the Thomas Steel bond portfolio. As part of the strategy, you will have to enter into a currency swap as the fixed-rate yen payer. The swap will neutralize the dual-currency bond position but will unfortunately increase the credit risk exposure of the portfolio."

Skinner has also spoken to Orval Mann, the senior economist with Director Securities, about his expectations for the bond portfolio. Mann has also provided some advice to Skinner in the following comment:

"I know you are expecting a general increase in interest rates but I disagree with your assessment of the interest rate shift. I believe interest rates are going to decrease. Therefore, you will want to synthetically remove the call features of any callable bonds in your portfolio by purchasing a payer interest rate swaption."

21.1. The duration of Swap A and Swap B would be *closest* to:

	Swap A	Swap B
A.	−2.50	−3.25
B.	−2.88	−3.50
C.	−2.50	−3.50
D.	−2.88	−3.25

21.2. Determine the notional principal required for Skinner to achieve a portfolio duration of 4.5 using the longer duration swap, and then determine the notional principal required for Skinner to achieve a portfolio duration of 5.5 using the shorter duration swap.

	Duration of 4.5	Duration of 5.5
A.	$457 million	$320 million
B.	$492 million	$278 million
C.	$457 million	$278 million
D.	$492 million	$320 million

21.3. Critically evaluate Mann's suggested strategy in the event that interest rates move counter to Skinner's expectations.
A. Mann is incorrect; callable bonds should be offset by selling a payer swaption.
B. Mann is incorrect; callable bonds should be offset by purchasing a receiver swaption.
C. Mann is incorrect; callable bonds should be offset by selling a receiver swaption.
D. Mann's statement is correct.

21.4. After his long conversation with Director Securities' senior economist, Orval Mann, Skinner has completely changed his outlook on interest rates and has decided to extend the duration of his portfolio. The *best* strategy to accomplish this objective using swaps would be to enter into a swap to pay:
A. fixed and receive fixed.
B. floating and receive fixed.
C. floating and receive floating.
D. fixed and receive floating.

21.5. Skinner has been consulting with Dwayne Barter, a client of Director Securities and CFO of a large corporation. Barter is interested in using interest rate swaps to convert his firm's floating rate debt to fixed rate debt. Barter is planning to enter into a swap to pay a fixed rate and receive a floating rate in exchange. Which of the following is the *most accurate* statement Skinner could make regarding such a transaction? The swap would:

    A. increase the cash flow risk of Barter's firm.

    B. reduce both the cash flow risk and market value risk of Barter's firm.

    C. increase both the cash flow risk and market value risk of Barter's firm.

    D. increase the market value risk of Barter's firm.

21.6. Evaluate the appropriateness of Michaels' suggested strategy to offset the bond portfolio exposure to the dual currency bond, and also evaluate Michaels' assessment of the swap portion of the transaction.

	Strategy	Swap
A.	Appropriate	Incorrect
B.	Inappropriate	Correct
C.	Appropriate	Correct
D.	Inappropriate	Incorrect

Questions 22.1–22.6 relate to the Glendale Foundation.

Bart Hope, CFA, is the chief investment officer of Glendale Foundation, which supports a wide variety of child-related causes. Total assets of the Foundation Trust are $2.3 billion. The Foundation's current asset mix is 55% stocks, 35% bonds, and 10% cash (T-bills earn 3.5%). The foundation currently funds $126.5 million annually for a variety of programs for children. This spending rate is forecasted to remain constant. Hope believes that the future inflation rate will equal the current cash yield. Hope does not envision any major capital expenditure program for the foreseeable future.

The investment portfolio of the Foundation has underperformed its benchmarks over the past three years. Hope believes corrective action is needed to address the poor performance problem. Hope wants to evaluate the possibility of adding alternative assets to improve the Foundation's risk/return profile. In particular, Hope is interested in venture capital and hedge funds. Hope's staff generated the following figure, which reviews the relevant metrics to make the asset mix decision. The overall cost of investing the assets is 75 basis points.

Figure 1: Expected Returns, Risk Parameters, and Correlations for Asset Classes Under Consideration

	Mean Return	Volatility	Correlation		
			1	2	3
1. Glendale's portfolio	12.1%	10.0%	1.00		
2. Venture capital	11.4%	18.9%	0.50	1.00	
3. Hedge funds	13.5%	10.3%	0.75	0.25	1.00

One of the members of Hope's staff, Rene Meyer, has included a report on the key attributes of investing in venture capital funds. The report includes the following sections:

Structure: Indirect venture capital investments are achieved by pooling the funds of multiple investors into a limited liability company (LLC). The investors are limited partners who allow a general partner to control the investments for a period of 7 to 10 years. The general partner also invests capital, earning a management fee of 1.5 to 2.5% of invested capital and a carried interest fee which is generally 20% of the fund profits after the limited partners' capital investments have been recovered.

Strategy: Because initial public offerings are a primary exit strategy of venture capital investing, the correlation between public equity markets and returns on venture capital investments are positive. Therefore, the primary focus of any venture capital investment undertaken by Glendale should be long-term return enhancement rather than significant diversification. In addition, Glendale must make sure that all of the committed capital is available for the required up front cash distribution to the general partner at the beginning of the investment period.

In making a hedge fund allocation decision, Hope understands that there is no one index to benchmark against, but she expects Glendale's equities, as well as venture capital and hedge fund sectors, to outperform the S&P 500 Index. Hope also recognizes there are several unique strategies within the hedge fund group that have very different risk/reward trade-offs.

Jen Clark, another member of Hope's staff, has identified four hedge funds as potential investment opportunities for the Glendale Foundation. Figure 2 lists the funds under consideration and their most recent securities trades.

Figure 2: Hedge Fund Trades

Fund W	Fund X	Fund Y	Fund Z
The fund recently purchased the stock of TVN company after it announced that it had accepted a cash tender offer from RHR corporation. The fund took a short position in RHR that was equal in value to the long TVN position.	Fund X purchased the stock of four companies within the chemical manufacturing industry while simultaneously selling short the stock of three companies in the transportation industry. The relative size of the trades left the fund with a net short exposure.	A long position was taken in Burg Inc., a grocery store chain. At the same time, a short position was taken in a second grocery store chain, TRE Corp. The overall beta of the trades was equal to 0.01 and the net investment was equal to zero.	The fund purchased a long position in an S&P 500 Index, funding the purchase with a short position in a broad based index tracking the Japanese market. Fund Z expects the S&P to rise and the Japanese market to decline over the next year.

While Clark is presenting the hedge funds, Hope comments that he is concerned with the potential difficulties in measuring hedge fund manager performance. Glendale's charter has fairly strict requirements regarding the performance assessment of asset managers that control the assets of the foundation. Hope believes the funds being presented may be difficult to track against a benchmark index as required by Glendale's charter.

22.1.   State whether an asset-only approach (AO) or an asset-liability management approach (ALM) would be *most appropriate* for the Glendale Foundation, and calculate the return objective of the Glendale Foundation portfolio.

	Asset allocation	Return objective
A.	AO	9%
B.	ALM	10%
C.	AO	10%
D.	ALM	9%

22.2.   Which of the following statements describing processes for identifying potential asset classes for Glendale Foundation's portfolio is *least appropriate*? Hope has:
   A. considered asset classes with a low correlation of returns to the Foundation's existing investment portfolio.
   B. grouped together into one equity class both domestic and international equities.
   C. considered all of the relevant asset groups in developing the Foundation's portfolio.
   D. considered the liquidity factor of all the asset classes under consideration.

22.3.   Based on the data provided in Figure 1 and the Sharpe ratios of Glendale's portfolio, hedge funds, and venture capital, indicate whether adding venture capital or hedge funds to the Glendale Foundation portfolio would allow the foundation to achieve a superior efficient frontier (calculations required).

	Venture capital	Hedge funds
A.	Yes	Yes
B.	No	No
C.	Yes	No
D.	No	Yes

22.4.   One of Hope's staff members has written a report on the proposed private equity investment. Determine whether the comments in the report related to the structure and strategy of Glendale's private equity investment are *correct* or *incorrect*.

	Structure	Strategy
A.	Correct	Correct
B.	Correct	Incorrect
C.	Incorrect	Correct
D.	Incorrect	Incorrect

22.5. Determine which of the hedge funds identified by Clark and listed in Figure 2 *most likely* follows an equity market neutral strategy and which of the funds *most likely* follows a hedged equity strategy.

Equity market neutral	Hedged equity
A. Fund Z	Fund X
B. Fund Z	Fund W
C. Fund Y	Fund X
D. Fund Y	Fund W

22.6. Which of the following is *least likely* to be a reason for Hope's concern over the ability to track hedge fund manager performance against a benchmark index as required by the Glendale Foundation charter?

A. Prices used to compute the hedge fund index returns suffer from stale prices, causing artificially low risk and correlation estimates.

B. Indexes available for comparison remove the historical returns of hedge funds that have been dissolved at the request of fund shareholders.

C. The weight of each hedge fund included in the indexes is determined using the relative value of total assets under management.

D. When a hedge fund is added to the available indexes, the fund's historical returns are added to the historical returns of the index, artificially improving overall performance.

Questions 23.1–23.6 relate to Kevin Travis and Barton Emerging Markets Equity Fund.

Kevin Travis, CFA, has managed the highly successful Barton Aggressive Growth Fund for the past four years, using a top down/demographic approach. Barton Investment Management believes that Travis can use the investment management skills he developed at the Barton Aggressive Growth Fund to turn around the underperforming Barton Emerging Markets Equity Fund (EMF). Travis has begun to review the economic environments of the countries the EMF is invested in and reallocate assets to those geographic regions or countries that show the most promise for appreciation.

As part of his "top down" discipline, Travis looks at the shape of the yield curve of the country to provide him information on the current course of fiscal and monetary policy. Two of the countries Travis is considering are Turkey and Greece. When asked by Travis, the Barton international fixed income analyst prepares the following figure, with the current yield curves for both the Turkish and Greek fixed income markets.

Figure 1: Current Yield Curves

	1 month	3 month	6 month	1 year	3 year	5 year	10 year
Turkey	5.7	5.8	5.9	6.0	6.0	6.1	6.1
Greece	8.2	7.7	6.9	5.9	5.3	5.0	4.8

While managing the Barton Aggressive Growth Fund, Travis purchased a few Thai equities for his fund that performed very well. Travis wonders whether the Thai economy is pro-growth, or if those returns were just a consequence of the growth of the Asian "miracle" and not to be repeated. Mary Schwartz, the Asian analyst assigned to the EMF, does the basic research on the Thailand economy and delivers Figure 2, which includes historical and expected data, to Travis.

Figure 2: Thai Economic Statistics 2001-09E

(Baht in millions)	2001	2002	2003	2004	2005	2006	2007	2008E	2009E
Gov't Surplus (Deficit) as % GDP	(13)	(7)	(3)	(3)	1	5	7	9	8
Current Account Surplus (Deficit) as % GDP	(4)	(3)	(2)	1	3	2	4	4	3
Baht Revenue – Thai National Industries	37	40	45	78	82	87	95	111	128
Tariff Receipts – Baht	80	76	71	65	60	55	50	48	40
Number of Hospitals & Schools Built	23	26	24	28	32	35	37	40	35
Tax Collection as % GDP	35	36	33	36	38	35	38	35	34
Investment as % GDP	30	31	32	34	37	39	39	38	40

Travis tells Schwartz that Thailand sounds like it is a good candidate for increased investment by the EMF, but he would like to verify the trend growth rate of the Thai GDP, which he estimates is 8.9%. Schwartz hands Travis the following estimated labor inputs and productivity inputs for the Thai economy.

Figure 3: Thai Estimated Labor Inputs and Labor Productivity Inputs

Growth in potential labor force	3.5%
Growth from capital inputs	2.5%
Growth from increased productivity – capital goods	1.9%

Currently, 18% and 3% of EMF assets are invested in China and the Czech Republic, respectively. Travis has decided that Sung Li Ltd., a Chinese Electronics company, and Kopin Brew Ltd., a Czech brewing company, have attractive fundamentals and merit more research. Travis believes that since the equities will be denominated in the currencies of China (renminbi) and Czechoslovakia (koruna), currency returns versus the U.S. dollar will be an important part of the total rate of return. Because of an expected decline in U.S. interest rates over the next year, the U.S. dollar is expected to weaken. Travis is very happy picking up this excess return from his foreign currency exposure, until he finds out that the Chinese and Czechoslovakian governments peg the renminbi and the koruna to the dollar and the euro, respectively. Travis worries that if he buys Sung Li Ltd. or Kopin Brew Ltd. equities, a significant devaluation of the renminbi or koruna could devastate his returns. Schwartz hands Travis the following figure of Chinese government versus U.S. Treasury spreads and Czechoslovakian government vs. U.K. government spreads.

Figure 4: 5-Year Price Spreads – Renminbi and Koruna

5-year bonds (Spreads in Basis Points)	Jan	Feb	Mar	Apr	May	Jun	Jul
Chinese gov't vs. US Treasury spreads	5	3	5	2	4	1	2
Czech gov't vs. UK gov't Gilt spreads	10	7	15	20	25	30	47

Travis believes there are two primary factors that drive equity valuations in every country – earnings growth and interest rates. To formulate a preliminary opinion on whether a country merits additional research, Travis uses the checklist method of forecasting. In an attempt to obtain a short-term (i.e. next six months) forecast of the attractiveness of the Australian equity market, Travis gathers the following facts.

Figure 5: Australian Checklist of Forecast Factors

GDP Sector	Six Month Growth Rate Trend
Consumer spending	Growth rate accelerating from 2% to 4%
Business investment	Deceleration from 2% to 1% due to lower commodity prices
Government spending	Accelerating due to growth in tax receipts from 2% to 3.5%
Central bank	Benign monetary policy; no trend to higher interest rates

As part of the asset "basket clause" of the EMF, Travis is allowed to invest 5% of the EMF assets in non-emerging markets fixed-income securities. His choice of investment vehicles for use in the "basket clause" are the highly liquid United Kingdom Index-Linked-Gilts (ILGs). His international fixed income salesman assures Travis that yields from ILGs accurately reflect inflation in all conditions.

23.1. Based on the two yield curves shown in Figure 1, indicate the *most likely* condition of monetary and fiscal policy (loose or tight) in each country.

Turkey (monetary)	Greece (fiscal)
A. Loose	Tight
B. Loose	Loose
C. Tight	Tight
D. Tight	Loose

23.2. Based on the information in Figure 2, indicate whether Thailand has a pro-growth structural policy and whether rapid growth of the Thai economy will always equate to strong returns on the Thai stock market.

Thai pro-growth gov't	Strong Thai market returns
A. Yes	Yes
B. Yes	No
C. No	Yes
D. No	No

23.3. Assuming that Travis' estimate of the Thai GDP growth rate is accurate, calculate the Thai GDP growth rate from increased actual labor force participation (LFP).
    A. 1.0%
    B. 2.9%
    C. 3.5%
    D. 4.5%

23.4. Determine the risk of currency devaluation for Sung Li Ltd. and Kopin Brew Ltd. Assume that all other economic factors stay the same.

Sung Li Ltd.	Kopin Brew Ltd.
A. High risk	High risk
B. High risk	Low risk
C. Low risk	High risk
D. Low risk	Low risk

23.5. Forecast the short-term outlook of the Australian equity market for either positive or negative economic returns based solely on the factors given in Figure 5. Cite the major weakness of the checklist approach to forecasting.

Equity market returns	Major weakness of checklist approach
A. Positive	Complex and time consuming
B. Negative	Subjective
C. Positive	Subjective
D. Negative	Complex and time consuming

23.6.   Travis is concerned that one of two scenarios is likely in the U.K.: a strong economy (with higher short-term interest rates), or a consensus expectation of higher inflation in the fixed income market. Indicate the *most likely* effect of either scenario on ILG yields.

	Strong economy	Higher inflation expectation
A.	Higher yields	Higher yields
B.	Higher yields	Lower yields
C.	Lower yields	Higher yields
D.	Lower yields	Lower yields

END OF AFTERNOON SESSION

PRACTICE EXAM 3
SCORE SHEET

MORNING SESSION		
Topic	Question	Points
Portfolio Management	1A	14
Portfolio Management	1B	6
Portfolio Management	2	9
Portfolio Management	3	8
Asset Valuation	4A	6
Asset Valuation	4B	3
Asset Valuation	4C	2
Asset Valuation	4D	3
Asset Valuation	4E	4
Asset Valuation	5A	3
Asset Valuation	5B	4
Asset Valuation	5C	3
Asset Valuation	6A	3
Asset Valuation	6B	6
Portfolio Management	7A	10
Portfolio Management	7B	8
Portfolio Management	7C	6
Portfolio Management	8A	6
Portfolio Management	8B	5
Portfolio Management	8C	4
Portfolio Management	9A	6
Portfolio Management	9B	4
Portfolio Management	10A	4
Portfolio Management	10B	6
Portfolio Management	11A	12
Portfolio Management	11B	8
Portfolio Management	11C	6
Portfolio Management	12A	4

MORNING SESSION (CONTINUED).		
Topic	Question	Points
Portfolio Management	12B	4
Portfolio Management	12C	4
Portfolio Management	13	9
Total		180

AFTERNOON SESSION		
Ethical and Professional Standards	14	18
Ethical and Professional Standards	15	18
Portfolio Management	16	18
Asset Valuation	17	18
Asset Valuation	18	18
Asset Valuation	19	18
Asset Valuation	20	18
Asset Valuation	21	18
Portfolio Management	22	18
Portfolio Management	23	18
Total		180

PRACTICE EXAM 3
SCORE SHEET

MORNING SESSION		
Question	Max. Points	Your Approx. Score
1A	14	
1B	6	
2	9	
3	8	
4A	6	
4B	3	
4C	2	
4D	3	
4E	4	
5A	3	
5B	4	
5C	3	
6A	3	
6B	6	
7A	10	
7B	8	
7C	6	
8A	6	
8B	5	
8C	4	
9A	6	
9B	4	
10A	4	
10B	6	
11A	12	
11B	8	
11C	6	
12A	4	

MORNING SESSION (CONTINUED)		
Question	Max. Points	Your Approx. Score
12B	4	
12C	4	
13	9	
Total	180	

AFTERNOON SESSION		
Question	Max. Points	Your Approx. Score
14	18	
15	18	
16	18	
17	18	
18	18	
19	18	
20	18	
21	18	
22	18	
23	18	
Total	180	

Certain Passing Score: 252 of 360 (70%)
Probable Passing Score: 234

Please note that we write these exams to be as challenging and representative as possible. However, due to the relaxed conditions that most candidates apply when they "take" these tests (i.e., "I'm getting a little tired, I think I'll go to the refrigerator and get a snack"), you should adjust your score downward by 10–15% to get a more accurate measure of the score you would have actually received on exam day. Also, you must be honest with yourself for your score on this exam to have any meaning. Don't assume, for example, that if your answer is close, the graders will be generous with points.

PRACTICE EXAM 3
MORNING SESSION

Questions 1 and 2 relate to Reggie Perlin. A total of 29 minutes is allocated to these questions. *Candidates should answer these questions in the order presented.*

Blake McCurdy, CFA, is a new portfolio manager for Diego Investment Counseling, LLC. McCurdy has been asked to evaluate the portfolio of Reggie Perlin, 58 years old. Perlin is a retired inventor with a retirement account portfolio worth $10 million. Under the structure of Perlin's retirement account, any income or capital gains are not taxable until the funds are withdrawn from the portfolio. The portfolio is currently allocated 40% to small capitalization stocks with the remainder in cash. As a result of several inventions, Perlin receives a monthly royalty check, which he will continue to receive until his death. The royalty payment is adjusted annually for inflation, and currently is set at $18,000 per month.

In the past year, Perlin married a 35-year-old woman. His previous wife died five years ago, and he has three children aged 25 to 31 years old. Perlin has informed McCurdy that he would like to have a balance of $20 million in his portfolio when he turns 65 in seven years time. Perlin is willing to take only the risk necessary to achieve the $20 million target. Upon his 65th birthday, Perlin plans to withdraw all assets from his retirement account portfolio and divide the after-tax proceeds among his wife and children.

Perlin is currently subject to an income tax rate of 30%. Perlin has no debt and needs $12,600 per month after taxes to live on. Once he distributes his portfolio, Perlin believes his royalty income will be more than adequate to cover his cost of living and any other needs that might arise.

QUESTION 1 HAS TWO PARTS FOR A TOTAL OF 20 MINUTES

A.   **Prepare** an investment policy statement using the objectives and constraints format for Perlin, based solely on the information provided to this point.

Answer Question 1A in the template provided.

(14 minutes)

B.   **Evaluate** the current portfolio's asset allocation against the investment policy developed in Part A.

(6 minutes)

©2008 Schweser

Template for Question 1A

Note: Your response should include appropriate content for each objective and constraint based on Perlin's current situation.

Objectives	Comments
1.	
2.	

Constraints	Comments
1.	
2.	
3.	
4.	
5.	

QUESTION 2 HAS ONE PART FOR A TOTAL OF 9 MINUTES

McCurdy has developed the four asset allocation alternatives provided in Figure 1 for Perlin. **Recommend** the one alternative portfolio in Figure 1 that is the *most appropriate* strategic asset allocation for Perlin. **Justify** your response with *four* reasons.

Figure 1: Proposed Asset Allocation

Asset Class	Yield	Return	Alternative Portfolios Asset Allocation Percentages (%)			
			A	B	C	D
Cash & equivalents	3.0%	3.0%	1	2	10	2
U.S. Treasury notes	5.0%	5.0%	0	3	0	0
Municipal bonds (AA)	4.7%	4.7%	0	15	0	0
Corporate bonds (AA)	6.5%	6.5%	25	5	0	24
Large-cap stocks	2.0%	10.0%	20	20	20	24
Small-cap stocks	0.5%	12.0%	25	25	25	30
International stocks	1.0%	11.0%	10	10	15	5
REIT	5.0%	10.0%	10	10	15	0
Venture capital fund	0.0%	20.0%	9	10	15	15
			100	100	100	100
Expected annual total return (%)			10.56	10.34	11.45	11.17
Expected standard deviation (%)			12.10	11.50	14.10	14.10

(9 minutes)

QUESTION 3 HAS ONE PART FOR A TOTAL OF 8 MINUTES

Diego Investment Counseling has previously used a traditional approach to determine investors' "personality" classifications. The portfolio manager has categorized the investor based on the initial and periodic personal interview(s) with the investor and a review of past investment activity. While Diego believes past client risk assessments to be accurate, McCurdy's supervisor now believes this traditional approach needs to be supplemented by a questionnaire approach to better determine investors' "personality types." To facilitate the development of the new questionnaires, McCurdy has been reviewing notes from past client interviews. Excerpts from four different client interviews are listed below.

1. "In general, I don't like to see much turnover in my account since I don't like to take advantage of market timing strategies. Those strategies seem likely to have a low probability of actually making money. What I find more important is preserving the value of my portfolio against inflation."

2. "Most of the time I don't want to be bothered with stock tips from my broker. I read the same research they read, and I often think the analysts writing the reports don't have a clue what they are talking about. The majority of my investments have been selected using my own careful research, but there are a few stocks in my portfolio that I just had a feeling about so I bought them."

3. "I like to have broad access to quality reports from analysts and economic researchers so I can stay abreast of key market developments. I do not appreciate, however, receiving calls from my stockbroker regarding the latest investment strategy that is also being sold to everyone else in the market. Most of the time the recommended strategy is too risky and doesn't fit with my portfolio."

4. "I need to have access to market information quickly so I can keep up-to-date on where the hot money is. I read research occasionally but the analysts are usually talking over my head about some boring blue-chip company. Everyone in my investment club generally agrees that the analysts are overrated. I like my portfolio to be reasonably liquid so I can move funds quickly."

For each of the client excerpts, **identify** and **justify** the primary personality type appropriate to the excerpt.

(8 minutes)

QUESTION 4 HAS FIVE PARTS FOR A TOTAL OF 18 MINUTES

Max Cady is the Chairman of the investment committee of Mitchum University (MU). The MU endowment is currently invested primarily in stocks (65% of assets) and bonds (25% of assets) with the remainder in cash. Cady would like to further diversify the MU endowment by adding an asset class—commodities. In particular, Cady is interested in gaining exposure to the energy sector. Rising energy costs have been a budgetary problem for MU, and Cady would like to derive some benefit from higher energy prices. Cady is uncertain as to how MU could best add the desired exposure to energy, and he has contacted Greg Peck, CFA, who serves as a consultant to the MU endowment.

Peck has suggested three alternatives:

1. Trading futures contracts on oil or some other energy-related commodity.

2. Overweighting energy stocks in the existing MU portfolio.

3. Buying exchange traded funds (ETFs) related to the energy sector.

Peck suggested an ETF based on the Goldman Sachs Commodity Index (GSCI). Cady is familiar with ETFs but is less knowledgeable about commodity futures contracts. Peck has provided Cady with a breakdown of commodity futures returns over the past 30 days for three upcoming oil futures contracts, shown in Figure 1.

Contract Maturity	Futures Price June 15	Futures Price May 15	Change in Spot Price
July	$63.25	$62.55	$0.50
October	$62.35	$61.70	$0.50
January	$61.75	$61.20	$0.50

Cady is evaluating his alternatives.

A. For each of the three alternatives suggested by Peck, **select** whether the approach is a direct or an indirect commodity investment, and **comment** on how well each alternative could achieve Cady's objective of higher exposure to energy-related commodities.

(6 minutes)

Answer Question 4A in the template provided.

B.   **Calculate** the roll return, for the period May 15 to June 15, for the oil futures contracts maturing in July, October, and January, based on the numbers given in Figure 1.

(3 minutes)

Answer Question 4B in the template provided.

C.   **Identify** the current oil futures pricing situation as backwardation or contango, and **justify** your response.

(2 minutes)

Answer Question 4C in the template provided.

D.   Cady has been reviewing the recent performance of the GSCI, and has found that for the last 12 months, the GSCI has had a roll return of 6.4% and a spot return of 10.2%. If the collateral return on the GSCI over the past 12 months was 7.1%, **calculate** the total return on the GSCI. **Comment** on the weighting of different commodity sectors within the GSCI.

(3 minutes)

E.   **Discuss** the potential benefits to the MU endowment of adding energy-related commodities as an asset class, in terms of:
   i. Inflation hedging.
   ii. Diversification.

(4 minutes)

Template for Question 4A

Alternative	Type (circle one)	Comment
Futures contracts	Direct Indirect	
Energy stocks	Direct Indirect	
ETFs	Direct Indirect	

Template for Question 4B

Contract	Roll yield calculation
July	
October	
January	

Template for Question 4C

Futures pricing	Justification
Backwardation Contango	

QUESTION 5 HAS THREE PARTS FOR A TOTAL OF 10 MINUTES

Juan Ketter, CFA, conducts reviews of real estate fund managers and commingled real estate funds (CREFs) for Fund Evaluation Inc. (FEI). Ketter just completed his evaluation of the Von Wilstrom Real Estate Mutual Fund, which has a stated objective to hold apartment REITs exclusively. In an internal memorandum, FEI states that based on an analysis of returns and standard deviation of real estate fund benchmarks, indirect investment in real estate is twice as risky as direct investment in real estate.

A summary of the performance of the Fund and various benchmarks is provided below:

Figure 1: Performance Statistics

	Average Return	Standard Deviation
Von Wilstrom Fund	12%	28%
NAREIT index	20%	20%
NCREIF index	13%	10%
Apartment REITs	10%	30%
Office REITs	14%	26%

Ketter's supervisor, Eileen Davies, concludes that the Von Wilstrom Fund performed poorly during the evaluation period.

A.   **State** whether Ketter should agree or disagree with the FEI memorandum that indirect investment in real estate is twice as risky as direct investment. **Justify** your response with *two* reasons.

Answer Question 5A in the template provided.

(3 minutes)

B.   **Explain** *one* strength and *one* weakness of using the NCREIF index as a benchmark for the performance of closed-end CREFs.

Answer Question 5B in the template provided.

(4 minutes)

C. **Indicate** whether Ketter should agree or disagree with Davies's conclusion about the performance of the Von Wilstrom Fund, and **justify** your response with *one* supporting reason.

Answer Question 5C in the template provided.

(3 minutes)

Template for Question 5A

FEI Memo	Justification
Agree

Disagree | |

Template for Question 5B

Strength/ Weakness	Explanation
Strength	
Weakness	

Template for Question 5C

Decision	Justification
Agree

Disagree | |

QUESTION 6 HAS TWO PARTS FOR A TOTAL OF 9 MINUTES

Creative Capital Partners (CCP) is a private equity investment firm that invests in closely-held businesses in the U.S. and European markets. CCP is set up as a limited partnership and has approximately 30 limited partners at any given time. George Newman, CFA, is a principal with CCP and has been asked by a group of existing limited partners and potential new limited partners to explain the private equity market in general and to describe the due diligence process used by the firm to evaluate investment opportunities. Newman makes the following comments regarding the private equity market:

> "The private equity market can be divided into two main stages, which include the formative and expansion stage. Within the formative stage, seed stage companies are characterized by small levels of investment, usually provided by the founder and his or her family. Seed stage companies have unproven ideas that must be converted into a marketable product. Venture capital funds and strategic partners generally provide the capital to move the company through the start-up phase to the expansion stage, at which point revenues begin to flow into the company. Once the company is well into the expansion stage, 'Angel' investors commonly provide additional capital to assist the company in preparing for its initial public offering."

A. **Evaluate** Newman's comments to the group of limited partners regarding the private equity market.

(3 minutes)

B. Newman has decided to provide the group of limited partners with information on the due diligence process related to three areas. **Identify** and **explain** *one* due diligence consideration related to each of the following areas:
   i. Evaluation of prospects for market success.
   ii. Operational review.
   iii. Financial/legal review.

Answer Question 6B in the template provided.

(6 minutes)

Template for Question 6B

Due Diligence Area	Consideration	Explanation
Evaluation of prospects for market success		
Operational review		
Financial/legal review		

QUESTION 7 HAS THREE PARTS FOR A TOTAL OF 24 MINUTES

The Sterling Foundation is evaluating its equity portfolio performance over the past year. For the third consecutive year, the portfolio has posted a double digit overall return. Still, the trustees of the foundation would like a more detailed analysis of their returns. The portfolio is allocated into three segments—domestic large capitalization stocks, domestic small capitalization stocks, and international stocks. The Rawls Group, a consulting firm, makes the asset allocation decision among the three segments at the beginning of each year, and then selects a new manager for each segment. The segment weights and returns for the past year are provided in the following table.

	Weights		Returns	
Asset Class	Actual	Benchmark	Actual	Benchmark
Large cap stocks	0.60	0.50	12.5%	10.0%
Small cap stocks	0.25	0.30	16.0%	18.5%
International stocks	0.15	0.20	10.0%	9.0%
	1.00	1.00		

In order to help evaluate the foundation's equity performance, the trustees have asked for an attribution analysis.

A.   **Calculate** the overall returns over the past year for both the Sterling Foundation equity portfolio and the benchmark portfolio, and **state** whether Sterling has outperformed or underperformed the benchmark.

Answer Question 7A in the template provided.

(10 minutes)

B.   **Calculate** both the allocation effect and the selection effect of Sterling's performance relative to the benchmark.

Answer Question 7B in the template provided.

(8 minutes)

C. Based on your answers to Parts A and B, **evaluate** Sterling's
performance relative to the benchmark.

(6 minutes)

Template for Question 7A

Portfolio	Calculation	Return
Sterling		
Benchmark		
Circle One		
Outperform Underperform		

Template for Question 7B

Effect	Calculation	Final Answer
Allocation effect		
Selection effect		

Questions 8 and 9 relate to Smith Hospital. A total of 29 minutes is allocated to these questions. *Candidates should answer these questions in the order presented.*

Smith Hospital is a publicly traded company that operates acute care hospitals across the United States. A national nursing shortage has hindered Smith's ability to take full advantage of growth opportunities. Smith Hospital also suffers from high employee turnover, a problem plaguing the entire health care industry. To attract and retain qualified nurses, Smith offers a variety of benefits including a defined benefit pension plan. Smith's defined benefit pension plan was created fifteen years ago and its assets are currently valued at $100 million. At present, 80% of the plan is invested in equities, with the remaining 20% invested in bonds. Benefit payments are fixed after the employee retires. Figure 1 provides details about the Smith Hospital Pension Plan.

Figure 1: Smith Hospital Pension Plan for 2007

	2007
Average active participants' age	31 years old
Ratio of active to inactive participants	8 to 1
Actuarial value of plan assets	$99 million
Average employment service	5.5 years
Beta of the pension plan's equity component	0.75

Sarah Weekly, CFA is the Chief Financial Officer for Smith Hospital and oversees the company's pension plan. Weekly believes that the Smith Hospital Pension Plan's asset allocation affects the overall company's risk profile. Weekly created figures 2 and 3 to evaluate the company's risk profile. In addition, Weekly calculated the following asset allocation for the pension plan benchmark:

- Nominal Bonds – 85%
- Real Rate Bonds – 5%
- Equities – 10%

In a meeting with upper management, Weekly proposed that the assets of the pension plan be indexed to the benchmark. Weekly designed the benchmark to be low risk. Weekly also proposed that the company begin a defined contribution plan to assist in the nurse recruiting process by increasing employee benefits. Figure 2 provides data to calculate the company's weighted average cost of capital (WACC).

Figure 2: Smith Hospital WACC Data

	2007
Market value of operating assets	$500 million
Market value of debt	$200 million
Market value of equity	$300 million
Risk free rate	4%
Market risk premium	7%
Smith Hospital's Beta	1.00
Estimated Core WACC	8.2%

Figure 3 provides a risk analysis of various pension plan asset mixes for the overall company.

Figure 3: Risk analysis of Smith Hospital Pension Plan

Equity Percentage	Pension Asset Beta	Total Asset Beta	Smith Equity Beta
0%	0.00	0.400	0.80
80%	?	0.500	1.00
100%	0.75	0.525	1.05

QUESTION 8 HAS THREE PARTS FOR A TOTAL OF 15 MINUTES

A.   **Discuss** three reasons the benchmark calculated by Weekly is *not* appropriate for the Smith Hospital Pension Plan. (Refer to Figure 1.)

(6 minutes)

Answer Question 8A in the template provided.

B.   **Calculate** Smith Hospital's estimated core WACC adjusted for the company's pension plan assets. Ignore income taxes. (Refer to figures 1 and 2.)

(5 minutes)

Answer Question 8B in the template provided.

C.   **Discuss** *four* effects of using Smith Hospital's estimated core WACC (given in Figure 2) rather than the estimated core WACC adjusted for the company's pension plan assets (calculated in Part B) in the capital budgeting process.

(4 minutes)

Template for Question 8A

Benchmark discussion
1.
2.
3.

Template for Question 8B

	Market Value	Beta		Market Value	Beta
Operating assets (core)	500	?	Debt	200	0
Pension assets	100	?	Pension liabilities	100	0
			Equity	300	1.0
Total assets	600	0.5	Total liabilities & equity	600	0.5

Estimated core WACC adjusted for pension assets = ?

QUESTION 9 HAS TWO PARTS FOR A TOTAL OF 10 MINUTES

A.   **Discuss** the effect that alternative pension plan asset allocations will have on Smith Hospital's valuation and its optimal capital structure. Specifically, review the following alternative allocations: (Refer to Exhibit 3)
   - 100% equity allocation.
   - 0% equity allocation.

(6 minutes)

Answer Question 9A in the template provided.

B.   **Comment** on Weekly's decision to add a defined contribution plan. Specifically, address the key features of the defined contribution plan from the perspective of:
   - Smith Hospital.
   - Employee.

(4 minutes)

Answer Question 9B in the template provided.

Template for Question 9A

1. 100% Equities	Valuation:
	Optimal capital structure:
2. 0% Equities	Valuation:
	Optimal capital structure:

Template for Question 9B

1. Smith Hospital	
2. Employee	

QUESTION 10 HAS TWO PARTS FOR A TOTAL OF 10 MINUTES

Hugo Gamez, CFA, manages portfolios for high net worth investors. Gamez established an aggressive asset mix that includes a 10% allocation to international investments for his clients willing to accept greater risk. However, Gamez' international equity investments are only in developed markets, with no exposure to emerging markets. The recent strong performance produced by emerging market equities has sparked client interest in the investment class. Gamez is impressed with the fact that emerging market countries account for 85% of the world's population and 48% of the global economic output. However, Gamez is concerned about the high risk level of emerging market investments and whether they would be suitable for his clients. After reviewing figures 1 and 2, Gamez states that as a result of the lack of diversification benefits, the rationale for investing in emerging markets no longer holds and thus precludes adding any emerging market equities to client portfolios.

Figure 1: Data from 2001 through 2005

Correlation	MSCI Emerging	MSCI World ex-U.S.	U.S. Large Cap	U.S. Small Cap	Annualized Returns	Standard Deviation
MSCI Emerging	1.00				19.3%	21.0%
MSCI World ex-U.S.	0.87	1.00			4.9%	15.6%
US Large Cap	0.81	0.88	1.00		0.5%	14.9%
US Small Cap	0.83	0.83	0.84	1.00	8.2%	19.2%

Figure 2: Data from 1996 through 2000

Correlation	MSCI Emerging	MSCI World ex-U.S.	U.S. Large Cap	U.S. Small Cap	Annualized Returns	Standard Deviation
MSCI Emerging	1.00				−4.2%	27.2%
MSCI World ex-U.S.	0.82	1.00			7.5%	15.1%
U.S. Large Cap	0.71	0.78	1.00		18.3%	16.0%
U.S. Small Cap	0.67	0.67	0.65	1.00	10.3%	21.3%

A.   **Identify** *four* reasons for the higher correlation between the emerging market and developed market investment returns over the past ten years. (Refer to figures 1 and 2.)

(4 minutes)

B.   **State** whether you agree or disagree with Gamez' statement that the rationale for investing in emerging markets no longer holds and **defend** your selection. (Refer to Exhibits 1 and 2) **No calculations required.**

(6 minutes)

Answer Question 10B in the template provided.

Template for 10B

Circle one	Defend your selection
Agree Disagree	

QUESTION 11 HAS THREE PARTS FOR A TOTAL OF 26 MINUTES

Great Northern Company, a U.S.-based global manufacturer of consumer products, recently established a foundation to provide financial and leadership support for nonprofit organizations dedicated to improving the quality of life in the communities where Great Northern Company operates. The Foundation will contribute to the global social concerns found in their home communities through grants, volunteerism and leadership. The Foundation has been established in the country of Grik. Great Northern selected Grik for both the amount of business conducted in the country and the fact that Grik levies no taxes on foundations, unlike some other countries.

Great Northern funded the Foundation with $1.5 billion in cash and will make annual contributions based on the company's profitability. The Board of Directors has determined that the Foundation should be viewed as a perpetual institution. The Foundation's investments must pass a socially responsible screen developed by its Board of Trustees. In addition, the Board requires that the portfolio invest 60% of its assets overseas to meet the constraint of investing in communities where Great Northern operates. The Foundation expects to fund annual grants totaling 4.7% of total assets. In addition to the spending requirement, the Board wants to earn 2% above the inflation rate. The total return objective is the most important goal. If necessary, the grants will be paid from either contributions or from the Foundation assets.

The Board of Trustees hired a consulting firm, which has provided five possible asset allocations including eight potential asset classes. The consultant provided the table below highlighting the income and return expectations for each portfolio. The expected inflation rate is 3%. The Board established a guideline that a minimum of 5% is required to be invested in any one asset class.

Figure 1: Great Northern Foundation's Strategic Asset Allocation

Asset Class	*Alternative Portfolios Asset Allocation Percentages (%)*				
	A	*B*	*C*	*D*	*E*
U.S. stocks	5.0	5.0	5.0	5.0	5.0
International stocks	30.0	5.0	15.0	20.0	20.0
U.S. fixed income	5.0	5.0	5.0	5.0	20.0
International fixed income	30.0	55.0	45.0	20.0	40.0
Private equity	7.0	5.0	5.0	15.0	5.0
Real estate	13.0	15.0	15.0	20.0	5.0
Hedge funds	5.0	5.0	5.0	10.0	5.0
Natural resources	5.0	5.0	5.0	5.0	0.0
Current income (%)	4.0	5.3	4.8	3.5	5.0
Total return (%)	11.2	9.8	10.3	12.9	10.0

A.   **Prepare** an investment policy statement using the objectives and constraints format for the Great Northern Foundation's portfolio.

Answer Question 11A in the template provided.

(12 minutes)

B. Based on Figure 1 and the objectives and constraints determined in Part A, **select** the best asset allocation for Great Northern Foundation's portfolio. **Support** your conclusion with *three* reasons.

(8 minutes)

C. **Discuss** *three* potential problems with Great Northern Foundation's policy allocation developed in Part B.

(6 minutes)

Template for 11A

Objectives	Comments
1.	
2.	

Constraints	Comments
1.	
2.	
3.	
4.	
5.	

QUESTION 12 HAS THREE PARTS FOR A TOTAL OF 12 MINUTES

The Board of Directors for Shark Mutual Funds is conducting its scheduled annual meeting. An agenda item for the meeting is the discussion of best execution. The Board hired an outside consultant to review the mutual funds' trading execution. The Board is hoping the consultant will help Shark Mutual Funds comply with guidelines established in the last SEC audit of Shark Mutual Funds.

In attendance are John Sullivan, CFA, head equity trader, and Susan Ullom, CFA, head of equities for Shark Mutual Funds. The consultant's presentation praised the company's trading effort. She stated that for 92% of the buy tickets, the purchase price for the security was less than the value-weighted average price (VWAP) and that for 95% of the sell tickets, the selling price for the security was greater than the VWAP. Sullivan was happy with the results, especially in light of the fact that Shark's mutual funds range in style from momentum investing to value investing. However, these results are in direct conflict with Ullom's perceptions of Shark's trading efficiency. Ullom and her portfolio management staff have criticized the trading effort for the poor execution prices. Ullom believes that poor trading has contributed to the Funds' underperformance with respect to their benchmarks.

A.   **Discuss** *two* problems with the consultant's use of the VWAP benchmark as the *correct* pricing benchmark for Shark's mutual funds.

(4 minutes)

B.   Trades can be motivated by value or by news. **Describe** each type of trade, and **identify** the *most important* factor for each trading strategy.

(4 minutes)

C.   A Board member questions the consultant as to how best execution can be quantified. **Explain** what is meant by best execution.

(4 minutes)

QUESTION 13 IS COMPOSED OF ONE PART FOR A TOTAL OF 9 MINUTES

Bill Thacker, CFA is a portfolio manager for Andrews Advisors, a U.S.-based firm. Thacker is discussing with junior employees how to construct and revise investment policy statements. During their meeting, Thacker makes the following comments:

"Many investors will use a mental accounting approach where investment goals are segregated. For example, an investor might say they have one portfolio for retirement and one for their child's college expenses, the latter to which they definitely want to make maximum allowable contributions. Any funds left over can be allocated to the retirement fund. For this type of investor, a fixed horizon strategy would not be suitable because it would not ensure funding of the child's education."

"An investment policy statement should be reviewed and considered for possible revision when an investor experiences a change in personal circumstances or when external conditions change significantly. For example, a change in tax laws may trigger an investment policy statement review."

"Investors classified as individualistic investors tend to be very conservative. They can also be very difficult clients to work with because they do their own research and are very confident in their decisions."

State whether or not *each* of these comments is correct. If incorrect, **explain** why.

Answer Question 13 in the template provided.

(9 minutes)

Template for Question 13

Comment	Is the statement correct or incorrect? (circle one)	Explanation, if incorrect
"Many investors will use a mental accounting approach where investment goals are segregated. For example, an investor might say they have one portfolio for retirement and one for their child's college expenses, the latter to which they definitely want to make maximum allowable contributions. Any funds left over can be allocated to the retirement fund. For this type of investor, a fixed horizon strategy would not be suitable because it would not ensure funding of the child's education."	Correct Incorrect	
"An investment policy statement should be reviewed and considered for possible revision when an investor experiences a change in personal circumstances or when external conditions change significantly. For example, a change in tax laws may trigger an investment policy statement review."	Correct Incorrect	

Comment	Is the statement correct or incorrect? (circle one)	Explanation, if incorrect
"Investors classified as individualistic investors tend to be very conservative. They can also be very difficult clients to work with because they do their own research and are very confident in their decisions."	Correct Incorrect	

END OF MORNING SESSION

PRACTICE EXAM 3
AFTERNOON SESSION

Questions 14.1–14.6 relate to Cindy Hatcher and Bernhardt Capital.

Cindy Hatcher, CFA, has spent the last ten years as a portfolio manager with Bernhardt Capital. While working for Bernhardt, Hatcher was responsible for maintaining and improving the company's code of ethics and guidelines for ethical money management. As a result of Hatcher's efforts, Bernhardt saw a dramatic decline in the number of complaints received from their individual and institutional customers.

One of Bernhardt's direct competitors, Smith Investments, is keenly aware of Hatcher's reputation for ethical business practices and has offered her a job as their compliance officer. Hatcher has been apprised of several potential ethical problems at Smith that she will be directly responsible for fixing through implementation of policies and procedures that will prevent ethical dilemmas. The management at Smith is willing to grant Hatcher the authority to construct and implement policies to eliminate the ethical problems at the company.

Hatcher agrees to accept the position with Smith and resigns from employment with Bernhardt. As her first initiative with the company, Hatcher distributes to all employees at Smith a survey intended to acquaint her with the company's common business practices. Her goal is to identify those factors that are most likely to interfere with Smith's compliance with the CFA Institute's Code of Ethics and Standards of Practice. After collecting and analyzing the anonymous responses to the survey, Hatcher has identified the following four issues as the most frequently cited questionable business practices:

1. Many Smith employees have relatives who are clients of the firm. For relatives' accounts where the Smith employee does not have beneficial ownership, trades are generally executed in conjunction with trades for other discretionary accounts held at the firm. Only in accounts where the Smith employee has beneficial ownership are trades delayed until all discretionary account trading is completed.

2. Many of Smith's employees either personally own or maintain, through a family member, beneficial ownership of stocks that are also held in accounts for many of the firm's clients. While the company maintains a strict disclosure policy to the firm of such beneficial ownership and an "at will" disclosure policy to its clients, employees are not barred from trading these securities for their personal benefit even if their clients also own or have a direct or indirect financial interest in the same securities.

3. Account managers meet weekly to discuss the issues and concerns of the client portfolios managed at the firm. During the meetings it is not unusual for individual clients to be identified and discussed. Information regarding the client's holdings and investment strategy is discussed as well as personal needs related to the client's portfolio. The meetings are held in order to provide guidance and continuing education to all of the firm's account managers.

4. At the suggestion of fixed-income analysts at the firm, most of the portfolio managers working for Smith have been adding B-rated corporate fixed-income securities to their portfolios. Analysts originally made (and continue to make) the suggestion due to the attractive yield potential offered by this class of investments. Smith's portfolio managers were thrilled with the idea since the returns on many of the portfolios' equity positions have been stifled by high profile accounting scandals.

Management at Smith Investments has been pleased with Hatcher's efforts so far but is concerned about the firm's ability to maintain compliance with the CFA Institute's Global Investment Performance Standards (GIPS®). The managing director of the firm, Erich Prince, has made the following comments to Hatcher:

> "I am concerned that we will not be able to claim compliance with GIPS at the end of the year since our new information system has inhibited our ability to include terminated portfolios in the historical record up to the last full measurement period before they were terminated. Also, we are unable to regroup portfolios that utilize hedging into separate composites from those that do not utilize hedging. These portfolios are currently grouped according to traditional value and growth strategies based on the capitalization of portfolio holdings (i.e., large vs. small)."

Hatcher eases Prince's mind by telling him she will "ensure full compliance with GIPS by the end of the quarter."

14.1. Which of the following *best* describes a policy that Hatcher could implement to eliminate violations of the CFA Institute Code and Standards in conjunction with trades placed for relatives of the employees of Smith Investments?
    A. Implement a policy prohibiting trades in accounts belonging to relatives of Smith employees.
    B. Restrict trades on relatives' accounts until all other trades have been placed for Smith's other clients.
    C. Require approval by a senior manager with no relationship to the account before placing any trades for the account.
    D. No new policy is necessary since the current policy doesn't violate the Code and Standards.

14.2. Hatcher is concerned about Smith's policies related to disclosure of beneficial ownership of securities. Determine if Smith's disclosure policies are in violation of the CFA Institute Code and Standards and suggest a strategy to eliminate the violation if one exists.
   A. The policy violates the Code and Standards and can be fixed by barring employees from trading the conflicting securities.
   B. The policy violates the Code and Standards and can be fixed by requiring written disclosure to clients regarding Smith employees with beneficial ownership of conflicting securities.
   C. The policy violates the Code and Standards and can be fixed by requiring account managers to refer new clients to a different account manager if their portfolios contain securities for which the account manager is also a beneficial owner.
   D. This particular policy does not violate the Code and Standards.

14.3. Which of the following procedures should Hatcher enact to ensure that Smith Investments is in compliance with Standard IV(B.5) Preservation of Confidentiality? Prohibit:
   A. discussion of clients' individual needs at the weekly meetings of account managers.
   B. discussion of clients' holdings and investment strategy at the weekly meetings of account managers.
   C. identification of clients being discussed at the weekly meetings of account managers.
   D. the weekly meetings of account managers altogether.

14.4. Smith's portfolio managers have been adding B-rated corporate fixed-income securities to their portfolios at the recommendation of the firm's fixed-income analysts. With regard to this situation, Smith's employees have violated the CFA Institute's Code and Standards for which of the following reasons?
   A. Fixed-income analysts are recommending debt securities that are below an investment grade credit rating.
   B. Portfolio managers have failed to consider the investment policy statement of each portfolio before adding the fixed-income securities to the portfolios.
   C. Fixed-income analysts have failed to provide a detailed description of the investment characteristics of the corporate fixed-income securities to the portfolio managers.
   D. Portfolio managers have violated the fair dealing standard by adding the fixed-income securities to most of the portfolios and not all of the portfolios.

14.5. Has Hatcher violated, either directly or indirectly, the CFA Institute Code of Ethics and Standards of Practice?

A. Hatcher violated Standard III(E) Responsibilities of Supervisors by accepting the position with the knowledge that violations were occurring at Smith.

B. Hatcher violated Standard III(E) Responsibilities of Supervisors by failing to make an adequate effort to uncover potential violations at Smith Investments.

C. Hatcher violated Standard III(B) Duty to Employer by accepting a position with a firm that is in direct competition with Bernhardt.

D. Hatcher has not violated the code or standards.

14.6. Evaluate Martin Prince's comments about Smith's ability to maintain compliance with the Global Investment Performance Standards (GIPS). Are Prince's statements regarding terminated portfolios and hedging strategies correct or incorrect?

	Terminated portfolios	Hedging strategies
A.	Incorrect	Incorrect
B.	Correct	Incorrect
C.	Correct	Correct
D.	Incorrect	Correct

Questions 15.1–15.6 relate to Harold Chang and Woodlock Management Group.

Harold Chang, CFA, has been the lead portfolio manager for the Woodlock Management Group (WMG) for the last five years. WMG runs several equity and fixed income portfolios, all of which are authorized to use derivatives as long as such positions are consistent with the portfolio's strategy. The WMG Equity Opportunities Fund takes advantage of long and short profit opportunities in equity securities. The fund's positions are often a relatively large percentage of the issuer's outstanding shares and fund trades frequently move securities prices. Chang runs the Equity Opportunities Fund and is concerned that his performance for the last three quarters has put his position as lead manager in jeopardy. Over the last three quarters, Chang has been underperforming his benchmark by an increasing margin and is determined to reduce the degree of underperformance before the end of the next quarter. Accordingly, Chang makes the following transactions for the fund:

Transaction 1: Chang discovers that the implied volatility of call options on GreenCo is too high. As a result, Chang shorts a large position in the stock options while simultaneously taking a long position in GreenCo stock, using the funds from the short position to partially pay for the long stock. The GreenCo purchase caused the share price to move up slightly. After several months, the GreenCo stock position has accumulated a large unrealized gain. Chang sells a portion of the GreenCo position to rebalance the portfolio.

Transaction 2: Chang takes a long position in a forward contract on the common stock of HNH Corp, a small pharmaceutical firm based in the U.S. Chang subsequently entered buy orders for HNH shares to be executed on the New York and London stock exchanges. The trades are large enough that the company's share price rises as a result of the trades. Chang reverses the forward position for a large profit after the HNH shares are purchased for the fund. The HNH shares are held for a month and then sold for another large profit.

Richard Stirr, CFA, who is also a portfolio manager for WMG, runs the firm's Fixed Income Fund. Stirr is known for his ability to generate excess returns above his benchmark, even in declining markets. Stirr is convinced that even though he has only been with WMG for two and a half years, he will be named lead portfolio manager if he can keep his performance figures strong through the next quarter. To achieve this positive performance, Stirr enters into the following transactions for the fund:

Transaction 3: Stirr decides to take a short forward position on the senior bonds of ONB Corporation, which Stirr currently owns in his Fixed Income Fund. Stirr made his decision after overhearing two of his firm's investment bankers discussing an unannounced bond offering for ONB that will subordinate all of its outstanding debt. As expected, the price of the ONB bonds falls when the upcoming offering is announced. Stirr delivers the bonds to settle the forward contract, preventing large losses for his investors.

Transaction 4: Sitrr has noticed that in a foreign bond market, participants are slow to react to new information relevant to the value of their country's sovereign debt securities. Stirr, along with other investors, knows that an announcement from his firm regarding the sovereign bonds will be made the following day. Stirr doesn't know for sure, but expects the news to be positive, and prepares to enter a purchase order. When the positive news is released, Stirr is the first to act, making a large purchase before other investors and selling the position after other market participants react and move the sovereign bond price higher.

Because of their experience with derivatives instruments, Chang and Stirr are asked to provide investment advice for Cherry Creek, LLC, a commodities trading advisor. Cherry Creek uses managed futures strategies that incorporate long and short positions in commodity futures to generate returns uncorrelated with securities markets. The firm has asked Chang and Stirr to help extend their reach to include equity and fixed income derivatives strategies. Chang has been investing with Cherry Creek since its inception and has accepted increased shares in his Cherry Creek account as compensation for his advice. Chang has not disclosed his arrangement with Cherry Creek since he meets with the firm only during his personal time. Stirr declines any formal compensation but instead requests that Cherry Creek refer their clients requesting traditional investment services to WMG. Cherry Creek agrees to the arrangement.

Three months have passed since the transactions made by Chang and Stirr occurred. Both managers met their performance goals and are preparing to present their results to clients via an electronic newsletter published every quarter. The managers want to ensure their newsletters are in compliance with CFA Institute Standards of Professional Conduct. Chang states, "in order to comply with the Standards, we are required to disclose, in detail, the process used to analyze and select portfolio holdings, the method used to construct our portfolios, and any changes that have been made to the overall investment process. In addition, we must include in the newsletter all factors used to make each portfolio decision over the last quarter and an assessment of the portfolio's risks." Stirr responds by claiming, "we must also clearly indicate that projections included in our report are not factual evidence but rather conjecture based on our own statistical analysis. However, I believe we can reduce the amount of information included in the report from what you have suggested and instead issue more of a summary report as long as we maintain a full report in our internal records."

15.1.   Determine whether Chang has violated any CFA Institute Standards of Professional Conduct with respect to Transaction 1 and Transaction 2.

	Transaction 1	Transaction 2
A.	No	No
B.	No	Yes
C.	Yes	No
D.	Yes	Yes

15.2.   Determine whether Stirr has violated any CFA Institute Standards of Professional Conduct with respect to Transaction 3 and Transaction 4.

	Transaction 3	Transaction 4
A.	No	No
B.	No	Yes
C.	Yes	No
D.	Yes	Yes

15.3.   According to CFA Institute Standards of Professional Conduct, which of the following statements regarding Chang's arrangement with Cherry Creek, LLC is *most accurate*? Chang's arrangement:
A. does not violate any Standards.
B. violates the Standards because he has not obtained written consent from WMG to enter into the agreement.
C. violates the Standards because he has misrepresented his ability to provide professional advice to Cherry Creek.
D. violates the Standards because he has engaged in a form of market manipulation and engaged in professional misconduct.

15.4.   According to CFA Institute Standards of Professional Conduct, which of the following statements regarding Stirr's arrangement with Cherry Creek, LLC is *most accurate*? Stirr's arrangement:
A. does not violate any Standards.
B. need only be disclosed to WMG to be acceptable.
C. need only be disclosed to clients and prospects to be acceptable.
D. is acceptable only if disclosed to WMG and to clients and prospective clients.

15.5. Determine whether Chang's comments regarding the disclosure of investment processes used to manage WMG's portfolios and the disclosure of factors used to make portfolio decisions over the last quarter are *most likely* correct or incorrect.

	Investment processes	Decision factors
A.	Correct	Correct
B.	Correct	Incorrect
C.	Incorrect	Correct
D.	Incorrect	Incorrect

15.6. Determine whether Stirr's comments regarding the use of projections in the report and the length of the report are *most likely* correct or incorrect.

	Projections	Length of report
A.	Correct	Correct
B.	Correct	Incorrect
C.	Incorrect	Correct
D.	Incorrect	Incorrect

Questions 16.1–16.6 relate to Dan Draper.

Dan Draper, CFA is a portfolio manager at Madison Securities. Draper is analyzing several portfolios which have just been assigned to him. In each case, there is a clear statement of portfolio objectives and constraints, as well as an initial strategic asset allocation. However, Draper has found that all of the portfolios have experienced changes in asset values. As a result, the current allocations have drifted away from the initial allocation. Draper is considering various rebalancing strategies that would keep the portfolios in line with their proposed asset allocation targets.

Draper spoke to Peter Sterling, a colleague at Madison, about calendar rebalancing. During their conversation, Sterling made the following comments:

Comment 1:   Calendar rebalancing will be most efficient when the rebalancing frequency considers the volatility of the asset classes in the portfolio.

Comment 2:   Calendar rebalancing on an annual basis will typically minimize market impact relative to more frequent rebalancing.

Draper believes that a percentage-of-portfolio rebalancing strategy will be preferable to calendar rebalancing, but he is uncertain as to how to set the corridor widths to trigger rebalancing for each asset class. As an example, Draper is evaluating the Rogers Corp. pension plan, whose portfolio is described in Figure 1.

Figure 1: Rogers Corp Pension Plan

Asset Class	Expected Return	Standard Deviation	Average Transaction Cost	Correlation With Other Assets in Portfolio
U.S. small-cap stocks	10%	15%	0.30%	0.21
Emerging market stocks	14%	22%	0.40%	0.10
Real estate limited part-nership	16%	10%	3.00%	0.16
U.S. government bonds	6%	2%	0.05%	0.14

Draper has been reviewing Madison files on four high net worth individuals, each of whom has a $1 million portfolio. He hopes to gain insight as to appropriate rebalancing strategies for these clients. His research so far shows:

Client A is 60 years old, and wants to be sure of having at least $800,000 upon his retirement. His risk tolerance drops dramatically whenever his portfolio declines in value. He agrees with the Madison stock market outlook, which is for a long term bull market with few reversals.

Client B is 35 years old, and wants to hold stocks regardless of the value of her portfolio. She also agrees with the Madison stock market outlook.

Client C is 40 years old, and her risk tolerance varies proportionately with the value of her portfolio. She does not agree with the Madison stock market outlook, but expects a choppy stock market, marked by numerous reversals, over the coming months.

Client D is 38 years old, and needs $500,000 for a business venture he plans to start two years from now. If his portfolio appreciated by 20%, his risk tolerance would increase by 30%. He expects a choppy stock market, marked by numerous reversals, over the coming months.

16.1.   Indicate whether Sterling's comments related to calendar rebalancing are correct or incorrect.

Comment 1	Comment 2
A. Correct	Correct
B. Correct	Incorrect
C. Incorrect	Correct
D. Incorrect	Incorrect

16.2.   Draper believes that the risk tolerance for tracking error relative to the target asset mix and the volatility of any other asset classes in a portfolio are important factors in determining an appropriate rebalancing corridor. Assuming all other factors are equal, the optimal rebalancing corridor will be wider when:
   A. the risk tolerance for tracking error is high and the volatility of other asset classes is low.
   B. the risk tolerance for tracking error is high and the volatility of other asset classes is high.
   C. the risk tolerance for tracking error is low and the volatility of other asset classes is low.
   D. the risk tolerance for tracking error is low and the volatility of other asset classes is high.

16.3.   Based on the information provided in Figure 1, which asset class of the Rogers pension plan should have the narrowest rebalancing corridor width?
   A. U.S. small cap stocks.
   B. Emerging market stocks.
   C. Real estate limited partnership.
   D. U.S. government bonds.

16.4.   In selecting a rebalancing strategy for his clients, Draper would *most likely* select a constant mix strategy for:
        A. Client A.
        B. Client B.
        C. Client C.
        D. Client D.

16.5.   A constant proportion strategy with a floor greater than zero and a multiplier equal to one is also known as a:
        A. buy and hold strategy.
        B. concave strategy.
        C. selling insurance strategy.
        D. constant mix strategy.

16.6.   Which of the following statements is *most* accurate regarding rebalancing strategies? The constant:
        A. proportion strategy has a concave payoff curve and a multiplier greater than 1.
        B. proportion strategy has a convex payoff curve and a multiplier less than 1.
        C. mix strategy has a concave payoff curve and a multiplier less than 1.
        D. mix strategy has a convex payoff curve and a multiplier greater than 1.

Questions 17.1–17.6 relate to the Huey Long Endowment.

The Huey Long Endowment was established to improve the health of underserved people in the state of Louisiana. The Endowment has total assets of $1.4 billion. A Board of Directors oversees the Endowment's activities. Figure 1 details the Endowment's strategic asset allocation and allowable asset class ranges.

Figure 1: Strategic Asset Allocation and Ranges

	Current Policy Allocation	Allowable Ranges	
		Minimum	Maximum
United States (U.S.) equity	37%	42%	72%
Developed non-U.S. equity	20%	(Equities combined)	
Core fixed income	8%	8%	38%
High yield fixed income	9%	(Fixed income combined)	
U.S. Treasury TIPS	6%		
Absolute return	15%	5%	35%
Private equity	3%	(Alternative investments combined)	
Real estate	2%		

The Endowment invested the entire Developed non-U.S. equity category in Germany. Rather than passively indexing to the German market via the DAX index, the Board hired a firm to provide additional value through enhanced indexing. Figure 2 provides the return and risk statistics of the Endowment's enhanced indexing compared to the passive index.

Figure 2: Return and Risk of Enhanced Index Firm and DAX

	Return	Beta	Active Risk
Enhanced indexing	13.5%	1.05	1.5%
DAX index	13.0%	1.00	
German risk-free rate	1.0%	0	
U.S. equity	18.3%	1.15	5.1%
U.S. equity benchmark	16.1%	1.00	

The Board fired a money manager in the "U.S. equity" category for poor 5-year performance and hired a consultant to conduct a money manager search. The consultant came back with a recommendation of two potential U.S. equity money managers, Lane Capital Management and Parker Investment Counsel. The consultant classified the investment strategy of both companies as core multi-cap. The consultant provided the Board with the data in Figures 3, 4, and 5 for their consideration in making a final selection.

Figure 3: Suggested Portfolio Percentages Based on Market Capitalization

	Giant	Large	Medium	Small	Micro
Lane Capital Management	11.5%	53.1%	27.2%	8.2%	0%
Parker Investment Counsel	42.4%	35.0%	17.4%	4.1%	1.1%
Core multi-cap benchmark	41.2%	31.2%	19.6%	6.4%	1.6%

Figure 4: Returns and Risk (Percentage Values)

	2003	2004	2005	2006	2007	5-Year Average	Standard Deviation	Active Risk	Misfit Risk
Lane Capital Management	−6.9	−15.4	37.7	15.4	9.7	6.5	12.3	2.7	1.5
Parker Investment Counsel	−9.3	−14.3	32.6	13.1	6.3	4.4	14.5	1.0	0
Core multi-cap benchmark	−11.5	−21.6	30.7	11.7	6.1	1.5	15.0	NA	NA
Value multi-cap benchmark	−4.8	−16.1	31.1	16.7	6.6	5.4	13.9	NA	NA
Growth multi-cap benchmark	−20.7	−28.0	30.3	6.4	5.1	−3.6	16.6	NA	NA
Treasury bill	3.5	1.6	1.0	1.4	3.2	2.1	0.6	NA	NA

Figure 5: Portfolio Analysis

	Lane	Parker	Core Multi-cap Benchmark
Number of stocks	50	250	3000
Weighted-average market cap	$15 billion	$29 billion	$27 billion
Dividend yield	2.7%	1.7%	1.6%
Price-to-earnings	14.5	18.2	18.1
Price-to-book	1.9	2.7	2.8
EPS growth (5-year projected)	7%	14%	14%
Portfolio turnover	100%	60%	8%
Sector Breakdown:			
Healthcare	14.4%	15.5%	12.1%
Technology	6.4%	14.6%	12.8%
Finance	26.6%	21.2%	23.1%
Energy	12.3%	7.0%	7.8%
Materials	3.0%	3.8%	4.5%
Industrials	8.8%	8.3%	8.1%
Telecom	6.0%	3.0%	2.9%
Utilities	8.5%	2.0%	3.4%
Consumer discretionary	0%	17.6%	18.3%
Staples	14.0%	7.0%	7.0%

During the selection discussion, a board member posed a question concerning the difference between returns-based and holdings-based style analyses. The consultant provided the following two explanations:

Statement 1: Returns-based style analysis is cost effective, but it requires the correct index be used to evaluate the manager.

Statement 2: Holdings-based style analysis is a true reflection of a portfolio manager's security selection process, but it is more data intensive than returns-based analysis.

The board also questioned each company about their sell criteria. Each company's response follows:

Lane: Our company uses a number of different sell criteria. The firm's analysts spend a great amount of effort selecting new investment ideas. A target price is established and fundamentals are continually evaluated. As new ideas present themselves, those stocks we deem fully valued are sold. This process leads to a low turnover ratio.

Parker: Our firm focuses on stocks that have the ability to generate consistent growth. If a company misses its earnings expectations four quarters in a row, the stock is sold. In addition, any stock that falls 20% below its purchase price is automatically sold. We believe in diversification and maintain a minimum weighting for each sector equal to 50% of the index's sector weighting. If the portfolio's sector weighting is greater than 150% of the index's weighting, stocks in that sector are sold to bring the allocation into compliance.

17.1. Based on Figures 1 and 2, the information ratio for the Endowment's total equity allocation is *closest* to:
A. 0.5.
B. 1.0.
C. 1.5.
D. 2.0.

17.2. Based on Figure 2, state whether the board should continue enhanced indexing or use the passive DAX index and state (yes or no) whether the board could fully replicate the DAX by investing in 30 stocks.

Selection	DAX replication
A. Enhanced indexing	Yes
B. DAX	Yes
C. Enhanced indexing	No
D. DAX	No

17.3. Based on Figures 3 through 5, state whether Lane or Parker is *most appropriate* for the core multi-cap investment strategy, and based solely on the Sharpe ratio (for the 5-year average returns), state whether Lane or Parker should be selected.

Investment strategy	Selection
A. Lane	Lane
B. Parker	Lane
C. Lane	Parker
D. Parker	Parker

17.4. Based on the 5-year average returns provided in Figure 4, calculate the total active risk for Lane and the true active return for Parker.

	Lane's total active risk	Parker's true active return
A.	2.1%	2.9%
B.	3.1%	2.9%
C.	2.1%	8.0%
D.	3.1%	8.0%

17.5. Indicate whether the consultant's statements concerning returns-based and holdings-based style analyses are correct or incorrect.

	Statement 1	Statement 2
A.	Correct	Correct
B.	Incorrect	Correct
C.	Correct	Incorrect
D.	Incorrect	Incorrect

17.6. Indicate whether or not the sell criteria discussion presented by each company warrants a red flag in the selection process.

	Lane	Parker
A.	Yes	Yes
B.	No	Yes
C.	Yes	No
D.	No	No

Questions 18.1–18.6 relate to Cardinal Fixed Income Management.

Joan Weaver, CFA and Kim McNally, CFA are analysts for Cardinal Fixed Income Management, located in the southeastern United States. Cardinal provides investment advisory services to pension funds, endowments, and other institutions throughout the U.S. and Canada. Cardinal recommends investments in investment grade corporate and government bonds.

Cardinal has largely advocated the use of passive approaches to bond investments, where the predominant holding consists of an indexed or enhanced index bond portfolio. They are exploring, however, the possibility of using a greater degree of active management to increase excess returns. The analysts have made the following statements.

- Weaver: "An advantage of both enhanced indexing by matching primary risk factors and enhanced indexing by minor risk factor mismatching is that there is the potential for excess returns, but the duration of the portfolio is matched with that of the index, thereby limiting tracking error due to interest rate risk."
- McNally: "The use of active management by larger risk factor mismatches typically involves large duration mismatches from the index, in an effort to capitalize on interest rate forecasts."

As part of their increased emphasis on active bond management, Cardinal has retained the services of consulting economists, John Dobson and Mike Martinez, to provide expectational input on factors such as interest rate levels, interest rate volatility, and credit spreads. During their presentations, Dobson states that he believes long-term interest rates should fall over the next year, but that short-term rates should gradually increase. Martinez forecasts that interest rate volatility should increase over the near term. Weaver and McNally are currently advising an institutional client that wishes to maintain the duration of its bond portfolio at 6.7. In light of Dobson's and Martinez's forecasts, they are considering the following three bonds.

	Annualized Bond Yield	Bond Maturity in years	Semiannual Coupon Payment
Bond A	6.2%	5.25	$3.10
Bond B	6.6%	8.50	$3.30
Bond C	7.1%	19.75	$3.55

McNally estimates that the client's targeted duration can be achieved with a single investment in Bond B, referred to as Portfolio 1, or by investing in both Bonds A and C, referred to as Portfolio 2.

Weaver and McNally next examine an investment in a semiannual coupon bond newly issued by the Manix Corporation, a firm with a credit rating of AA by Moody's. The specifics of the bond purchase are provided below given Weaver's projections. It is Cardinal's policy that bonds be evaluated for purchase on a total return basis.

Investment horizon	1 year
Cost of funds for Cardinal	9.00%
Bond maturity in years	20 years
Initial annualized bond yield	6.50%
Reinvestment rate for coupon	5.00%
Annual coupon rate paid semiannually	6.50%
Projected annualized yield to maturity at end of investment horizon	6.00%

One of Cardinal's clients, the Johnson Investment Fund, has instructed Weaver and McNally to recommend the appropriate debt investment for $125,000,000 in funds. Johnson is willing to invest an additional 15% of the portfolio using leverage. Johnson requires that the portfolio duration not exceed 5.5. Weaver recommends that Johnson invest in bonds with a duration of 5.2. The maximum allowable leverage will be used and the borrowed funds will have a duration of 0.8.

Weaver and McNally are discussing the changes that have occurred in the bond market and its current composition. The analysts make the following comments.

- Weaver: "Due to the increasing sophistication of bond issuers, the amount of bonds with call and put options has increased over the years. These bonds therefore sell at a discount relative to bullets."
- McNally: "Putable bonds are quite attractive when interest rates rise. However, we should be careful if we invest in bonds that are putable because valuation models often fail to account for the credit risk of the issuer."

Another client, Blair Portfolio Managers, has asked Cardinal to provide advice on duration management. Last year, their portfolio of had a market value of $3,010,444 and a dollar duration of $108,000. The current figures for the portfolio are provided below.

	Market Value	Duration	Dollar Duration
Bond 1	$940,000	3.8	$35,720
Bond 2	$820,000	2.8	$22,960
Bond 3	$780,000	4.7	$36,660
Bond 4	$621,000	3.5	$21,735

Weaver has asked Palmer to make a recommendation on the best way to readjust the portfolio's current dollar duration back to last year's dollar duration.

18.1.   Regarding their statements on the relative duration positions of various approaches to enhanced index bond management, are Weaver and McNally correct?

	Weaver	McNally
A.	No	No
B.	No	Yes
C.	Yes	No
D.	Yes	Yes

18.2.   Considering the forecasts by Dobson and Martinez in isolation, which of the following provides the *most* appropriate strategy?

	Position given Dobson's forecast	Position given Martinez's forecast
A.	Portfolio 1	Underweight callable bonds
B.	Portfolio 1	Overweight callable bonds
C.	Portfolio 2	Underweight callable bonds
D.	Portfolio 2	Overweight callable bonds

18.3.   The expected bond equivalent yield for the Manix Bond, using total return analysis, is *closest* to:
A. 5.62%.
B. 11.86%.
C. 12.12%.
D. 12.20%.

18.4.   Does Weaver's recommended investment for the Johnson Investment Fund violate the investment guidelines?
A. No, the duration of the portfolio is 5.1.
B. No, the duration of the portfolio is 5.2.
C. Yes, the duration of the portfolio is 5.9.
D. Yes, the duration of the portfolio is 6.1.

18.5. Regarding their statements on bonds with options, are Weaver and McNally correct?

	Weaver	McNally
A.	No	No
B.	No	Yes
C.	Yes	No
D.	Yes	Yes

18.6. To adjust the dollar duration of the Blair portfolio back to last year's level, Palmer should recommend that Blair rebalance each bond to:
   A. 0.92 of its current value.
   B. 0.95 of its current value.
   C. 1.05 of its current value.
   D. 1.08 of its current value.

Questions 19.1–19.6 relate to Ethan Edwards and Searcher Securities.

Ethan Edwards, CFA, is a fixed income portfolio manager for Searcher Securities. Edwards has been reviewing the pension fund of Cicatrix Corp., a large account with $55 million in fixed income securities. He is considering proposing a contingent immunization strategy to the trustees of the Cicatrix pension fund. The average age of Cicatrix employees covered by the plan is only 41. In a recent meeting, the trustees of the plan informed Edwards that a 6.0% return was an acceptable minimum for the next six years.

The Cicatrix pension bond portfolio was set up in a classical immunization strategy four years ago. At that time the objective was to fund a $75 million liability in 10 years. The allocation was a barbell strategy using zero-coupon bonds with half of the bonds maturing in 4 years and half maturing in 15 years. The 4-year bonds are now maturing, and Edwards is hoping to use the proceeds to create a contingent immunized portfolio. Edwards plans to once again use a barbell structure, with half of the portfolio invested in maturities shorter than the 6-year time horizon set by the trustees and the other half in the original 15-year bonds.

One of the trustees of the Cicatrix pension fund asked Edwards about whether rebalancing the portfolio was a concern when using classical immunization strategies. Edwards responded by claiming that as the yield curve shifts and time passes, the portfolio will need to be rebalanced. Edwards also stated that the costs to rebalance are high but can be mitigated by limiting the investment universe to highly liquid securities.

Another trustee asked Edwards to assess the feasibility of pursuing a multiple liability immunization strategy for the fund and report his findings. Among other items, Edwards' response contained the following information:

- Assuming parallel shifts in interest rates, multiple liability immunization is possible for the Cicatrix pension fund so long as the asset portfolio used to immunize the liability stream has a duration equal to the duration of the liability stream.
- As an alternative to multiple liability immunization, the Cicatrix pension fund could fund the upcoming liabilities through a cash flow matching strategy. A cash flow matching strategy would be free from immunization risk, and typically would require less capital to fund the pension liabilities.

19.1. Determine what risk exposure existed at the time Cicatrix initially set up the classical immunization strategy four years ago, and determine what type of security should replace the maturing 4-year bonds to properly maintain a classical immunization strategy.

    Initial risk exposure   Reinvestment
- A. Reinvestment risk   1-year zero coupon bond
- B. Price risk   1-year zero coupon bond
- C. Reinvestment risk   2-year zero coupon bond
- D. Price risk   2-year zero coupon bond

19.2. In order to minimize immunization risk in the event of a nonparallel interest rate shift, which of the following portfolio structures is preferable (assuming the entire portfolio will be restructured)?
   A. Employing a barbell strategy with maturities highly dispersed around the 6-year horizon.
   B. Buying zero coupon bonds maturing in six years.
   C. Buying a series of 6-month T-bills.
   D. Buying high coupon bonds with a duration of six years.

19.3. Determine whether Edwards is correct or incorrect with regard to his statement about the conditions requiring portfolio rebalancing to maintain an immunization strategy and his statement about methods to reduce the costs of rebalancing.

	Conditions	Cost reduction
A.	Correct	Correct
B.	Incorrect	Correct
C.	Correct	Incorrect
D.	Incorrect	Incorrect

19.4. Edwards estimates that the currently available return for a 6-year time horizon is 7.25%. What is the required terminal value of the portfolio, assuming semiannual compounding, and what is the amount of assets needed today to achieve that required terminal value?

	Required terminal value	Assets required today
A.	$78.42 million	$51.15 million
B.	$78.42 million	$55.00 million
C.	$84.32 million	$55.00 million
D.	$84.32 million	$59.14 million

19.5. Evaluate Edwards' comment regarding the duration of the asset portfolio in multiple liability immunization. Edwards is:
   A. incorrect, because the immunization strategy does not require the duration of the asset portfolio to match the duration of the pension liabilities.
   B. incorrect, because the immunization strategy requires that the duration of the asset portfolio is greater than the duration of the pension liabilities.
   C. incorrect, because the immunization strategy requires that the duration of the asset portfolio is less than the duration of the pension liabilities.
   D. correct, because the immunization strategy requires the duration of the asset portfolio to match the duration of the pension liabilities.

19.6.   Determine whether Edwards' comments regarding the immunization risk
and capital requirements for a cash flow matching strategy are correct or
incorrect.

	Immunization risk	Capital requirements
A.	Correct	Correct
B.	Incorrect	Correct
C.	Correct	Incorrect
D.	Incorrect	Incorrect

Questions 20.1–20.6 relate to Joseph Armett and Crowwer Investment Strategists.

Joseph Armett, CFA, a U.S.-based investor, has developed a substantial global personal investments portfolio. The portfolio is performing reasonably well, but Armstrong is concerned about a variety of risks to which the portfolio is exposed.

Armett has hired Crowwer Investment Strategists to present various risk management alternatives. Specifically, Armett is interested in how to protect his portfolio of French stocks against currency risks and, also, how to hedge its current value.

Crowwer has been focusing on Armett's portfolio of French stocks. Here are some particulars regarding this portfolio:

* Total valuation is €12.5 million.
* Portfolio beta is 1.12 relative to the Paris CAC Index.
* Current CAC index value is 3,450.
* CAC futures beta = 1.0.
* Exchange rate currently is $1.04/€.
* Yield curves are essentially flat—dollar and euro interest rates and dividend yield are all equal to 3.8%.

Crowwer has also been discussing with Armett the fine points of some other types of risk to be considered, along with some of the factors to consider when hedging the future value of a foreign investment.

Armett has also asked Crowwer to advise him of his alternatives if he desires to hedge multicurrency portfolios.

20.1. Armett wishes to protect against a decline in the French stock market, but not the euro.
   * Size of Paris CAC index contracts is €10 times the Paris CAC index.
   * There are futures contracts quoted with a March delivery.

   How many futures contracts should Armett buy/sell in order to hedge the French stock market risk?
   A. Buy 406 futures contracts.
   B. Buy 362 futures contracts.
   C. Sell 406 futures contracts.
   D. Sell 362 futures contracts.

20.2. Armett has now decided there is a greater concern about the depreciation of the euro, and is no longer as concerned about the strength of the French stock market.
- Size of Paris CAC index contracts is €10 times the Paris CAC index.
- There are futures contracts quoted with a March delivery.

How many euros should Armett sell forward?
A. Sell €12.5 million forward.
B. Sell €14 million forward.
C. Sell 14 contracts forward.
D. Selling forward is not an effective strategy to accomplish the objective.

20.3. Consider the following scenario. Armstrong is heavily invested in bonds but becomes bullish on the French stock market. With the use of futures and options, he can immediately act on his desire to change his asset allocation to more heavily emphasize French equities. He purchases stock index futures or options and thereafter slowly switches his portfolio from bonds to equities. Which of the following is *least likely* to be a reason for using this strategy as opposed to immediately shifting the portfolio allocation?
A. Lower transactions costs.
B. Allows him the time to select the best stocks.
C. Locks in potential profits on his anticipated stock market gains.
D. Reduction in overall portfolio risk.

20.4. It has been explained to Armett that, in order to hedge multicurrency portfolios, a cross-hedge approach works best. Which of the following statements regarding cross-hedging is *least accurate?*
A. In a multicurrency portfolio, it is important to hedge each currency individually.
B. A U.S. investor would use a futures position in an alternative currency to hedge currency risk, due to possible correlation of some currencies.
C. The goal is to write contracts on currencies that are closely correlated with the investment currencies.
D. Currency hedging can lower the portfolio's volatility.

20.5. Crowwer has recently advised Armett to consider insuring some of his portfolios against currency risks using currency options. Currency options are useful in protecting against unfavorable currency movements, chiefly because:
A. they not only hedge risk, but they also can create profit opportunities in the case of unfavorable currency moves.
B. they have symmetrical risk-return characteristics.
C. volatility is lessened.
D. in the event of a favorable currency move, the options can simply expire.

20.6. The basic approach to the use of currency futures contracts to protect the portfolio against currency risk is to:
   A. sell contracts equal to the foreign value of the portfolio.
   B. hedge currency risk of the present cash position.
   C. select the proper hedge ratio.
   D. employ a currency overlay approach.

Questions 21.1–21.6 are related to Milson Investment Advisors.

Milson Investment Advisors (MIA) specializes in managing fixed income portfolios for institutional clients. Many of MIA's clients are able to take on substantial portfolio risk and therefore the firm's funds invest in all credit qualities and in international markets. Among its investments, MIA currently holds positions in the debt of Bauer Inc., Enertech Company, and SBK Company.

Bauer Inc. is a heavy equipment manufacturer in Germany. The company finances a significant amount of its fixed assets using bonds. Bauer's current debt outstanding is in the form of noncallable bonds issued two years ago at a coupon rate of 7.2% and a maturity of 15 years. Bauer expects German interest rates to decline by as much as 200 basis points (bp) over the next year and would like to take advantage of the decline. The company has decided to enter into a 2-year interest rate swap with semiannual payments, a swap rate of 5.8%, and a floating rate based on 6-month EURIBOR. The duration of the fixed side of the swap is 1.2. Analysts at MIA have made the following comments regarding Bauer's swap plan:

- The duration of the swap from the perspective of Bauer is equal to 0.95.
- By entering into the swap, the duration of Bauer's long-term liabilities will become smaller causing the value of the firm's equity to become more sensitive to changes in interest rates.

Enertech Company is a U.S. based provider of electricity and natural gas. The company uses a large proportion of floating rate notes to finance its operations. The current interest rate on Enertech's floating rate notes, based on 6-month LIBOR plus 150bp, is 5.5%. To hedge its interest rate risk, Enertech has decided to enter into a long interest rate collar. The cap and the floor underlying the collar have maturities of two years, with settlement dates in arrears every six months. The strike rate for the cap is 5.5% and for the floor is 4.5%, based on 6-month LIBOR, which is forecast to be 5.2%, 6.1%, 4.1%, and 3.8%, in 6, 12, 18, and 24 months, respectively. Each settlement period consists of 180 days. Analysts at MIA are interested in assessing the attributes of the collar.

SBK Company builds oil tankers and other large ships in Norway. The firm has several long-term bond issues outstanding with fixed interest rates ranging from 5.0% to 7.5% and maturities ranging from 5 to 12 years. Several years ago, SBK took the pay floating side of a swap with a rate of 6.0%, a floating rate based on LIBOR, and a tenor of eight years. The firm now believes interest rates may increase in 6 months, but is not 100% confident in this assumption. To hedge the risk of an interest rate increase, given its interest rate uncertainty, the firm has sold a payer interest rate swaption with a maturity of 6 months, an underlying swap rate of 6.0%, and a floating rate based on LIBOR.

MIA is considering investing in the debt of Rio Corp, a Brazilian energy company. The investment would be in Rio's floating rate notes, currently paying a coupon of

8.0%. MIA's economists are forecasting an interest rate decline in Brazil over the short term.

21.1.   Given Bauer Inc.'s expectations regarding German interest rates, which of the following represents the effective interest rate the firm will pay on its liabilities after entering into the swap?
A. Fixed rate of 5.8%.
B. Fixed rate of 13.0%.
C. EURIBOR plus 140bp.
D. EURIBOR less 140bp.

21.2.   Are the MIA analysts' comments regarding the duration of the Bauer Inc. swap and the effects of the swap on the company's balance sheet correct?

	Swap duration	Balance sheet effects
A.	No	No
B.	No	Yes
C.	Yes	No
D.	Yes	Yes

21.3.   Which of the following is *closest* to the payoff from Enertech's collar that will occur 24 months from now?
A. Enertech will make a payment of $0.0020 per dollar of notional principal.
B. Enertech will make a payment of $0.0035 per dollar of notional principal.
C. Enertech will receive a payment of $0.0020 per dollar of notional principal.
D. Enertech will receive a payment of $0.0035 per dollar of notional principal.

21.4.   Which of the following is *closest* to the effective interest rate that Enertech will make 18 months from now assuming the notional principal of the collar is equal to the outstanding principal on the firm's floating rate notes?
A. 2.8%.
B. 3.5%.
C. 3.8%.
D. 4.0%.

21.5.   Which of the following statements correctly assesses SBK's swaption strategy to mitigate the risk of an interest rate increase? If interest rates increase:
A. the strategy will increase the market risk of SBK's debt.
B. the strategy will increase the cash flow risk of SBK's debt.
C. the strategy will effectively hedge the interest rate increase.
D. the swaption will be worthless to SBK and have no impact on the firm.

21.6. Which of the following strategies would *best* hedge the risk of MIA's investment in the Rio Corp. floating rate notes?
   A. Sell an interest rate call with a strike rate of 8.0%.
   B. Sell an interest rate put with a strike rate of 7.0%.
   C. Purchase an interest rate call with a strike rate of 9.0%.
   D. Purchase an interest rate put with a strike rate of 7.0%.

Questions 22.1–22.6 relate to Arthur Campbell and Campbell Asset Management.

Arthur Campbell, CFA, is the founder of Campbell Capital Management (CCM), a money management firm focused solely on high net worth individuals. Campbell started CCM two years ago after a 25-year career with a large bank trust department. CCM provides portfolios tailored to match the unique situation of each individual client. All of CCM's clientele have balanced portfolios. CCM does not use derivatives or exotic instruments to manage any of its portfolios. CCM's equity style is defined as growth at a reasonable price (GARP). Most of CCM's portfolios are managed under one of the following three approaches:

- Aggressive (10 accounts): 70% stocks and 30% bonds.
- Moderate (4 accounts): 50% stocks and 50% bonds.
- Conservative (25 accounts): 30% stocks and 70% bonds.

CCM has recently added the following two clients:

1. Harold Moss, a long-time acquaintance of Campbell. Campbell and Moss agree to an investment policy statement in which Moss' portfolio will be managed under CCM's Aggressive approach but will have significantly greater exposure to technology stocks than a typical CCM aggressive portfolio.

2. Richard Bateman is a successful businessman with a $5 million portfolio. Bateman wants his portfolio managed using a conservative approach, and he specifically states that no options or futures are to be used.

A current client, Stan North, has decided to retire. North would like to reduce his risk exposure from aggressive to conservative. CCM moves North's account, including its historical performance, to the conservative composite. At the end of 2007, CCM reports the moderate portfolio composite performance but does not include the associated number of accounts.

CCM reported the 2007 returns on its conservative composite as shown in Figure 1:

Figure 1: CCM Conservative Composite Returns: Year Ending December 31, 2007

	Market Value 12/31/2006	Asset Mix	Returns
Stocks	$95,875,000	30%	8.5%
Bonds	$182,000,000	70%	5.2%
Cash	$47,125,000	0%	3.4%
Total	$325,000,000		

The data shown in Figure 2 relates to portfolio transactions from the 2nd quarter of 2007.

Figure 2: CCM Equity Returns for the Second Quarter of 2007

	Moss Portfolio	*North Portfolio*
Market value 3/31/2007	$2,500,000	$7,400,000
Cash inflows (outflows)		
4/30/2007	$300,000	
5/31/2007		($3,200,000)
Market value 6/30/2007	$3,100,000	$4,500,000

22.1. Campbell wants CCM's composites to be compliant with the Global Investment Performance Standards (GIPS)®. Indicate (yes or no) whether the Moss and the Bateman accounts should to be added to CCM's aggressive and conservative composites, respectively, to remain compliant with GIPS.

    Moss   Bateman
A. Yes   Yes
B. No   Yes
C. Yes   No
D. No   No

22.2. CCM established three types of composites: aggressive, moderate, and conservative. State whether CCM's composites are *correctly* defined according to GIPS.
A. No, CCM must define an equity and fixed-income benchmark.
B. No, CCM must quantify risk parameters.
C. Yes, if CCM establishes a tight allowable range.
D. Yes, CCM has correctly stated its composites.

22.3. Using GIPS, state whether CCM *correctly* or *incorrectly* dealt with the change in North's account and whether CCM *correctly* or *incorrectly* dealt with the performance presentation of the moderate composite.

    North account   Moderate composite
A. Correct   Correct
B. Incorrect   Correct
C. Correct   Incorrect
D. Incorrect   Incorrect

22.4. Which of the following statements concerning CCM's performance presentation is **FALSE**? According to GIPS standards:

A. external verification of CCM's performance measurement policies is required.

B. internal verification that CCM's account objectives are consistent with the composite's definition is required.

C. CCM must provide data concerning the use of leverage and derivatives.

D. CCM must provide a complete list of accounts opened and closed during the period.

22.5. Based on Figure 1, use the strategic asset allocation method to calculate the annual return of the bond category for the conservative composite.

A. 4.5%.

B. 4.7%.

C. 4.8%.

D. 5.2%.

22.6. Based on Figure 2 and using the modified Dietz method, calculate the equity performance of both the Moss and the North portfolios for the second quarter of 2007.

	Moss	North
A.	10.7%	4.1%
B.	11.1%	4.7%
C.	10.7%	4.7%
D.	11.1%	4.1%

Questions 23.1–23.6 relate to Paul Dennon and Apple Markets Associates.

Paul Dennon is senior manager at Apple Markets Associates, an investment advisory firm. Dennon has been examining portfolio risk using traditional methods such as the portfolio variance and beta. He has ranked portfolios from least risky to most risky using the traditional methods.

Recently, Dennon has become more interested in employing value at risk (VAR) to determine the amount of money clients could potentially lose under various scenarios. To examine VAR, Paul selects a fund run solely for Apple's largest client—the Jude Fund. The client has $100 million invested in the portfolio. Using the variance/covariance method, the mean return on the portfolio is expected to be 10% and the standard deviation is expected to be 10%. Over the past 100 days, daily losses to the Jude Fund on its 10 worst days were (all are losses in millions): 20, 18, 16, 15, 12, 11, 10, 9, 6, and 5. Dennon also ran a Monte Carlo simulation (over 10,000 scenarios). The following table provides the results of the simulation:

Figure 1: Monte Carlo Simulation Data

Percentiles	1%	2.5%	5%	10%	50%	95%	97.5%
Jude Fund returns	−25%	−20%	−18%	−12%	10%	15%	20%

The top row of the table reports the percentage of simulations that had returns below those reported in the second row. For example, 95% of the simulations provided a return of 15% or less, and 97.5% of the simulations provided a return of 20% or less.

Dennon's supervisor, Peggy Lane, has become concerned that Dennon's use of VAR in his portfolio management practice is inappropriate and has called a meeting with him. Lane begins by asking Dennon to justify his use of the VAR methodology and explain why the estimated VAR varies depending on the method used to calculate it. Dennon presents Lane with the following table detailing VAR estimates for another Apple client, the York Pension Plan.

Figure 2: Estimates Using Different VAR Methods for the York Pension Plan

VAR Method	Estimate	Dennon's Comments
Historical	$19 million	Future volatility for the York Pension Plan holdings is expected to be greater than what the portfolio experienced in the past. This VAR estimate reflects a narrower distribution of returns than what can be expected in future periods.
Analytical (variance/ covariance)	$26 million	Since this method assumes normally distributed returns but the returns on the York Pension Plan are actually negatively skewed, the analytical estimate of VAR is biased upward.
Monte Carlo simulation	$33 million	This method allows for any distributional assumption necessary and also considers the interaction of asset returns to provide a forward-looking estimate of VAR for the York Pension Plan. If normal distributions were assumed and a very large number of simulations were run, this method would converge to a VAR estimate of $19 million.

To round out the analytical process, Lane suggests that Dennon also incorporate a system of evaluating portfolio performance. Dennon agrees to the suggestion and computes several performance ratios on the York Pension Plan portfolio to discuss with Lane. The performance figures are included in the following table. Note that the minimum acceptable return is equal to the risk-free rate.

Figure 3: Performance Ratios for the York Pension Plan

Ratio	2007	2006	2005
Sharpe	0.85	0.86	0.85
RoMAD	1.0	1.2	1.5
Sortino	0.73	0.81	0.88

23.1. Using the variance/covariance method, the value at risk in the Jude Fund with 97.5% probability will be *closest* to:
A. $10 million.
B. $90 million.
C. $20 million.
D. $80 million.

23.2. Using the historical data over the past 100 days, the value at risk on any single day in the Jude Fund with 95% probability is *closest* to:
A. $5 million.
B. $20 million.
C. $12 million.
D. $10 million.

23.3. Using the Monte Carlo simulation method, the value at risk in the Jude Fund with 95% probability is *closest* to:
A. $25 million.
B. $20 million.
C. $18 million.
D. $15 million.

23.4. Evaluate Dennon's comments regarding the VAR estimates provided by the historical and analytical VAR methods, and state whether you agree or disagree with his comments.

	Historical	Analytical
A.	Disagree	Disagree
B.	Disagree	Agree
C.	Agree	Agree
D.	Agree	Disagree

23.5. Which of the following correctly assesses Dennon's comment regarding the Monte Carlo Simulation method of estimating VAR?
A. Monte Carlo VAR analysis is limited to normal or near-normal distribution assumptions for input variables.
B. The convergence value for the Monte Carlo model should have been stated as $26 million rather than $19 million.
C. Complex interactions among variables within a Monte Carlo model cannot be captured and reflected in the model's output.
D. Outputs from the Monte Carlo model are not forward looking since the major assumptions used in the model are based on historical data.

23.6. Using the performance evaluation information compiled by Dennon, determine which of the following statements is *most likely* correct with regard to the York Pension Plan? Over the last three years, the:
A. annual excess return earned on the plan's assets has increased dramatically.
B. maximum drawdown that an investor must accept for a given return has decreased.
C. amount of capital at risk relative to the return earned on the plan assets has decreased.
D. probability that the plan will experience a return less than the risk-free return has increased.

END OF AFTERNOON SESSION

PRACTICE EXAM 1
MORNING SESSION ANSWERS

The following answers are not the detailed guideline answers found in the CFA study guide, but rather the guideline answers a grader would refer to in grading a candidate's exam.

QUESTION 1 (8 points)

Source: Study Sessions 3 and 4

A.   4 points—Allow 1 point each for identifying any two of the following and 1 point each for the supporting discussion. (Study Session 3, LOS 11.b)

        1/n diversification bias: Malloy chose to divide his retirement assets equally among all of the offered asset classes. This plainly reflects 1/n diversification bias. If his employer had offered 3 or 30 options, Malloy would likely have invested in all of the choices.

        Status quo bias: Malloy maintains his initial asset allocation (even with annual rebalancing to the initial allocation), which reflects a status quo bias of endorsing his initial asset allocation choice.

        Endorsement effect: The support here is weaker than the other two effects, but the equal allocation across all offered asset classes suggests that Malloy is assuming that his employer is making an implicit suggestion of an appropriate asset allocation based on the investment choices offered.

B.   4 points—Allow 1 point each for identifying the correct effect of the following factors and 1 point each for the supporting comments. (Study Session 4, LOS 16.b,d)

Factor	Effect on discretionary wealth to total assets ratio	Comments
Inheritance from family member	Increase	In receiving the inheritance, Malloy's discretionary wealth to total assets ratio increases, allowing for a more aggressive asset allocation.
Desire to avoid "outliving his assets"	Decrease	Malloy's desire to avoid "outliving his assets" would decrease the ratio, because in order to offset the uncertainty of his remaining life, Malloy would need to adopt a more conservative asset allocation, including a safety cushion. This safety cushion would reduce discretionary wealth. Note that in Malloy's situation, his concern is somewhat unfounded – he probably has plenty of assets to cover his expenses for the rest of his life. However, the portfolio manager must respond to his stated concern.

QUESTION 2 (8 points)

Source: Study Session 4

8 points—1 point for higher/lower, 1 point for justification. (Study Session 4, LOS 15.m)

Asset	Allocation should be: (circle one)	Justification
Bond fund	Lower	Malloy has little need of low-risk securities or current income in his retirement account. The bond fund allocation should be minimal.
Balanced fund	Lower	Again, Malloy has little need of low-risk securities or current income in his retirement account. Including this fund as well as the core and bond funds is redundant anyway.
Core fund	Higher	Malloy needs capital appreciation potential, so he should allocate more funds to the equity options available in his retirement plan.
Growth fund	Higher	Malloy needs capital appreciation potential, so he should allocate more funds to the equity options available in his retirement plan.

QUESTION 3 (19 points)

Source: Study Session 5

A.   13 points (Study Session 4, LOS 15.j,l)

Investment Policy Statement

Objectives	Comments
1. Risk	(3 points) Malloy can accept moderate to high levels of risk in his portfolio. The income needs are relatively low, and the time horizon should be 20+ years (1 point). While the income needs might limit risk slightly, the long time horizon argues for higher levels of risk being acceptable (1 point). Malloy's stated objective of maximizing capital appreciation after meeting the income requirements implies a willingness to bear higher levels of risk (1 point).
2. Return	(10 points) 1 point—The daughter's law school expenses can be paid out of annual net income. 2 points—After Malloy retires, the portfolio must generate annual after-tax income of $150,000, or [$150,000 / (1 − 0.3)] = $214,286 pre tax. 1 point—In order to allow for a 5% withdrawal to cover his after-tax living expenses, the value of the portfolio upon Malloy's retirement would need to be $214,286 / 0.05 = 4,285,720. 2 points—The expected values of the Venture Capital partnership and the New York Condo are given, so the value of retirement account + cash bequest would need to be: $4,285,720 − 1,000,000 − 400,000 = $2,885,720 2 points—Return required on retirement account and bequest for the next eight years: $[2,885,720 / (800,000 + 750,000)]^{1/8} − 1 = 0.081$ 2 points—Most of the income needs can probably be met from yield, but if necessary some invasion of principal could occur to cover occasional shortfalls. A total return approach is appropriate.

Source: Study Session 5

B.   6 points (Study Session 4, LOS 15.k,l)

Constraints	Comments
i. Time horizon	3 part time horizon (1 point)—Three years until wife retires. (1 point)—Five more years until Malloy retires. (1 point)—Post retirement 15+ years.
ii. Liquidity	(1 point)—For first three years, income needs are met outside of portfolio: $(300,000 \times 0.7) + 40,000 - 180,000 - 65,000 = \$5,000$ (1 point)—For next five years, income needs are met outside of portfolio: $[(300,000 - 90,000) \times 0.7] + 40,000 - 180,000 = \$7,000$ (1 point)—After Malloy's retirement, he plans to withdraw 5% annually.

QUESTION 4 (18 points)

Source: Study Session 3

A.   9 points—1 point for listing each risk/cost and 2 points for a complete discussion of each. (Study Session 3, LOS 13.c)

Fundamental risk for Engles is the possibility that after buying Offshore's stock, an event unique to the company negatively impacts the stock's performance without an offsetting decline in Coastal's stock.

Noise trader risk (also known as irrational traders compared with arbitrageurs or rational traders) is the risk that the mispricing of Offshore worsens in the short run. The mispricing could continue as investors become more pessimistic about Offshore's outlook in the short term. In turn, investors of HiLo could force HiLo to liquidate their position early if steep losses result in a loss of investor confidence in HiLo's investment ability.

Implementation costs refer to costs of learning about the mispricing or the shorting cost in the arbitrage process. In other words, any cost that makes it less attractive to establish a short position instead of a long one. For example, fees charged for borrowing stock, or the larger cost of not being able to find shares to borrow at any price, are costs that should be considered.

Source: Study Session 3

B.   9 points—1 point for noting that any pair of securities with an R^2 greater than 25% would be acceptable as "best (perfect) substitutes." (Study Session 3, LOS 13.a)

Limiting factors:
1.   Arbitrageurs are risk averse and have short horizons. (2 points)
2.   The noise trader risk is systematic. (2 points)

The limiting factors ensure that: (allow 2 points each for any two of the following)

* The mispricing will not be wiped out by a single arbitrageur taking a large position in the mispriced security.
* A large number of small investors are prevented from exploiting the mispricing.
* Implementation costs may be so large as to prohibit small investors from participating in the arbitrage.

From the behavioral point of view, irrational trading can have a substantial and long-lived impact on stock prices. This supports behavioral finance's contention that financial phenomena can be better understood using models in which some agents are not fully rational. This viewpoint is in direct contradiction to the efficient market hypothesis.

QUESTION 5 (15 points)

Source: Study Session 17

A.   9 points (Study Session 17, LOS 45.a,e,h,i)

1 point each for correctly identifying whether the statement is correct or incorrect.

2 points for each explanation.

0 points possible if the correct/incorrect decision is wrong.

Comment	Is the statement correct or incorrect? (circle one)	Explanation, if incorrect
"Although withholding taxes are frequently assessed by foreign governments on dividends and interest, the presence of domestic tax credits means that they are no longer a significant obstacle to international investing."	Incorrect	The withholding taxes assessed by foreign governments can be a significant obstacle to international investing. Although the taxes are often paid back to the investor after a period of time, the delay creates an opportunity cost. In some countries, the taxes are not paid back but are mitigated by tax credits provided by the domestic government. However, the credits do not benefit investors who are tax-exempt in the domestic country (e.g. foundations).

"I would recommend that the return on a stock be compared to global sector benchmarks because industry factors have increased in importance for explaining stock returns. In fact, I believe that diversifying across borders is no longer necessary as long as the investor has adequate industry representation."	Incorrect	It is true that industry factors have increased in importance for explaining stock returns and that as a result, global sector benchmarks are often recommended for performance evaluation. However, an investor should still diversify across borders. Consider for example an Italian investor. If he or she were to diversify across industries but invest only in Italian companies, they would still be exposed to the Italian country factor risk. Further, not all industries will be present in Italy and those that are may not be the best investment. The contemporary investor would be wise to diversify across both countries and industries (global investing) instead of just diversifying across countries (international investing).
"Differing governmental monetary and fiscal policies cause bond market correlations to be low, often lower than that between equity markets. As a result, adding global bonds to global equity portfolios can improve the performance of a global efficient frontier, especially for lower risk portfolios."	Correct	Note: It is usually the case that CFAI does not require you to provide an explanation when the statement is correct. The discussion below is to help you better understand the material. The factors that cause bond market correlations to be low are differing governmental fiscal and monetary policies. If a government has unusually high budget deficits or extremely high interest rates, the country's bond market and currency will tend to move independently of other countries. Hence the correlation between domestic and foreign bonds will tend to be low, especially when foreign bond returns are measured in U.S. dollar terms. The correlations between international bond markets can be quite low, often lower than that between international stock markets. Therefore, adding international bonds to a global portfolio offers opportunities for lower risk and higher return, especially for lower risk portfolios.

Source: Study Session 17

B.   6 points (Study Session 17, LOS 45.b,c)

4 points for calculating the contribution of currency risk.

2 points —to obtain the return in domestic currency (DC = the euro) terms, we use the following formula that considers the stock return in yen terms as well as the exchange rate change:

RDC = 12% + 5% + (12% × 5%) = 17.60%

To calculate the contribution of currency risk, we must first calculate the risk of the stock in euro terms. The risk of the Japanese stock in euro terms must consider the risk of the Japanese stock in yen terms, the risk of the yen, and the correlation between the yen and the Japanese stock.

The variance (2 points) and standard deviation (1 point) of the Japanese stock in domestic currency (DC = the euro) terms is:

$$\sigma_{DC}^2 = 0.29^2 + 0.14^2 + 2(0.29)(0.14)(0.3) = 0.1281$$

$$\sigma_{DC} = \sqrt{0.1281} = 0.3579 = 35.79\%$$

1 point—the contribution of currency risk is the difference between the asset risk in euro terms and the asset risk in yen terms:

contribution of currency risk = 35.79% − 29.00% = 6.79%

Note that this is much less than the 14% that might otherwise be expected as being the risk from the yen-euro exchange rate.

QUESTION 6 (25 points)

Source: Study Session 11

A.   6 points (Study Session 11, LOS 34.b)—one point each for any six of the following eight due diligence discussions:

Due diligence
1. Market Opportunity—Understand the markets being considered for investment. Determine whether active management can continue to generate a positive alpha in the future.
2. Investment Process—Identify those managers with best practices and a competitive advantage among the managers under consideration.
3. Organization—Determine whether the manager has low historical personnel turnover, adequate succession plans, and fair compensation.
4. People—Conduct an interview with all the principals of the firm under consideration. Speak with current and past clients. Determine whether the principals and employees are trustworthy and competent.
5. Terms & Structure—Evaluate the terms of the deal. Determine whether they are fair and reasonable based on the alternative investment category under consideration.
6. Service Providers—Ask about service providers such as lawyers, auditors, prime brokers, and lenders that deal with the manager.
7. Documents —Read and understand all documents.
8. Write-up—Make a written record of all the issues describe above.

Source: Study Session 11

B.   4 points (Study Session 11, LOS 34.d,f)

The financial advisor's recommendation is inappropriate. Although the hedge fund returns are higher than the managed futures and risk is lower, managed futures have a significantly lower correlation with the equity category. In fact, assuming a 10% or 20% weighting in managed futures rather than in hedge funds would result in a better risk/return profile for the overall Tokay Endowment portfolio.

Source: Study Session 11

C.   6 points (Study Session 11, LOS 34.f)

3 points for each:

1. Diversification benefit—Managed futures may perform best when Tokay's stock and bond investments are performing relatively poorly. Academic research suggests that historically when stocks and bonds have significant negative returns, the returns of managed futures are positive (2 points). In addition, managed futures have positive correlation with stocks and bonds when they report positive returns (1 point).

2. Liquidity—Managed futures provide Tokay Endowment the opportunity to swiftly respond to major price movements either upward or downward in the financial and commodity markets. The transaction does not require liquidation of other

investment holdings or adding to overall portfolio risk. (2 points) However, the transaction is highly leveraged. (1 point)

Source: Study Session 11

D.   9 points (Study Session 11, LOS 34.d,f,i)

1. Benchmarks (3 points)	Tokay Endowment can either develop custom benchmarks or use benchmarks provided by Cambridge Associates and Thomson Venture Economics. Tokay must be careful evaluating the historical performance of buyout funds. Benchmark pricing data may not accurately reflect the true volatility of buyout funds. Private equity markets evaluate investments using internal rate of return based cash flow analysis.
2. Investment characteristics (3 points)	Middle-market buyouts represent companies in their mature stage. The companies have a long track record and substantial revenues. Normally the company has only a few funds or perhaps only one fund providing investment capital. (Compare this with venture capital companies where several funds may take a position in the company.) The buyout fund is heavily involved in the management of the company and normally uses debt financing for the buyout. The failure rate of companies that are targeted by buyout funds is low. (Comparably, venture capital funds have a high failure rate with the companies they invest in.)
3. Impact on the overall portfolio's risk/return profile (3 points)	Capital is normally committed for a long period of time with the potential for future cash calls. The indirect investment approach provides greater liquidity compared to using a direct investment approach. Tokay is relying on the manager's skill in choosing and managing the portfolio of companies in the buyout fund to generate strong investment returns to a greater degree than other investment vehicles.

QUESTION 7 (8 points)

Source: Study Session 11

A.   4 points (Study Session 11, LOS 36.a)

Circle one	Support your conclusion
Contango	2 points—Angus Company deals with commodities (cattle) that are consumed over a short period of time as opposed to a commodity such as gold that is held as a long-term investment. Therefore, Angus' operations will experience high storage costs and additional benefits for holding the physical commodity of cattle. The benefits accruing to Angus from holding inventory are known as the convenience yield. With this information a simple formula describing the relationship between the forward and spot price is: forward price = spot price + interest rate + storage costs – convenience yield. The cattle industry is experiencing slowing demand for beef, and as a result, fewer cattle are being slaughtered causing herds (inventory) to increase. The high available inventory causes the convenience yield to be low. The low convenience yield results in the term structure of cattle prices to be contango. 1 point—Contango means that spot prices are lower than forward prices and/or that prices are lower for near term maturities compared to higher prices for longer term maturities. Backwardation is the opposite of contango and would result from shortages of cattle inventory.

Source: Study Session 11

B.   4 points (Study Session 11, LOS 36.c)

Hedging with futures can lead to basis risk because the standardized exchange-traded futures contracts may have characteristics different from the asset being hedged and are frequently not held until maturity. In comparison, forward contracts generally do not have basis risk because they are usually tailor-made and held until maturity. DVE Ranch faces two potential mismatches in using the feeder cattle futures contract to hedge:

1.   (2 points) The contract size: The feeder futures contract covers 50,000 pounds per contract, while DVE Ranch needs to hedge 90,000 pounds (600 × 150).

2.   (2 points) Maturity: Information about the exact time frame for the hedge or the available contract maturities was not provided. However, the maturity mismatch between a futures contract and the hedging time period must be considered.

Another issue can be asset mismatch. A futures contract matching the underlying asset may not exist. Thus, a contract which has a high correlation with the asset to be hedged should be used. Obviously, there will be some mismatch between the movement of the contract used and the asset hedged, resulting in basis risk.

QUESTION 8 (31 points)

Source: Study Session 5

A.   15 points (Study Session 5, LOS 21.i)

Commercial Bank Objectives (1 point each)	Discussion (2 points each)
1. Manage interest rate risk	Investment securities allow banks to adjust their interest sensitivity very quickly. The current portfolio, with a heavy weighting of long-term bonds, is positioned for a decreasing interest rate environment, while their economist is calling for increasing rates.
2. Liquidity management	Banks use the security portfolio as their primary source of liquidity and to reduce liquidity risk. Overall, First National's portfolio needs securities with greater liquidity, to offset a relatively high risk loan portfolio. The low-rated corporate securities may not be very liquid, and the CMO may also lack liquidity.
3. Income for yield	The security portfolio is an important contributor to a bank's earnings. First National is being too aggressive in their search for income and has created a low quality portfolio.
4. Manage credit risk	Banks use their security portfolio to adjust the bank's overall risk profile. In some scenarios, if the securities are more attractively priced, the bank may purchase more bonds rather than making loans. Currently, First National is assuming above average risks in its operations as well as in its securities portfolio.
5. Total return	Total return has historically been a nontraditional objective for banks. It measures the effectiveness of security portfolio management in terms of both interest earnings and capital gains. First National does not employ a total return approach.

Source: Study Session 5

B.   10 points (Study Session 5, LOS 21.i,j)

Constraints (1 point each)	Comments (1 point each)
1. Time horizon	The time horizon is relatively short given that funds may be needed to originate new loans or reposition the bank for changes in the interest rate environment.
2. Liquidity	Liquidity is an important issue to consider. First National may want to sell securities in its portfolio and use the proceeds to increase its loan portfolio. The Bank may also want to adjust its overall risk profile by buying or selling securities. In addition, the bank must be able to meet withdrawals from depositors.
3. Legal	Commercial banks must meet both state and federal legal requirements. Banks must use a fraction of their deposit funds to satisfy the legal reserve requirement. Capital adequacy ratios must be maintained.

| 4. Taxes | Taxes are a concern in managing the securities portfolio. However, overall operational profitability must be considered to determine the impact of taxes and any corresponding adjustments to the portfolio. |
| 5. Unique | Black does not have the time or resources needed to manage the portfolio. This makes active management of the portfolio or sophisticated trading strategies difficult to implement. |

Source: Study Session 5

C.   6 points (Study Session 5, LOS 21.j,n)

2 points each for any three of the following answers:

1. The tax-exempt income is equal to the total income earned from operations. The amount allocated to tax-exempt securities should be reduced. In addition, alternative minimum income tax may come into play, reducing the effect of the tax-exempt securities.

2. First National's loan portfolio carries an above average risk level, so the investment portfolio should invest in higher quality securities. However, the securities in the portfolio are low investment to below investment grade. The entire portfolio should have an A rating or better to offset the risks contained in the Bank's loan portfolio.

3. The investment portfolio is positioned to take advantage of lower interest rates with its high duration; however, the Bank's economist is forecasting higher interest rates.

4. The lower quality bonds could have a liquidity issue if the Bank needs to sell them. The bank may want to increase its loan exposure and would need to sell assets from the investment portfolio to provide the funding.

5. Black does not have the investment expertise or resources to manage the aggressive portfolio that has been created.

QUESTION 9 (14 points)

Source: Study Session 11

A.   6 points (Study Session 11, LOS 34.u,v)

2 points—If the company's prospects improve, both the market price of distressed bonds and the market price of the issuing company's stock will appreciate. Baker would profit on the bonds, but have some offsetting loss on the short stock position.

1 point—As the company's situation improves, the debt should appreciate more than the stock due to the debt's senior credit position.

2 points—Since the arbitrage is long bonds and short the stock, it will earn the difference between the accrued interest on the bonds versus any dividends paid on the stock. In a distressed situation, dividends will have probably been suspended.

1 point—Typically, to conserve cash, any company in a distressed situation will not quickly resume paying a dividend, allowing the distressed debt investor to earn the accrued interest without having to pay dividends on the short stock position.

Source: Study Session 11

B.   6 points (Study Session 11, LOS 34.u,v)

    i.   Event risk—2 points—can be a significant risk, but because the event is usually related to the specific company situation, this risk is not highly correlated with overall stock or bond market returns.

    ii.   Market liquidity risk—2 points—Lack of liquidity is a significant risk of distressed debt. There are few participants in the distressed debt markets. To motivate a transaction, the seller would be forced to lower her price significantly. In addition, implementing a successful business plan can take years. Investors must be willing to accept the long-term nature of distressed debt investing. Otherwise, full return potential of the investment will not be realized.

    iii.   Market risk—2 points—least important of the three, since most distressed debt returns are situation-specific and not highly correlated with market trends.

Source: Study Session 11

C.   2 points (Study Session 11, LOS 34.v)

J factor risk refers to the effect of the judge on the results of any bankruptcy proceeding. The judge may rule more in favor of debt or equity securityholders, and thus have a dramatic impact on their respective returns.

QUESTION 10 (12 points)

Source: Study Session 10

A.   6 points (Study Session 10, LOS 31.b)

alpha = [(5.0 − 6.5) + (−0.5 − −1.5) + (8.8 − 8.1) + (3.2 − 3.5)] / 4 = −0.025% (3 points)

information ratio = alpha/tracking error

information ratio = −0.025 / 1.4 = −0.01786 (3 points)

Source: Study Session 10

B.   6 points (Study Session 10, LOS 31.o)

$$\text{information coefficient} \sqrt{\text{breadth}}$$

$$\text{portfolio of 300 stocks} = 0.075\sqrt{300} = 1.30 \text{ (2 points)}$$

$$\text{portfolio of 500 stocks} = 0.053\sqrt{500} = 1.19 \text{ (2 points)}$$

Based on the Law of Fundamental Active Management, the portfolio of 300 stocks has a higher adjusted information ratio and should be selected.

Select the portfolio of 300 stocks (2 points)

           ©2008 Schweser

QUESTION 11 (12 points)

Source: Study Session 16

A.   9 points (Study Session 16, LOS 43.p)

1 point for each correct calculation for 9 points.

Performance Measure	Portfolio	Calculation	Value
Sharpe	1	$(0.42 - 0.06) / 1.2 =$	0.30
	2	$(0.25 - 0.06) / 0.4 =$	0.475
	3	$(0.16 - 0.06) / 0.2 =$	0.50
Treynor	1	$(0.42 - 0.06) / 1.8 =$	0.20
	2	$(0.25 - 0.06) / 1.2 =$	0.1583
	3	$(0.16 - 0.06) / 0.5 =$	0.20
Jensen	1	$[0.42 - (0.06 + 1.8(0.2 - 0.06)] =$	0.108
	2	$[0.25 - (0.06 + 1.2(0.2 - 0.06)] =$	0.022
	3	$[0.16 - (0.06 + 0.5(0.2 - 0.06)] =$	0.03

Source: Study Session 16

B.   3 points (Study Session 16, LOS 43.p)

1 point—Portfolio 3 had the best risk-adjusted returns.

1 point each for any of the following, for a total of 2 points.
- Portfolio 3 had the highest Sharpe ratio.
- Portfolio 3 had the highest Treynor measure.
- Portfolio 1 is not a well-diversified portfolio. Since both the Treynor and Jensen measures assume a diversified portfolio, the results of Portfolio 1 cannot be compared.

QUESTION 12 (10 points)

Source: Study Session 11

A.   3 points (Study Session 11, LOS 34.f)

Award one point for accept, and two points for justification.

Burg's Proposal	Justification
Accept	The new portfolio has higher risk adjusted returns. The Sharpe ratio of the current portfolio is $(7.1 - 4.0) / 12.1 = 0.2562$, while the Sharpe ratio for the proposed portfolio is $(8.0 - 4.0) / 12.4 = 0.3226$ Note: a justification of higher returns without addressing risk would only earn one point.

Source: Study Session 11

B.   4 points (Study Session 11, LOS 34.g)

Award one point for identifying the advantage/disadvantage and one point for brief explanation.

Issue	Direct Investment vs. REITs	Explanation
Portfolio diversification	**Advantage**	Direct investment offers higher diversification benefits than REITs. Returns on REITs have demonstrated a higher correlation with stock and bond returns historically.
Liquidity	**Disadvantage**	Direct investment offers poor liquidity – the Luther pension portfolio will have 0.15×60 = $9 million to invest in real estate. This is not enough to acquire any kind of diversified portfolio of properties. Also, transaction costs of getting into and out of specific properties will be much higher than investing in REITs.

Source: Study Session 11

C.   3 points (Study Session 11, LOS 34.e)

Award one point for unsmoothed and two points for justification.

NCREIF Index	Justification
Unsmoothed	The NCREIF index uses appraised values, due to the lack of daily trading data for real properties. These appraised values understate the volatility of real estate values, by smoothing the fluctuations. Unsmoothed index numbers are a more accurate reflection of the volatility of real estate values.

PRACTICE EXAM 1
AFTERNOON SESSION ANSWERS

To get detailed answer explanations with references to specific LOS and Schweser Study Notes content, and to get valuable feedback on how your score compares to those of other Level 3 candidates, use your Username and Password to gain Online Access at schweser.com and choose the left-hand menu item "Practice Exams Vol. 2."

13.1.	C	16.3.	B	19.5.	C
13.2.	B	16.4.	D	19.6.	D
13.3.	A	16.5.	A	20.1.	A
13.4.	B	16.6.	B	20.2.	C
13.5.	A	17.1.	B	20.3.	C
13.6.	C	17.2.	C	20.4.	B
14.1.	D	17.3.	D	20.5.	C
14.2.	D	17.4.	A	20.6.	A
14.3.	A	17.5.	C	21.1.	C
14.4.	C	17.6.	A	21.2.	B
14.5.	D	18.1.	B	21.3.	A
14.6.	B	18.2.	C	21.4.	A
15.1.	A	18.3.	B	21.5.	D
15.2.	C	18.4.	A	21.6.	A
15.3.	C	18.5.	D	22.1.	A
15.4.	B	18.6.	C	22.2.	C
15.5.	B	19.1.	D	22.3.	C
15.6.	D	19.2.	B	22.4.	A
16.1.	A	19.3.	A	22.5.	D
16.2.	D	19.4.	D	22.6.	B

PRACTICE EXAM 2
MORNING SESSION ANSWERS

Source: Study Session 14

A.   4 points (Study Session 14, LOS 41.l)

2 points —Algorithmic trading is designed to detect opportunities in changing market data and execute trades with controlled risk and costs.

2 points—Monitoring risks is an important function, for example, to avoid an unbalanced portfolio or unintentional exposure to a sector.

Algorithmic trading is not solely for the institutional buy-side investor, as some hedge funds and broker-dealers provide liquidity using algorithms.

Source: Study Session 14

B.   6 points—1 point for each algorithmic trading strategy and 1 point for each justification. (Study Session 14, LOS 41.m)

Template for 1B

Stock	Appropriate algorithmic trading strategy	Justification
1. Star	Implementation shortfall strategy	Although the Star trade is a small percentage of daily volume and has a narrow spread as a percentage of the last price, the urgency level is high. The high urgency level justifies an implementation shortfall strategy. narrow spread = $\dfrac{39.76-39.74}{39.75} = 0.0005$ small % of daily volume = $\dfrac{1,150,000}{11,500,000} = 10.0\%$

2. Moon	Use a broker or crossing system	The Moon trade's wide spread and large percentage of daily volume suggests a broker or crossing system should be used. In addition, the trade has a low urgency level. $\text{wide spread} = \dfrac{150.37-149.62}{150.00} = 0.005$ $\text{large \% of daily volume} = \dfrac{500,000}{2,200,000} = 22.7\%$
3. Sun	Simple participation strategy based on VWAP, TWAP, or another benchmark	The Sun trade has a narrow spread as percentage of last price, low urgency level, and trades at a small percentage of daily volume which makes the simple participation strategy best suited for this trade. $\text{narrow spread} = \dfrac{80.02-79.98}{80.00} = 0.0005$ $\text{small \% of daily volume} = \dfrac{500,000}{6,000,000} = 8.3\%$

Source: Study Session 14

C.   5 points (Study Session 14, LOS 41.l)

Circle one	Defend Your Selection
Inaccurate 1 point for correct selection	2 points—Rather than eliminating traders, algorithmic trading strategies will make them more productive. 2 points—The role of a trader has changed under algorithmic trading as greater emphasis is placed on strategic and tactical decision making rather than managing broker relationships. This does not mean the role of a trader would be eliminated.

QUESTION 2

Source: Study Session 17

A.   6 points (Study Session 17, LOS 49.i,l)

1 point each for correctly identifying whether the comment is consistent with the GIPS standards.

2 points for recommending the change necessary to bring the firm into compliance with the GIPS standards.

3 points for correctly identifying a comment as consistent with GIPS standards.

0 points possible if the yes/no decision is wrong.

Comment	Is the comment consistent with the requirements of GIPS? (circle one)	If not, recommend the change that will bring the firm into GIPS compliance
"We have not reported the performance for our real estate composite because we only have eight portfolios in it, which is less than the minimum number of portfolios required to form a composite. Once we have the required ten portfolios necessary for composite creation, we will begin reporting performance for the real estate composite."	No	There is no minimum required number of portfolios necessary for composite creation. The firm should report the performance of the composite. Perhaps Richardson was thinking of the requirement for reporting the number of portfolios in a composite. To be GIPS compliant, firms must report the number of portfolios in a composite, unless there are five or less portfolios in the composite.
"We have different policies for when portfolios are added to a composite. The time period for inclusion of new portfolios is longer for the private equity composite than it is for the small cap equity composite."	Yes	Note: It is usually the case that CFAI does not require you to provide an explanation when the statement is correct. The discussion below is to help you better understand the material. This policy is consistent with the GIPS standards. Depending on the type of asset, it can take several months to find a suitable investment for an investor's funds. Finding an investment in the private equity world can often take longer than in the case of publicly traded equity. It may also be the case that clients deposit their funds over an extended period. GIPS allows different portfolio inclusion policies for each of a firm's composites, as long as the policies are applied consistently within composites.

Source: Study Session 17

B. 6 points (Study Session 17, LOS 49.p)

   3 points for calculating the capital return.

   3 points for calculating the income return.

   To obtain the capital and income return, we must first calculate the capital employed (C_E), which utilizes the capital at the beginning of the period (C_0), the capital contribution, and the capital disbursement. If the capital contribution came at 0.43 into the quarter, then the manager had use of those funds for 0.57 of the quarter. We weight the capital contribution of $800,000 by this portion.

If the capital disbursement came at 0.87 into the quarter, then the manager lost use of these funds for 0.13 of the quarter. We weight the capital disbursement of $620,000 by 0.13 and subtract it as follows.

$$C_E = C_0 + \sum_{i=1}^{n} (CF_i \times w_i)$$

$$C_E = \$15,000,000 + \$800,000(0.57) - \$620,000(0.13) = \$15,375,400$$

To determine the capital return (R_C), we examine the capital gain or loss, capital expenditures, and sale of properties. Capital expenditures (E_C) are those used for improving a property and are subtracted because they will be reflected in the property's ending value and the manager should not receive credit for this additional value.

The proceeds from the sale of properties (S) are added in because the drop in ending property value from a sale should not be counted against a manager.

Using the figures from the example:

$$R_C = \frac{MV_1 - MV_0 - E_C + S}{C_E}$$

$$R_C = \frac{\$17,100,000 - \$16,300,000 - \$510,000 + \$930,000}{\$15,375,400} = 7.9\%$$

To determine the income return (R_i), we use the investment income (INC) minus the non-recoverable expenses (E_{NR}) minus debt interest (INT_D) minus property taxes (T_P). Essentially, we subtract the cost of doing business on a periodic basis from investment income as below.

$$R_i = \frac{INC - E_{NR} - INT_D - T_P}{C_E}$$
$$= \frac{\$546,000 - \$125,000 - \$78,000 - \$148,000}{\$15,375,400} = 1.3\%$$

The total return for the quarter is the sum of the capital return and the income return:

$$R_T = R_C + R_i = 7.9\% + 1.3\% = 9.2\%$$

QUESTION 3 (29 points)

Source: Study Session 5

A.   17 points (Study Session 5, LOS 21.i,j)

Compound return calculation: $(1.045)(1.04)(1.0035) - 1 = 9.06\%$

1 point—inflation adjustment (4%).

1 point—fee adjustment (0.35%).

1 point—multiplying, not adding terms.

1 point—return (9.06%).

Note that adding rather than multiplying would earn only 2 of 4 possible points.

Objectives	Comments
1. Return (3 points)	1 point—Total return approach should be used with current income requirements given highest priority, but not to the exclusion of long-term capital gains (must pay out $3.6 million this year). 1 point—Long-term return requirement is 9.06%. 1 point—Only 4.5% must be paid out. Remaining 4.56% will protect purchasing power and cover expenses.
2. Risk (2 points)	The fund needs to meet the $3.6 million income requirement, but so long as that need is met, the fund could accept more risk in the form of a slightly higher weighting to equity securities.

Constraints	Comments
1. Time horizon (2 points)	1 point—A long time horizon with annual reviews. 1 point—The $10 million athletic facility funding shortfall should be addressed
2. Liquidity (2 points)	1 point—Annual distribution of 4.5% of assets (do NOT add inflation to this 4.5%—the inflation adjustment is hopefully covered in the growth of assets to meet the total return requirement of 9.06%). 1 point—In four years time, the endowment must provide $10 million to fund the new athletic facility
3. Legal (1 point)	Prudent investor rule.
4. Taxes (1 point)	Tax exempt.
5. Unique (2 points)	The funding of the new athletic facility in four years. The bylaws requirement of investment only in U.S. domiciled securities.

Source: Study Sessions 5 and 7

B.   12 points (Study Session 5, LOS 21.i.j; Study Session 7, LOS 25.n)

The proposed allocation does not meet the income requirements because the portfolio yields only 3.38% as opposed to the 4.5% required. The yield would need to be increased, preferably without allowing the overall total return to fall below 9.06%.

2 points each for any of the following suggestions:
- Cash (T-bills) too high at 5.0%.
- US Treasury Notes too high relative to corporate bonds. More corporate bonds are needed to gain the additional yield.
- The allocation to corporate bonds is too low. In order to attain an average yield of 4.5%, you will need more of this high-yielding asset.
- The allocation to large-cap stocks is too low relative to small-cap stocks, again for the yield advantage. Alternatively, the suggestion could be that the allocation to small-cap stocks is too high relative to large cap stocks.
- Hedge funds offer a higher total return than venture capital, and so should have a higher allocation, given that no risk numbers are provided.
- The overall allocation to alternative asset classes is probably high given the income needs of the portfolio.

The question does not ask for a specific asset allocation, but as an example, the following allocation would meet the portfolio's objectives:

Asset	Yield	Return	Weight	Avg Yld	Avg return
T-bills	4.00%	4.00%	2.00%	0.08%	0.08%
U.S. Treasury notes	5.25%	5.25%	3.00%	0.16%	0.16%
Corporate bonds	7.00%	7.00%	45.00%	3.15%	3.15%
Large-cap stocks	2.00%	10.00%	25.00%	0.50%	2.50%
Small-cap stocks	0.50%	12.00%	5.00%	0.03%	0.60%
Hedge fund	0.00%	22.00%	5.00%	0.00%	1.10%
REIT	6.00%	11.00%	10.00%	0.60%	1.10%
Venture capital fund	0.00%	18.00%	5.00%	0.00%	0.90%
			100%	4.51%	9.59%

QUESTION 4 (6 points)

Source: Study Session 10

1. 2 points—Stone is incorrect. It is less likely that there will be pockets of inefficiency in large-cap stocks, since they are more widely researched.

2. 2 points—Stone is correct. An S&P index fund will overweight strong performing stocks. As these stocks increase in value, they become a larger part of the index. If there is a "reversion to the mean," the index fund would be overweighted in stocks that are likely to fall in value.

3. 2 points—Stone is incorrect. The small-cap sector is generally less efficient than the large-cap sector. Active strategies are more suited to small-cap stocks, where research is less complete and investors stand a better chance of benefiting from superior analysis. (Study Session 10, LOS 31.b,d,i)

QUESTION 5 (6 points)

Source: Study Session 4

2 points—Spontaneous investor.

2 points—Psychological profiling (includes behavioral finance and personality typing) helps the portfolio manager better understand unique needs of the investor.

2 points—The process plays an important role in setting individual risk tolerance and return objectives. (Study Session 4, LOS 15.b,d,e,f)

QUESTION 6 (12 points)

Source: Study Session 10

1 point for the accept or reject decision and 2 points for a good explanation (Study Session 10, LOS 32.a,b)

Accept or Reject (circle one)	Discussion
i. Reject	International benchmark indexes should be based on some measure of liquidity (i.e. float) not market capitalization.
i. Reject	International benchmark indexes should have a representative sample of companies that investors are able to invest in, but should not include all companies. For example, a $4 billion dollar fund cannot own a company with a $50 million market capitalization in any significant amount.
i. Reject	By constantly changing a benchmark index's makeup based on a company's market capitalization, a reconstitution effect is created, which in turn will make the index more difficult to outperform.
i. Accept	Benchmark indexes that rely on judgment are inferior. A benchmark index based on a fixed set of rules is preferred.

QUESTION 7 (16 points)

Source: Study Session 9

A.   4 points (Study Session 9, LOS 29.e)

3 points for calculation—The number of contracts is derived by:

$$\text{approx. number of contracts} = \frac{\left(D_T-D_I\right)P_I}{D_{CTD}P_{CTD}} \times \text{conversion factor for CTD bond}$$

$$= \frac{(5.0-6.8)\times 250,000,000}{6.5\times 100,000} \times 1.3 = -900.0 \text{ contracts}$$

1 point for numerator, 1 point for denominator, 1 point for correct answer

1 point—The contracts should be sold, as indicated by the minus sign in the formula. Mulder wants to decrease portfolio duration, which is accomplished by selling futures.

B.   3 points (Study Session 9, LOS 29.d)

1 point for any one of the following advantages—higher liquidity, lower transaction costs, or efficiency

1 point—Basis risk is the risk that the difference between the cash securities price and the futures price will change unexpectedly. If such a change occurs, the hedge may not perform as expected. This is especially a concern for futures hedges that will not be held until the maturity of the futures contract.

1 point—Any difference between the CTD security underlying the derivative and the security being hedged can give rise to basis risk. There is little information in the problem to indicate the potential for basis risk, but the CTD conversion factor of 1.3 might imply that the underlying differs from the hedged portfolio.

C.   5 points (Study Session 9, LOS 29.f)

	Credit forward at a contract spread of 250bp
i. the maximum potential loss to Mulder	1 point—the maximum loss would occur if the spread declined to zero (admittedly an unlikely event) 1 point—calculation: $\text{payoff} = (\text{spread at maturity} - \text{contract spread}) \times \text{notional principal} \times \text{risk factor}$ $= (0.0 - 0.025) \times \$10,000,000 \times 3 = -\$750,000$
ii. the payoff if the spread widens to 300bp at the maturity of the derivative	1 point— $\text{payoff} = (\text{spread at maturity} - \text{contract spread}) \times \text{notional principal} \times \text{risk factor}$ $= (0.030 - 0.025) \times \$10,000,000 \times 3 = \$150,000$
iii. the payoff if the spread narrows to 200bp at the maturity of the derivative	1 point—for noting that this would generate a loss 1 point—calculation: $\text{payoff} = (\text{spread at maturity} - \text{contract spread}) \times \text{notional principal} \times \text{risk factor}$ $= (0.020 - 0.025) \times \$10,000,000 \times 3 = -\$150,000$

D.   4 points (Study Session 9, LOS 29.f)

1 point—Credit default swaps offer significant flexibility.

1 point for supporting arguments:
*   Swaps are available for non-publicly traded securities
*   Swaps are negotiated independent of any exchange, and can be set up to match any needs of either party

1 point—seller of protection has no costs to establish their position.

1 point—seller is adding exposure to the credit risk, and thus leveraging their credit exposure

QUESTION 8 (8 points)

Source: Study Session 10

A. 4 points—1point each for correctly identifying the moral hazards and 1 point each for correctly suggesting a change in management's incentives. (Study Session 10, LOS 33.a,b)

Comment	Type of Moral Hazard	Change in Management's Incentives
"Because he has obtained the approval of several investment initiatives related to traditional wired network technologies, Baltus has managed to shift the majority of FRI investments away from wireless communications technology to the detriment of shareholders."	Entrenchment Strategy	Baltus is investing in older, less profitable ventures, that he is more comfortable with, to entrench his importance to the company and reduce his risk of being removed. The board of directors should increase the implicit incentive of job retention by more efficiently contracting with Baltus through an employment contract that has greater threat of dismissal for poor performance. In this case, less job security may be a better motivator than the performance-based pay which Baltus already receives.
"Korkov ... has convinced FRI's investment committee to invest in several media production ventures. The media companies FRI has invested in generally require long investment periods and have high levels of risk, making them relatively expensive capital projects that divert attention away from FRI's core operations."	Extravagant Investments	Korkov is taking expensive risks with shareholders' capital. If the risks pay off, he will be rewarded through his stock options. Korkov's interests may become more aligned with shareholders' interests if his compensation is more directly tied to the profitability of the firm rather than its stock performance. The long time horizon of the media ventures and the diversion from normal operations may cause FRI's current profitability to suffer. Closer alignment between Korkov's pay and FRI's current profitability may reduce his willingness to invest in the media ventures.

Source: Study Session 10

B. 4 points—1 point each for correctly explaining two incentives imposed by debt and 1 point each for correctly explaining two limitations of using debt to motivate management. (Study Session 10, LOS 33.e)

Incentives
* Managers must pay closer attention to free cash flows generated by the firm when leverage is increased in order to meet debt service payments and make profitable investments. If close attention is not paid, the firm will become internally illiquid. This can result in risk failure and subsequent termination of those managers who contributed to the failure.

- Managers are prevented from consuming perks or investing in unnecessary investment projects since excess free cash flow is removed from the firm.
- If managers do not manage the firm well and the debt goes into default, the firm's creditors effectively take control of the firm. Most managers desire to avoid working under the likely conservative and restrictive policies that would be instituted by controlling creditors.
- If managers are significant shareholders in the firm, increasing the number of debtholders increases the degree to which managers are residual claimants on the cash flows of the firm. Since the cash flows will be determined by management's actions, they will have greater incentive to act in the best interest of the shareholders (which is their own best interest).

Limitations
- *Cost of Illiquidity*—Increasing the level of debt too much can restrict the cash flows of the firm to the point that management cannot fund ongoing operations or invest in new profitable projects. Even if managers do act in the best interest of shareholders as a result of the increased debt level, unforeseen events that may be beyond management's control may negatively impact the already cash strapped firm. Capital markets may be unwilling to extend the needed funds to the poorly performing firm.
- *Bankruptcy Costs*—The costs of bankruptcy are high. Whether the firm enters into a Chapter 7 liquidation or a Chapter 11 reorganization, the stakeholders of the firm are likely to lose at least a portion of the value of their investment in the firm. Increasing the level of debt increases the risk of bankruptcy. If debt levels are pushed too high, the motivating effect is outweighed by the probability of default and eventual bankruptcy.

QUESTION 9 (24 points)

Source: Study Session 5

A.   12 points (Study Session 4, LOS 15.k,l)

Objectives	Comments
1. Return	1 point—Diamond has a normal need for long-term capital appreciation that any young person has. 2 points—Diamond has annual living expenses of $176,000 [$100,000 + mortgage payment (0.08 × 1,000,000 × 0.95)= $76,000] that exceed his current after-tax salary plus bonus [(150,000 + 50,000) × (1 − 0.3) = $140,000], so he also has a substantial income requirement to meet living expenses.
2. Risk	3 points—Diamond is in a very high-risk situation because of the high-risk nature of his employer's business and the financial exposure Diamond has to that business risk through his options and 401k plan. If Diamond were to lose his job, his financial situation would be severely compromised. His overall ability to tolerate risk is relatively high, given his long time horizon. However, the circumstances of his portfolio require that he carefully analyze risk prospects of decisions because of lack of adequate diversification.

Constraints	Comments
1. Liquidity	1 point—Diamond must have some liquidity because in the short-term his living expenses exceed his income.
2. Time horizon	1 point—Diamond is young and has a two-tiered time horizon—his remaining working life (long time horizon) and his eventual retirement years.
3. Taxes	1 point—In a 30% tax bracket, Diamond must be aware of tax consequences. He can sell his mutual fund and get a tax benefit. But he must be aware of the consequences of selling his appreciated Rome Corp. stock.
4. Legal	1 point—No particular issues.
5. Unique	2 points—Any discussion of Diamond's large mortgage and/or discussion of his over-exposure to the future of Rome Corp.

Source: Study Session 4

B.   6 points (Study Session 4, LOS 15.j,m)

2 points each for any three of the following:

3 Suggested Changes to Diamond's Current Asset Allocation
1. Sell the financial service mutual fund (Diamond already has too much exposure to one industry in his options and 401k). **Diversification is needed here.**
2. Sell at least some of the Rome stock held outside of the 401k plan. Diamond needs diversification from his options and 401k. Furthermore, his salary and bonus are tied to the company.
3. Any suggestion that Diamond should reduce risk by buying bonds or paying down his mortgage. He may also buy some longer term (low-risk) securities than the 3 month T-bills, to increase his income. Diamond has more than enough risk in his option and 401k holdings.
4. Any suggestion that Diamond add exposure to different industries in order to diversify whatever portion of his portfolio he elects to keep in equities.

Source: Study Session 4

C.   6 points (Study Session 4, LOS 19.d)

An equity collar uses a combination of call and put options to hedge the low basis stock holding.

2 points—A put option on Rome is purchased, with a strike price near the current market price ($45) to provide downside protection below the strike price of the put.

1 point—A call option on Rome is sold, usually with a strike price above the current market price, to allow for some upside potential.

1 point—The premium income from the call is used to offset some or all of the put premium paid. If Diamond wants to minimize the cost of the hedge, he will need to sell a call option with a lower strike price, thus surrendering a portion of his upside potential on the stock.

2 points—To avoid the "constructive sale" rules, Diamond must retain some risk in the Rome holding. The collar should cover only a portion of the 10,000 shares, no more than 85% based on IRS guidelines.

QUESTION 10 (4 points)

Source: Study Session 15

2 points for some attempt to increase the income requirement of the holdings by moving toward more bonds or bills to provide income needed to fund children's college education.

2 points for any attempt to further reduce Diamond's exposure to Rome stock now that his holdings have increased in value. There should be some discussion that the good fortune of Rome may not continue, or that Diamond should take advantage of the existing profit. (Study Session 15, LOS 42.c)

QUESTION 11 (12 points)

Source: Study Session 4

A.   9 points (Study Session 4, LOS 18.a,b)

Wealth Planning Options	Evaluation
1. Personal account	The assets in this account have an indefinite life (1 point), and Diamond has complete access and control over these funds (1 point). These funds are normally very tax inefficient. Diamond has zero availability of a valuation discount (1 point).
2. Tax-deferred pension vehicles	IRAs allow for withdrawal at age 59.5. Mandatory withdrawal is required at age 70.5 (1 point). The Diamonds have moderate access to the funds and a high degree of control (1 point). This is a very tax efficient vehicle, but no valuation discount is provided (1 point).
3. Charitable trust	The term of a charitable trust is normally less than 20 years (1 point). The Diamond's have no access to the funds and moderate control (1 point). The charitable trust is tax efficient. The charitable trust has no valuation discount for the transfer of assets (1 point).

Source: Study Session 4

B.   3 points   (Study Session 4, LOS 17.d)

   1 point—The Rome stock is low basis stock with a large unrealized gain, so tax planning is important.

   1 point—There would be no capital gains tax on the Rome stock, so Diamond would completely avoid any income tax on the substantial appreciation of the Rome shares.

   1 point—Diamond's estate would get the benefit of a deduction in the amount of the appreciated value of the stock, thus reducing his inheritance transfer tax liability.

QUESTION 12 (24 points)

Source: Study Sessions 5 and 7

A.   3 points for any of the following discrepancies totaling 15 points. (Study Session 5, LOS 21.i; Study Session 7, LOS 25.n)

Corrections	Discussion
1. Policy mix	The policy mix has too much equity exposure for a life insurance company portfolio. In particular, the international equity exposure is very aggressive. A maximum of 20% in equities with a maximum of 5% allocated to foreign investments.

2. Commodity listed as fixed income vehicle	5% of the total portfolio is allocated to commodities which may be appropriate given long-term concern over inflation. However, they are listed as a fixed income vehicle, seemingly reducing the risky nature of the investment. Real estate is also listed under fixed income vehicles. Both commodities and real estate should be classified as alternative investments.
3. Risk objective	The risk objective is not clearly defined. Simply stating "prudent risk should be taken" does not sufficiently clarify what risks are appropriate for the portfolio.
4. Legal considerations	The legal discussion is incorrect. All legal restrictions must be considered regardless of country specific regulations.
5. Taxes	ALL is concerned about after-tax returns. However, no mention of municipal bonds as a potential investment vehicle is made.
6. Return objective	Return objective does not discuss the importance of after-tax returns.
7. Benchmark	The passively managed large-capitalization equity component is being benchmarked to the small-capitalization Russell 2000 index.

Source: Study Session 15

B.   9 points (Study Session 15, LOS 42.h,j)

Constant mix:

1 point—Maintain exposure to stocks that is a constant proportion of portfolio value. This strategy buys stocks as they fall and sells stocks as they rise.

1 point—Best suited to investors whose risk tolerance remains constant despite changes in their wealth.

1 point—This strategy will outperform when markets are volatile with no significant trend.

Constant Proportion Portfolio Insurance:

1 point—A form of portfolio insurance strategy where a floor value for the portfolio is selected. As the value moves towards the floor, the exposure to risky assets is reduced until there is no risk at the floor value. A constant proportion strategy sells stocks as they fall and buys stocks as they rise.

1 point—Best suited to investors whose risk tolerance is very sensitive to changes in wealth.

1 point—This strategy will outperform when the market moves in a steady trend, either up or down.

Buy and Hold:

1 point—A passive strategy, where the assets are purchased and then held, with no rebalancing.

1 point—Best suited to investors whose risk tolerance increases as wealth increases, because the value will never go below the amount invested in the riskless asset, and will increase as the value of the risky asset increases.

1 point—The performance of this strategy will typically lie between the other two strategies, and its best performance would be in a market with a long term uptrend.

QUESTION 13 (12 points)

Source: Study Session 11

Any 4 of the following answers for a total of 12 points: (Study Session 11, LOS 34.s)

3 points—Returns: typically hedge funds only report return data monthly. The frequency of reporting could develop into a problem if:
  A. the frequency with which investor funds are allowed to exit or enter the hedge fund does not match the reporting frequency
  B. the calculation of the loss incurred from a fund's highest return to its lowest return (peak to trough–drawdown) does not include compounding
  C. the use of leverage affects asset weighting but not the return on the individual asset

3 points—Volatility and Downside Volatility: Most hedge fund strategies have a high degree of serial correlation, which causes excess smoothness of their returns. Since standard deviation makes an implicit assumption of serially uncorrelated returns, it incorrectly represents the actual risk of hedge funds. As a result of the problems with standard deviation, two alternative measures have been devised; downside deviation and drawdown.

3 points—Performance Appraisal Measures: The Sharpe ratio suffers from several limitations:
  A. The Sharpe ratio increases proportionally with time, e.g. annual is higher than monthly assuming serially uncorrelated returns.
  B. The Sharpe ratio is a poor measure if the hedge funds have skewed returns
  C. The Sharpe ratio is biased upward if the hedge fund holds illiquid securities
  D. The Sharpe ratio is biased upward if returns are serially correlated.
  E. The Sharpe ratio does not take correlations into account.
  F. The Sharpe ratio has no predictive power for the future performance of a hedge fund.
  G. The Sharpe ratio can be manipulated by altering the length of the measurement period, using derivatives to smooth returns, eliminating extreme returns, writing out-of-the-money call and put options to alter the hedge funds longer-term return profile.

3 points—*Correlations:* Correlation analysis assumes that asset prices have normally distributed returns. This assumption is necessary in order for regular correlation analysis to provide portfolio diversification benefits. If the returns are NOT normally distributed, then the inputs must be adjusted.

3 points—*Skewness and kurtosis:* Spare is only concerned with negative returns or downside risk. The most desirable hedge funds have a positive value of skewness. In addition, kurtosis may be an issue. If a hedge fund experiences extreme returns (mostly concerned with extreme negative returns), this should be a red flag to Spare. This is known as kurtosis.

3 points—*Consistency:* Spare should analyze the consistency of returns of hedge funds using a similar strategy. For each of the four strategies outlined above, Spare should review the consistency of the funds' returns. Spare should select the hedge fund with the greatest consistency of results within the selected hedge fund strategy.

PRACTICE EXAM 2
AFTERNOON SESSION ANSWERS

To get detailed answer explanations with references to specific LOS and Schweser Study Notes content, and to get valuable feedback on how your score compares to those of other Level 3 candidates, use your Username and Password to gain Online Access at schweser.com and choose the left-hand menu item "Practice Exams Vol. 2."

14.1. D	17.3. A	20.5. C
14.2. A	17.4. B	20.6. B
14.3. B	17.5. B	21.1. B
14.4. C	17.6. B	21.2. C
14.5. A	18.1. D	21.3. B
14.6. B	18.2. B	21.4. B
15.1. C	18.3. B	21.5. D
15.2. B	18.4. D	21.6. B
15.3. C	18.5. A	22.1. C
15.4. C	18.6. C	22.2. B
15.5. A	19.1. A	22.3. D
15.6. B	19.2. A	22.4. D
16.1. D	19.3. A	22.5. C
16.2. B	19.4. B	22.6. A
16.3. A	19.5. D	23.1. C
16.4. D	19.6. C	23.2. B
16.5. B	20.1. D	23.3. A
16.6. B	20.2. C	23.4. C
17.1. D	20.3. A	23.5. C
17.2. D	20.4. C	23.6. B

Practice Exam 3
Morning Session Answers

QUESTION 1 (20 points)

Source: Study Session 4

A.   14 points (Study Session 4, LOS 15.l)

Investment Policy Statement

Objectives	Comments
1. Risk	2 points—Perlin's monthly cash flow and debt-free situation suggest that the portfolio can take at least an average amount of risk. Although he currently has a high cash allocation, Perlin's investments in small-cap stocks suggest that Perlin is willing to assume a higher risk profile. Perlin has stated his willingness to assume the requisite level of risk in order to achieve his $20 million target within seven years, although he also stated he was unwilling to assume additional risk beyond that level. The overall risk tolerance is above average.
2. Return	2 points—The monthly cash flow meets Perlin's needs ($18,000 × 0.7 = $12,600 after tax). The return goal should focus on achieving Perlin's objective of $20 million in seven years. To achieve this objective, Perlin will need to grow his current assets at a 10.5% annual rate ($10 million × 1.105^7 = $20.1 million)

Constraints	Comments
1. Liquidity	2 points—Given the expectation of an ongoing income stream of considerable size, no liquidity needs appear to exist.
2. Time horizon	2 points—The horizon is seven years, as the portfolio will presumably be distributed at that time.
3. Taxes	2 points—Perlin's after-tax income needs are met by his royalty payment. Any gains for the next seven years will not be subject to taxes. Any taxes due on withdrawing the funds from his retirement account will be paid out of the gross distribution.
4. Legal	2 points—Investments under the management of an advisor will be governed by state law and the Prudent Investor rule.
5. Unique	2 points—The large portfolio and no apparent need for current income allow great freedom in developing the overall portfolio.

Source: Study Session 4

B.   6 points (Study Session 4, LOS 15.m)

> 2 points each for any three of the following:
> * The cash position is too high; more should be invested in stocks or other investment vehicles offering capital appreciation potential.

- The small-cap stock position is all right given the risk profile and portfolio flexibility.
- A greater allocation to stocks should be made—both to large-cap domestic and foreign stock with some exposure to emerging markets.
- The portfolio should be diversified into additional asset classes—bonds, real estate, and/or international investments.

QUESTION 2 (9 points)

Source: Study Session 4

1 point for recommending Portfolio A. (Study Session 4, LOS 15.m)

2 points each for any four of the following reasons:
- Portfolio A meets the required return of 10.5% (1 point) with the least risk (1 point).
- Portfolio B does not meet the return requirement (1 point)—the after-tax yield advantage offered by the municipal bonds is of no benefit in a non-taxable portfolio (1 point).
- Portfolio C meets the return requirement, but at higher risk (1 point) and with far too high an allocation to cash (1 point).
- Portfolio D meets the return requirement but is poorly diversified—the small-cap stocks and venture capital are likely to be highly correlated (1 point). More exposure to REITs or International Stocks is appropriate (1 point).
- Portfolio A offers the best risk-adjusted returns of the three portfolios that meet the required return (1 point).
  - Sharpe ratio (based off of cash yields) of (10.56 – 3.0) / 12.1 = 0.625 vs. 0.599 for Portfolio C and 0.579 for Portfolio D (1 point). Note that U.S. Treasury note yields could have also been used with the same result.
  - Portfolio C offers a better return than Portfolio D for the same level of risk (1 point).

QUESTION 3 (8 points)

Source: Study Session 4

1 point each for identification and 1 point for a brief description of the following personalities which provide insights into investor behavior: (Study Session 4, LOS 15.e,f)

1. Cautious investor – Very averse to losses; fears making bad investment decisions; has low portfolio turnover.

2. Individualist investor – Self-confident; obtains information from multiple sources; will sometimes exhibit independence in investment decision making.

3. Methodical investors – Rely on factual information; are disciplined in their approach; generally do not form emotional attachments to investments.

4. Spontaneous investors – Frequently readjust portfolio allocations and asset holdings; not investment experts but do not trust outside investment advice; follow trends in choosing investments.

QUESTION 4 (18 points)

Source: Study Session 11

A.   6 points

For each alternative, 1 point for direct/indirect; 1 point for comment
(Study Session 11, LOS 34.m)

Alternative	Type	Comment
Futures contracts	**Direct**	Direct exposure to energy commodity prices, either through purchasing the underlying asset itself or through derivatives such as futures contracts, provides the best exposure to changes in energy prices.
Energy stocks	**Indirect**	Overweighting energy stocks could provide some exposure to changes in energy prices, but many commodity producing firms hedge their exposure to price changes through the internal use of derivatives. This alternative would be the least likely to achieve Cady's objective for the MU endowment.
ETFs	**Indirect**	While an ETF investment is considered indirect, the suggested ETF based on the GSCI would give the MU endowment significant exposure to energy-related commodities. However, the GSCI does include non-energy related commodities as 30-40 percent of its weighting. This non-energy component would reduce the potential benefit sought by Cady.

Source: Study Session 11

B.   3 points (Study Session 11, LOS 34.n)

The roll return is the change in the futures price that is not attributable to changes in the spot price of the underlying asset. The calculation based on Figure 1 would be:

June 15 futures price – May 15 futures price – change in spot price

Award 1 point for each correct calculation

Contract	Roll return calculation
July	$63.25 – $62.55 – $0.50 = $0.20
October	$62.35 – $61.70 – $0.50 = $0.15
January	$61.75 – $61.20 – $0.50 = $0.05

Source: Study Session 11

C.   2 points (Study Session 11, LOS 34.n)

1 point for backwardation, 1 point for justification

Future pricing	Justification
Backwardation	When the contracts with longer maturities have lower futures prices, the market is said to be in backwardation. Because the January contracts are priced below the October contracts, and the October contracts are priced below the July contracts, the oil futures market is in backwardation.

Source: Study Session 11

D.   3 points (Study Session 11, LOS 34.e,n)

1 point—Total return = roll return + spot return + collateral return = 6.4 + 10.2 + 7.1 = 23.70%

1 point—The largest weighted sector in the GSCI is energy.

1 point—The GSCI does have exposure to non-energy related commodities, such as metals and agricultural products. The weights in the GSCI are based on a five-year moving average of world production for each commodity.

Source: Study Session 11

E.   4 points (Study Session 11, LOS 34.f,m,o)

  i.   Inflation hedging

      1 point—Commodities, and particularly energy-related commodities, have been shown to be effective as inflation hedges.

      1 point—Commodities offer the most benefit as inflation hedges when there are unexpected changes in the rate of inflation.

  ii. Diversification

      1 point—For the past 15 years, the correlation between commodity returns and stock/bond returns has been at or near zero, suggesting significant diversification benefits from adding commodities to a traditional portfolio such as MU's endowment.

      1 point—Adding energy-related commodities to the MU portfolio would certainly hedge some of the risk of higher energy costs, and alleviate some of the related budgetary issues.

QUESTION 5 (10 points)

Source: Study Session 11

A.   3 points (Study Session 11, LOS 34.g)

Award 1 point for disagree, and two points for justification.

FEI Memo	Justification
Disagree	First, the NCREIF (direct investment) is an unleveraged index, whereas REITs (indirect investment) are leveraged. Therefore, the NCREIF index does not include leveraged ownership of properties (understates the risk of most direct investments). Second, the NCREIF returns are calculated from property appraisals, which are usually done once per year. As a result, the appraisal values remain fairly stable over time. Therefore, the NCREIF index understates the true riskiness of direct investment. In contrast, REITs are publicly traded, securitized real estate assets. REIT returns are based on transactions.

Source: Study Session 11

B.   4 points (Study Session 11, LOS 34.e)

Award 2 points for a brief explanation of each.

Strength	The NCREIF index is an index of properties held by large institutions. CREFs manage real estate assets for large institutions (primarily pensions). In that sense, the NCREIF is an appropriate index for CREFs.
Weakness	Closed-end CREFs take leveraged positions in properties, and the NCREIF is an unleveraged index, which is a weakness of the NCREIF as a benchmark for closed-end CREF performance.

Source: Study Session 11

C.   3 points (Study Session 11, LOS 34.e,f)

Award 1 point for disagree, and 2 points for justification.

Decision	Justification
Disagree	While it is true that the Von Wilstrom Fund underperformed the NAREIT index, Ketter should point out that the Von Wilstrom Fund is an apartment REIT fund. It is not designed to be a well-diversified REIT fund (as represented by the NAREIT index). Therefore, the more appropriate benchmark for the Von Wilstrom Fund is the Apartment REIT component of the NAREIT index. Von Wilstrom's return was higher than the Apartment REIT index and its standard deviation was less than the Apartment REIT index. Therefore, the Von Wilstrom Fund performed well within its stated REIT objective.

QUESTION 6 (9 points)

Source: Study Session 11

A.   3 points (Study Session 11, LOS 34.h,k)

1 point each for identifying the following errors in Newman's statement:
- Strategic partners (corporate partnerships that invest in private equity) do not generally invest until the venture is in the expansion stage.
- In the expansion stage, revenues are not just beginning to flow into the company. Initial revenues occur in the latter phases of the formative stage. In the expansion stage, financing is needed for expanding sales.
- "Angel" investors generally invest early on in the formative stage. Angel investors are often the first source of outside capital (thus they also face the highest level of risk).

Source: Study Session 11

B.   6 points (Study Session 11, LOS 34.b)

1 point for correctly identifying one consideration in each area and 1 point for correctly explaining the consideration.

Due Diligence Area	Consideration	Explanation
Evaluation of prospects for market success	Sales potential	An assessment of the business plan should help in assessing the future success in terms of what outlets exist for the firm's products, who its competitors are, and what level of sales can be expected.
	Qualifications and experience of management	This is one of the biggest factors in the success of a venture. In assessing qualifications, a background check using management's references and independent sources is warranted to determine the level of skill and experience possessed by management. This is an ongoing process.
	Commitment of management	Level of commitment can be assessed by evaluating management's percentage of ownership in the company (higher levels indicating greater commitment) and whether compensation incentives align owner and manager interests.
	Cash invested	Managers that have invested a greater proportion of their individual net worth in the venture tend to be more focused on the success of the company.
	Customers' opinions	If the company already has a product in the marketplace, customer opinions can provide valuable insight into the current and future success of the company.
	Identify current investors	If current investors in the venture include experts or professionals with expertise in a similar area as the venture's line of business, future success may be more probable.
Operational review	Expert confirmation of technology	Investors need to have independent experts confirm the validity of new technologies being introduced by the venture.
	Employment contracts	The success of the venture may depend on key employees currently employed with the company. Employment contracts should be assessed to determine if the venture will be able to retain those individuals that are key to its success.
	Intellectual property	If the venture's success depends on proprietary information or technology, investors should ensure that the firm has the exclusive rights to, and that the firm has or will obtain the proper protections for (i.e., patents), such information or technology.
Financial/legal review	Assess potential for dilution of interest	Stock options granted to existing managers have the potential to dilute the investor's capital in the venture. The investor will want to utilize contracts to ensure such dilution does not occur.
	Review of financial statements	Audited financial statements may not exist for the venture. Investors should carefully review tax returns and conduct their own audits of the firm's internal financial reports.

©2008 Schweser

QUESTION 7 (24 points)

Source: Study Session 16

A.   10 points (Study Session 16, LOS 43.k)

Portfolio	Calculation	Return
Sterling	$(0.6 \times 12.5) + (0.25 \times 16.0) + (0.15 \times 10.0) =$ 1 point 1 point 1 point	13.00% 1 point
Benchmark	$(0.5 \times 10.0) + (0.3 \times 18.5) + (0.2 \times 9.0) =$ 1 point 1 point 1 point	12.35% 1 point
Circle one		
Outperform 2 points		

Source: Study Session 16

B.   8 points (Study Session 16, LOS 43.e,l)

Effect	Calculation	Final Answer
Allocation effect	1 point $(0.6 - 0.5) \times (10.0 - 12.35)$ + 1 point $(0.25 - 0.30) \times (18.5 - 12.35)$ + 1 point $(0.15 - 0.20) \times (9.0 - 12.35) =$	−0.375% 1 point
Selection effect	1 point $[0.50 \times (12.5 - 10.0)]$ + 1 point $[0.3 \times (16.0 - 18.5)]$ + 1 point $[0.2 \times (10.0 - 9.0)] =$	0.70% 1 point

Source: Study Session 16

C.   6 points (Study Session 16, LOS 43.e,l)

3 points—The outperformance is due to the selection effect, or rather, the value added by the segment managers.

3 points—The consultants (Rawls Group) actually penalized performance through their asset allocation decisions.

QUESTION 8 (15 points)

A.   6 points—two points for each benchmark discussion. (Study Session 7, LOS 26.c)

Benchmark discussion
1. Smith Hospital has a very young workforce with an average age of 31. In addition, the ratio of active to inactive participants is very high indicating a long tail liability. To meet the future pension liability of the workforce, a greater percentage of assets must be invested in equities than is currently required by the benchmark. In other words, to meet the liability generated by the real growth component from future wages, Smith Hospital must invest a greater percentage of the plan's assets in equities.
2. The growth in future wages earned by the young workforce will have an inflation component. A substantial liability is created by this inflation component and will require a higher percentage of pension assets invested in Treasury inflation-protected securities (TIPS) or some other type of inflation-protected securities.
3. The high percentage allocated to nominal bonds may reduce the company's overall risk profile, but it will not generate the returns needed to cover the growing pension liability. The percentage allocated to nominal bonds must be reduced. As the percentage of inactive participants rises, a larger proportion of the pension plan's assets can be invested in nominal bonds since employee benefits are fixed after retirement.

Source: Study Session 5

B.   5 points (Study Session 5, LOS 22.b)

	Market Value	Beta		Market Value	Bet
Operating assets (core)	500	0.48**	Debt	200	0
Pension assets	100	0.60*	Pension liabilities	100	0
			Equity	300	1.0
Total assets	600	0.5	Total liabilities & equity	600	0.

1 point * (equity allocation) (pension plan equity beta) = 0.8 × 0.75 = 0.6

The total assets beta is calculated by adding the weighted average of the operating assets (core) beta and the weighted average of the pension assets beta. To solve for the operating assets (core) beta, the total assets beta equation is used with the known variables as follows:

2 points ** 0.5 = [(100/600) 0.6] + [(500/600) × ?] →
{0.5 − [(100/600) × 0.6)]} / (500/600) = 0.48

2 points—Estimated core WACC adjusted for pension assets = RFR + (market risk premium × operating asset beta) = 0.04 + (0.48 × 0.07) = 0.0736

Source: **Study Session 5**

C.   4 points (Study Session 5, LOS 22.b)

1 point—Any difference between the WACC for the core business and the core WACC adjusted for pension assets will affect the capital budgeting process. Thus, the capital budgeting process will be affected if Smith Hospital's management ignores any risk inherent with the pension plan asset allocation decision.

1 point—The core WACC of 8.2% is higher than the pension adjusted core WACC of 7.4%.

1 point—By overestimating the discount rate by 0.8%, management will exclude value-added projects.

1 point—The long term consequence for Smith Hospital of excluding value-added projects is a lower stock price.

QUESTION 9 (10 points)

Source: Study Session 5

A.   6 points (Study Session 5, LOS 22.c)

1. 100% Equities	1 point—Valuation: The greater exposure to equities in the Smith Hospital Pension Plan will increase the company's overall risk profile. The higher overall risk level for the company can result in a lower price to earnings ratio. The conundrum is that Smith Hospital Pension Plan must generate adequate returns to cover the growing future liability. The higher return requirement can only be met by increasing the percentage invested in equities.
	2 points—Optimal capital structure: The greater exposure to equities in the Smith Hospital Pension Plan will increase the total asset risk of the company. Assuming Smith's capital structure remains unchanged, the higher asset risk will result in higher equity risk. If management wants to hold equity risk at the previous level, the company must reduce its leverage.

2. 0% Equities	1 point—Valuation: The exclusion of equities in the Smith Hospital Pension Plan will lower the company's overall risk profile by eliminating stock market volatility from the pension plan. The lower overall company risk profile should produce a higher valuation assuming all other factors are held constant. However, eliminating equities from the pension plan's asset mix will most likely require Smith Hospital to make higher future contributions as a result of lower investment returns from the pension plan. Higher pension contributions will lower the company's future cash flow. Lower investment returns from the pension plan will also eventually translate into lower earnings for Smith Hospital as its pension expense increases. Yet, the precise impact on Smith's future earnings is difficult to determine due to the numerous required assumptions such as the extent of employee turnover. The higher the level of employee turnover the lower the amount of pension contribution that is required.
	2 points—Optimal capital structure: The lower exposure to equities in the Smith Hospital Pension Plan will reduce the total asset risk of the company. By reducing the pension plan's allocation to equities, the company can increase its leverage and still maintain its previous risk profile. The additional leverage can be used to invest in valued added projects.

Source: Study Session 5

B. 4 points (Study Session 5, LOS 21.a)

1. Smith Hospital	1 point—Smith Hospital must contribute the amount owed to the employee on an annual basis.
	1 point: Smith Hospital must provide the employee a diversified selection of investment instruments.
2. Employee	1 point—The employee is responsible for all investment decisions and performance.
	1 point—The employee owns the assets and can move them if he or she leaves the company.

QUESTION 10 (10 points)

Source: Study Session 17

A.   4 points—1 point for any of the reasons given below for a total of four points.
(Study Session 17, LOS 47.b,c)

Over the last ten years, many emerging market liberalizations have occurred that give
foreign investors a greater opportunity to invest in emerging market equity securities.
These market liberalizations also give investors located in the emerging countries the
ability to transact in foreign equity securities. However, this liberalization process does
not guarantee that market integration will occur, either because investors do not accept
the changes as permanent or foreign investors have access to the emerging market
through other means. The general and specific market integrations that account for the
higher correlation between the emerging market and developed market investment
returns include:

1.   Government reforms in emerging markets.

2.   Corporate governance reforms in emerging markets.

3.   Stronger trade relationships have resulted in a more integrated world economy
(globalization).

4.   The greater number of companies with international operations.

5.   The emerging markets have a more developed trading process that leads to fair and
accurate pricing.

6.   Efficient trading processes that lead to lower transaction cost and higher quantities
of shares being traded without affecting the price.

7.   Solid investment returns have attracted foreign capital flows which are helping to
expand the emerging market economies.

8.   Lower systematic risk has reduced the cost of capital of emerging market firms.
The lower cost of capital leads to greater investment opportunities for the firm.

9.   The emerging markets have implemented disciplined monetary policies that have
reduced inflation rates.

10. The emerging markets have a more diversified economic base.

11. Emerging market countries have enjoyed higher and more sustainable GDP
growth.

12. Fiscal and monetary management have reduced external borrowing requirements.

Source: **Study Session 17**

B.   6 points (Study Session 17, LOS 47.c and LOS 48.e)

Circle one	Defend your selection
Disagree 1 point	3 points: 1 point—Gamez is correct that the higher correlation between emerging markets and developed markets will reduce diversification benefits, but so long as the correlation is less than perfect, there will still be benefits to diversifying into these markets. 1 point—Further, the standard deviation of emerging market investment returns has been lowered from 27.2% to 21.0%. 1 point—The benefits of the lower standard deviation will likely offset the higher correlation. In other words, emerging market investments still provide attractive diversification benefits. 2 points—Gamez did not consider the return portion of the risk/return trade-off. The outstanding growth opportunities presented by emerging market equities must be considered to evaluate their investment merits. The higher growth rates generated by emerging markets are being realized through a combination of improved domestic economies and strong international trade. In addition, emerging market fiscal and monetary policies are supportive of their growth opportunities.

QUESTION 11 (26 points)

Source: Study Session 5

A.   12 points (Study Session 5, LOS 21.j)

Objectives	Comments
1. Returns	1 point for discussing the 4.7% payout requirement. 1 point for discussing the return objective of $(1.047 \times 1.02 \times 1.03) - 1 = 10.0\%$. This total return is the most important goal of the Foundation.
2. Risk	1 point for discussing that, to meet the return objective, the Foundation must be willing to accept a relatively high risk level.

Constraints	Comments
1. Liquidity	1 point—The liquidity requirements for the Foundation are the anticipated 4.7% payout and any unanticipated needs for cash in excess of contributions made by the Foundation.
2. Time horizon	1 point—The foundation's time horizon is long-term.
3. Taxes	1 point—Foundation is tax exempt, however: 1 point—In some countries, taxes may impact the performance of a foundation
4. Legal	1 point—The Foundation will be subject to legal and regulatory constraints of Grik. These constraints may establish standards of prudence, and may also address consistency of foundation investments with stated objectives of foundation. In the U.S., for example, tax laws impose a graduated series of excise taxes if a private foundation invests in a manner that jeopardizes carrying out its tax-exempt purposes.
5. Unique	2 points—The Foundation requires all investments to pass a socially acceptable screen. 2 points—The Foundation requires 60% of its assets be invested in foreign countries in which the company does business.

Source: Study Session 7

B.   8 points (Study Session 7, LOS 25.m,n)

2 points—Portfolio C is the best choice.

2 points each for any of the following reasons:

Income: Portfolio C generates 4.8% in current income (1 point), which exceeds the 4.7% payout requirement (1 point).

Total return: Portfolio C generates 10.3% in total return (1 point), which exceeds the total return requirement (1 point).

Foreign investment: Portfolio C meets the 60% foreign investment constraint.

Diversification: Portfolio C meets the 5% minimum investment in all asset classes requirement.

An answer that took the approach of rejecting the other portfolios without addressing the issues above favoring Portfolio C could earn a maximum of four points, 1 point each for any of the following:

Portfolio A does not meet the current income requirement.

Portfolio B does not meet the total return requirement.

Portfolio D violates the 60% foreign investment requirement.

Portfolio E violates the 5% minimum asset class investment requirement.

Source: Study Session 17

C.   6 points (Study Session 17, LOS 45.a,g)

2 points each for any of the following for a total of 6 points:

The social screening process could impact the total return expectations by screening out certain investments that, while socially unacceptable to the foundation, may have large total return potential.

The 60% international investment requirement stipulates that the investments must be in countries where Great Northern does business. This may impact the return expectations generated by the consultant. The countries in which Great Northern does business may have significantly lower available returns than what is available elsewhere.

The current income requirement can only be met with a 45% investment in the international fixed income asset class. If interest rates unexpectedly rise in the foreign countries where Great Northern operates, the large exposure to this asset class would negatively impact the portfolio's overall performance.

QUESTION 12 (12 points)

Source: Study Session 14

A.   4 points (Study Session 14, LOS 41.h)

2 points—Measuring execution costs by implementing a VWAP benchmark can lead to higher trading costs as traders attempt to time orders based on the benchmark. For example, if a trader buying shares recognizes the security is moving higher as the market closing approaches, he may wait for the next trading day rather than purchase the full position by day's end. The next day the trader is able to finish buying the security in the VWAP range rather than incur a higher price relative to the VWAP the previous day. This is good for the trader's performance measurement, but the portfolio's performance suffers as shares are purchased at higher prices than could have been obtained the previous day.

2 points—The VWAP becomes an ineffective measure of trading if the trade orders are delivered to the trading desk just after the opening bell. The trade is compared with a VWAP calculated over the full day, while the actual trade is not. This may help or hurt the trader's measured performance.

Source: Study Session 14

B.   4 points (Study Session 14, LOS 41.j,k)

1 point—Trades motivated by value are represented by the Graham and Dodd process of fundamental, price-oriented valuation.

1 point—Trades motivated by news/information reflect the use of new information and changing expectations. ·

1 point—The most important factor in value trades is price, as the trader seeks to buy the stock below its intrinsic value.

1 point—The most important factor in news trades is time, as the trader rushes to complete the trade before the news/information spreads across the market.

Source: Study Session 14

C.   4 points (Study Session 14, LOS 41.n,o)

Any of the following answers for a total of 4 points:

1 point—Best execution depends on knowing ex ante the execution costs.

1 point—Best execution carries with it a fiduciary responsibility.

2 points—Best execution should be viewed as a procedure. This certainly includes the trade price, but also involves the timing of trades, the trading mechanism used, the commission charged, and even the trading strategy employed.

2 points—Best execution is difficult to measure in a dynamic environment, thus a benchmark is required.

2 points—The concept of best execution is challenged by numerous market practices, such as selecting preferred brokers to deal with, or paying for order flow, both of which arise as competitive responses to established markets.

QUESTION 13 (9 points)

Source: Study Session 4

1 point each for correctly identifying whether the statement is correct or incorrect.

2 points for each explanation.

0 points possible if the correct/incorrect decision is wrong.

(Study Session 4, LOS 15.c,f,h and LOS 20.d)

Comment	Is the statement correct or incorrect? (circle one)	Explanation, if incorrect
"Many investors will use a mental accounting approach where investment goals are segregated. For example, an investor might say they have one portfolio for retirement and one for their child's college expenses, the latter to which they definitely want to make maximum allowable contributions. Any funds left over can be allocated to the retirement fund. For this type of investor, a fixed horizon strategy would not be suitable because it would not ensure funding of the child's education."	**Incorrect**	The statement regarding mental accounting is correct. Mental accounting refers to the brain's tendency to classify activities into separate categories or accounts (e.g., winning investments, losing investments; daughter's education account, retirement account, etc.). The investor treats the accounts as if they were independent, ignoring the interrelationships that exist across the accounts in the portfolio. However, the statement regarding the fixed horizon strategy is incorrect. In a fixed horizon strategy, the present value of the investment goal is invested in riskless zero coupon bonds. This strategy will ensure funding of the child's education.

Comment	Is the statement correct or incorrect? (circle one)	Explanation, if incorrect
"An investment policy statement should be reviewed and considered for possible revision when an investor experiences a change in personal circumstances or when external conditions change significantly. For example, a change in tax laws may trigger an investment policy statement review."	Correct	Note: It is often the case that CFAI does not require you to provide an explanation when the statement is correct. The discussion below is to help you better understand the material. An investment policy statement should be reviewed and considered for possible revision when an investor experiences a change in personal circumstances or when external conditions change significantly. Examples of the former include: a change in marital status, health, and income. Examples of the latter include: a change in tax laws, capital market expectations, and asset availability. A large loss in the portfolio could also trigger an investment policy statement review.
"Investors classified as individualistic investors tend to be very conservative. They can also be very difficult clients to work with because they do their own research and are very confident in their decisions."	Incorrect	The investor type he is describing is a methodical investor. Methodical and individualistic investors have similar characteristics (they do their own research and are very confident in their decisions) but methodical investors are more risk averse than individualistic investors.

PRACTICE EXAM 3
AFTERNOON SESSION ANSWERS

To get detailed answer explanations with references to specific LOS and Schweser Study Notes content, and to get valuable feedback on how your score compares to those of other Level 3 candidates, use your Username and Password to gain Online Access at schweser.com and choose the left-hand menu item "Practice Exams Vol. 2."

14.1.	D	17.3.	B	20.5.	D
14.2.	B	17.4.	B	20.6.	A
14.3.	C	17.5.	C	21.1.	C
14.4.	B	17.6.	C	21.2.	D
14.5.	D	18.1.	C	21.3.	A
14.6.	B	18.2.	C	21.4.	B
15.1.	B	18.3.	B	21.5.	B
15.2.	C	18.4.	C	21.6.	D
15.3.	B	18.5.	B	22.1.	B
15.4.	D	18.6.	A	22.2.	C
15.5.	B	19.1.	A	22.3.	B
15.6.	A	19.2.	B	22.4.	A
16.1.	B	19.3.	A	22.5.	C
16.2.	A	19.4.	A	22.6.	B
16.3.	B	19.5.	D	23.1.	A
16.4.	C	19.6.	C	23.2.	C
16.5.	A	20.1.	C	23.3.	C
16.6.	C	20.2.	A	23.4.	D
17.1.	A	20.3.	D	23.5.	B
17.2.	A	20.4.	A	23.6.	D